Smarter Outsourcing

Jean-Louis Bravard

FT Prentice Hall

FINANCIAL TIMES

In an increasingly competitive world, we believe it's quality of thinking that will give you the edge – an idea that opens new doors, a technique that solves a problem, or an insight that simply makes sense of it all. The more you know, the smarter and faster you can go.

That's why we work with the best minds in business and finance to bring cutting-edge thinking and best learning practice to a global market.

Under a range of leading imprints, including *Financial Times Prentice Hall*, we create world-class print publications and electronic products bringing our readers knowledge, skills and understanding which can be applied whether studying or at work.

To find out more about our business publications, or tell us about the books you'd like to find, you can visit us at **www.pearsoned.co.uk**

PEARSON
Education

Smarter Outsourcing

An executive guide to understanding, planning and exploiting successful outsourcing relationships

Jean-Louis Bravard and Robert Morgan

Prentice Hall

FINANCIAL TIMES

An imprint of **Pearson Education**

Harlow, England • London • New York • Boston • San Francisco • Toronto • Sydney • Singapore • Hong Kong
Tokyo • Seoul • Taipei • New Delhi • Cape Town • Madrid • Mexico City • Amsterdam • Munich • Paris • Milan

PEARSON EDUCATION LIMITED

Edinburgh Gate
Harlow CM20 2JE
Tel: +44 (0)1279 623623
Fax: +44 (0)1279 431059
Website: www.pearsoned.co.uk

First published in Great Britain in 2006

© Pearson Education Limited 2006

ISBN-13: 978-0-273-70560-4
ISBN-10: 0-273-70560-1

British Library Cataloguing in Publication Data
A catalogue record for this book can be obtained from the British Library

Library of Congress Cataloging-in-Publication Data
Bravard, Jean-Louis.
    Smarter outsourcing : an executive guide to understanding, planning and exploiting
successful outsourcing relationships / Jean-Louis Bravard and Robert Morgan.
      p. cm.
    Includes index.
    ISBN-13: 978-0-273-70560-4
    ISBN-10: 0-273-70560-1
      1. Contracting out—Management. I. Morgan, Robert. II. Title.

    HD2365.B736 2006
    58.4'058—dc26

                                                                    2005054668

10 9 8 7 6 5 4 3 2 1
10 09 08 07 06

Typeset in 9pt Stone Serif by 70
Printed and bound in Great Britain by Henry Ling Ltd., Dorchester

The Publisher's policy is to use paper manufactured from sustainable forests.

Contents

Foreword: A letter from the authors

'The world is always ready to receive talent with open arms.' That's really what outsourcing is.

Craig Barrett, CEO Intel

Experience around the world shows that roughly two-thirds of outsourcing agreements fail to deliver the targeted benefits or create the hoped-for value for shareholders. The reason often given for this level of failure is that outsourcing is an 'immature' activity – a rationale that neatly absolves the senior management involved of any blame.

Maybe a little too neatly. The failure rate for mergers and acquisitions (M&A) is every bit as high as for outsourcing, but nobody tries to claim that M&A is 'immature'. Every month brings news of a CEO losing his or her job following a failed attempt at transformation through acquisition.

In short, the responsibility for both success and failure in M&A is laid at the door of the CEO and the board. The same should be true of outsourcing.

Outsourcing: the sharpest tool in the box

Why? Because outsourcing and M&A are not ends in themselves, but simply tools available to the board in its drive to achieve the organization's chosen strategy. A surgeon whose patient dies will not get away with blaming an 'immature' scalpel. Likewise, a board whose outsourcing agreement fails can blame whoever it likes – but knows that the real responsibility lies closer to home.

This responsibility is all the greater since outsourcing is a tool of enormous power and precision. Used correctly, it can play a pivotal role in a fundamental organizational transformation encompassing people, processes, culture and costs. It can improve commercial focus and reshape the balance sheet while maximizing agility and keeping options open for the future. At its best, it can put the CEO in effective control of the company's share price. This is why outsourcing is not a management tool, but an executive tool. In fact, we believe it is the smartest and sharpest executive tool.

Outsourcing's albatross

However, it is a tool that comes with baggage. Frequent misuse, misrepresentation and misunderstanding of the outsourcing concept has lumbered the very word itself with undeserved negative connotations. In the popular consciousness, outsourcing is something that exports jobs, rides roughshod over employees' lives and creates windfall profits for faceless companies. It is, in a word, a bad thing.

This is, quite simply, rubbish. As a tool, outsourcing – as with M&A – is neither intrinsically good nor bad. But the way it is applied has a fundamental impact on how it affects organizations and people. If the board takes an arbitrary decision to outsource a function or process, and then abdicates responsibility for communicating, implementing and managing that change, the impact will be disastrous. But planned, coherent and openly communicated outsourcing, driven by a firm commitment at the topmost levels of the organization, can demonstrably transform performance, enhance shareholder value, sharpen competitive edge and vastly boost the well-being and career prospects of employees – not least among those transferred to an outsourcing provider.

A question of understanding

So, how can the CEO exploit this tool to its fullest advantage? First, by understanding what it is and what it can do. Secondly, by knowing how to manage and motivate outsourcing relationships in a way that safeguards the business's own interests, while at the same time getting the best from the outsourcing partner in terms of investment, expertise and innovation.

Thirdly, and perhaps most crucially, by understanding the limits of what outsourcing can achieve. At first sight outsourcing initiatives might look like attractive point solutions to specific problems. But point solutions are almost never what a business really needs.

Invariably, what is actually required to transform corporate performance is a fundamental change in the organization's underlying philosophy and culture. Bringing an outsourcing provider's sophistication and focus to bear will drive cultural change. But cultural renewal throughout the business will only happen if it is driven remorselessly by the executive board – and no amount of outsourcing will paper over the cultural cracks on its own.

Why we have written this book

That – in a nutshell – is our view of outsourcing. But why have we gone to the time and effort of encapsulating it in book form? The straight answer is that we could see the need for executives to truly understand the potential of, and to demystify the misconceptions and folklore associated with, the concept of outsourcing.

The idea for this book was born in the Spring of 2003, when the two authors visited a highly respected specialist business bookshop in the City of London. We found that the store contained every possible book you could wish to read on management, but that not a single volume on outsourcing was displayed or catalogued. There were books on fairly recent areas such as the management of operational risk or weather derivatives, but nothing on outsourcing information technology (IT) or business process outsourcing (BPO) – despite the fact that Ross Perot had invented IT outsourcing back in 1962, over 40 years ago.

Having identified this gap, we weighed up the considerable time and effort needed to ensure that senior executives and even financial analysts could, perhaps for the first time, fully appreciate the merits and risks of a well-executed outsourcing strategy implemented through a well-planned and highly committed management and exploitation programme. We recognized that our complementary and intimate experiences on both the buy-side and sell-side of this controversial industry make us ideally qualified to collaborate on a book to bring CEOs a clear, balanced and unbiased view of the outsourcing process – presenting them with a truly practical and implementable road map, complete with all the right questions to ask and issues to consider at each stage.

From observation to road map

This very real need for greater understanding of outsourcing is the primary stimulus behind our decision to write this book. It is not a recipe book to help executives achieve quick, tactical outsourcing. Rather it is a collection of thoughts and opinions synthesized from considerable personal observation and experience – and then shaped to meet the very practical needs of CEOs and other senior executives.

Our starting point is that the sourcing of the capabilities in a business, far from being seen as operational 'plumbing', should be a real focus of attention at CEO and board level – and that outsourcing in particular should be approached with every bit as much planning, diligence and post-deal management as a large acquisition or divestiture.

As with M&A, success in outsourcing depends on the CEO and the board having staying power, clear objectives, clear timescales and an awareness that the journey does not stop when the contract is signed. The senior management behind successful major outsourcing transactions invariably grow in their collaboration skills during the sourcing journey. For their part, the service providers must learn to demonstrate the same level of executive maturity and commitment. And for the relationship to succeed, the creation of long-term value must encompass both firms – meaning their responsiveness and relationship must reach levels of intimacy that were unthinkable just a few years ago.

Power with responsibility

We have already pointed out that outsourcing is an extraordinarily powerful tool – arguably the most powerful available to a CEO. By the same token, it must be used with responsibility, care and commitment. We hope this book will help CEOs to do just that. If we succeed, we will not only help outsourcing to shake off its negative connotations, but also help to trigger a real uplift in both corporate performance and the job satisfaction of people across the world.

Jean-Louis Bravard and Robert Morgan
January 2006

About the authors

Jean-Louis Bravard (representing the sell-side) is an ex-investment banker who managed technology for a Wall Street company and was a firm advocate of outsourcing from the early 1990s. Today he is a relationship executive for one of the leading outsourcing vendors and has been at the origin of innumerable global and regional transactions.

Robert Morgan (representing the buy-side) founded a specialist outsourcing advisory consultancy more than a decade ago, which acts for companies considering outsourcing as part of a business transformation effort. It advises boards on how to design flexible strategic approaches, manage the outsourcing process, benchmark, and to realize the planned benefits envisaged from the deal.

List of abbreviations

4G – Fourth Generation
ATM – Automated Teller Machine
ASP – Application Service Provider
BPO – Business Process Outsourcing
BTO – Business Transformation Outsourcing
CEO –– Chief Executive Officer
CFO – Chief Financial Officer
CIO – Chief Information Officer
CIP – Continuous Improvement Programme
CMM – Capability Maturity Model
CRM – Customer Relationship Management
CSF – Critical Success Factor
EPOS – Electronic Point Of Sale
FAQs – Frequently Asked Questions
FSA – Financial Services Authority
FUD – Fear, Uncertainty, Doubt
GAAP – Generally Accepted Accounting Principles
GE – General Electric
HR – Human Resources
HRO – Human Resources Outsourcing
IAS – International Accounting Standards
IBS – International Banking System
ICT – Information Communications Technology
IOSCO – The International Organization of Securities Commissions
IP – Intellectual Property
IR – Investor Relations
IT – Information Technology
JV – Joint Venture
KPI – Key Performance Indicator
M&A – Mergers and Acquisitions
OEM – Original Equipment Manufacturer

PC – Personal Computer
PR – Public Relations
Q&A – Question and Answer
ROI – Return On Investment
SEC – Securities and Exchange Commission
SOX – Sarbanes-Oxley
SLA – Service Level Agreement
SME – Small and Medium-Sized Enterprise

Acknowledgements

The authors would like to thank the following family, friends and colleagues for their invaluable help and cooperation in producing this book:

- John Beedham
- Eibhlín Bravard
- Dan Brennan
- Charles Cox
- Pascal Deman
- Jemima Fitzgerald
- Stephen Francis
- Rachel Hirst
- Tim Kemp
- Judith Kent
- Ed Kirkby
- Mark Lewis
- Lisa Marriage
- Rick Marsland
- Peter Miller
- Margaret Morgan
- Phil Morris
- Jennifer Powell
- Daniela Zuin

Introduction:
Why you need to do this

Our long-term strategy is to outsource as much as we can, so our IT organization can concentrate on the things that will help us win in the marketplace.

Scott McNealy, Chairman and CEO, Sun Microsystems

What do you mean by outsourcing?

'Outsourcing' is a word loaded with connotations and preconceptions. Even dictionary definitions of it range from concise to exhaustive, and from superficial to off-beam. A few of them are shown in the accompanying box.

Outsourcing: what's in a word?

It seems a simple question to ask: 'What does outsourcing mean?' But the definitions presented in a random selection of today's English dictionaries and other sources suggest the answer is far more complicated than the question.

Here are a few:

Purchasing a significant percentage of intermediate components from outside suppliers.   *Bloomberg Financial Glossary*

The practice of subcontracting manufacturing work to outside, and especially foreign or non-union companies.   *Webster.com*

➤

> Work done for a company by people other than the company's full-time employees.   *investorwords.com*
>
> The procuring of services or products, such as the parts used in manufacturing a motor vehicle, from an outside supplier or manufacturer in order to cut costs.   *The American Heritage Dictionary of the English Language, 4th edn*
>
> The buying of parts of a product to be assembled elsewhere, as in purchasing cheap foreign parts rather than manufacturing them at home.   *Random House Unabridged Dictionary*, on Infoplease
>
> Paying another company to provide services which a company might otherwise have employed its own staff to perform, e.g. software development.   *The Free On-line Dictionary of Computing*
>
> Outsourcing is often defined as the delegation of non-core operations or jobs from internal production to an external entity (such as a subcontractor) that specializes in that operation. Outsourcing is a business decision that can be made for quality or financial reasons. The term also implies transferring jobs to another country, either by hiring local subcontractors or building a facility in an area where labor is cheap. It became a popular buzzword in business and management in the 1990s.   *Wikipedia*
>
> 1. Performance of a production activity that was previously done inside a firm or plant outside that firm or plant. 2. Manufacture of inputs to a production process, or a part of a process, in another location, especially in another country. 3. Another term for *fragmentation*.   *Deardorff's Glossary of International Economics*
>
> A practice used by different companies to reduce costs by transferring portions of work to outside suppliers rather than completing it internally.   *Investopedia.com*

The contrasts between these definitions – in terms of both their factual content and nuances – are striking. Since when did outsourcing imply using non-union labour? Or apply specifically to offshoring? Or only encompass manufacturing or production services? Does cost have to be a prime motivator?

There is a serious issue here for the CEO and board of any major business. All of these definitions do touch on some aspects of what outsourcing *should* be about. But the lack of consensus on what outsourcing actually means, even in independent published sources, and the range of interpretations placed on it by everyone from politicians to labour union leaders, make it critical to define your own thoughts and business objectives in order to determine exactly what outsourcing needs to do for your business.

And it can do a lot. If you want a quick primer in the power of strategic outsourcing, turn to the case study of BP on pages 199–204. For years, Sir John Browne at BP has used outsourcing as a strategic tool to reduce costs, increase effectiveness, mitigate risk, smooth the integration of acquisitions, ensure that the predicted cost savings match the market's expectations – and influence his company's share price.

For other CEOs, the first step towards doing the same lies in defining specifically what outsourcing means, before moving on to define what it can do.

Our definition

So, as people who have worked in outsourcing for decades, what do we understand by it? As a starting point, here is our basic definition. Outsourcing is . . .

- the contracted use and leverage of third-party resources, assets and skills,
- with guaranteed levels of quality, resilience and value to cost criteria and measurement
- to deliver services previously provided in-house
- possibly involving the transfer of existing staff to the service provider
- and/or transformation/rejuvenation of the business support processes and technology.

This book focuses not just on outsourcing, but on one specific type: **strategic outsourcing**, which is a sophisticated tool for achieving or exceeding *long-term* corporate objectives. This fits within the simple definition above. But it is differentiated by four main characteristics:

1 It involves a fundamental executive decision to reposition the business positively through a large-scale strategic change programme.

2 Mitigation of the associated risks through the contractual leverage of specialist third-party experience, resources, assets and skills.

3 Commitment to the concerted management and motivation of such relationships at every organizational level, especially by the executive team.

4   Focus on the key objective of ensuring that stakeholder value is created in a measurable and sustainable way.

So, what makes all this actually work in practice? The key concept for sustainable success in strategic outsourcing is often described thus: 'The basis of successful strategic outsourcing is visible and continuous executive sponsorship and commitment.'

As we shall explain in this book, this is almost right – but not quite. Remember – you are engaging in one of a number of contractually sophisticated business models with a third-party specialist and partner, and so it should read: 'The basis of successful strategic outsourcing is visible and continuous bilateral executive sponsorship and commitment.'

Using your M&A skills to best advantage

There is a hurdle to overcome before CEOs and board members can use outsourcing to achieve clearly defined strategic objectives. While you have heard a lot about major outsourcing, you often feel that you personally or corporately have little direct experience to bring to the fore in strategizing, planning, implementing and managing the process. Incorrect!

The answer is closer to home than you may think. The executive tool with clear parallels and disciplines of outsourcing is . . . M&A. This is an area where, unlike outsourcing, CEOs should feel they and their executive team instinctively know what to do. But in our view, if you understand how to effect large-scale and successful M&A, then you understand how to tackle all the key aspects of strategic outsourcing.

Why? M&A – in both acquiring and disposal – requires:

- solid strategic intent and a business case with demonstrable benefits and logic for the market, staff and other stakeholders;

- a detailed 'discovery' or due diligence period to establish current and future value, liabilities, consolidation synergies (people, assets, technology, cost savings, etc.) and leverage and exploitation strategies;

- an expert and controlled communications plan, with consistent and regular messages to all stakeholders including regulators, stock market and clients;

- visible and active executive sponsorship, engagement and commitment;

- a series of clear ROI statements with timeframes to contain market expectations and interest;
- careful consideration of the cultural integration issues;
- key metrics that are both relevant and rigorous;
- speed – without losing control or increasing risk;
- attention to ensure as little as possible disruption to maintaining and delivering everyday business.

All of these points are exactly true of strategic outsourcing. Still think that your personal skills should not be utilized to secure a successful and business-enabling outsourcing arrangement?

As with M&A, the CEO should expect to seek and exploit expert external advice to underwrite and facilitate the deal, getting the best from it for the business, and ensuring the best possible chance of demonstrable and measurable long-term success. Would you do a major acquisition without specialist advisers? Of course not!

Six principles for outsourcing success

Taking the need for committed leadership and the parallels with M&A, experience shows that applying six core principles underpinning successful M&A deals can help to ensure that outsourcing delivers at least its original business objectives and benefits. These six principles are illustrated in Figure 1.

These principles cannot actually guarantee achievement of the objectives, since that also requires continuing commitment and a sound grasp of the strategic and market context. But what applying these principles *will* do is swing the balance of probabilities away from failure to success. The rest is down to the CEO and board.

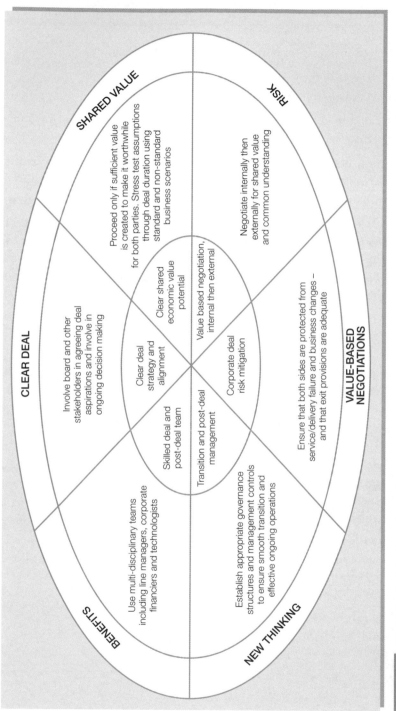

Figure 1   Six M&A principles for outsourcing success
Source: Adapted from McKinsey & Co.

Our approach in this book

Figure 1 forms the basis of the logical flow that we will follow in this publication. The first six chapters focus on issues related to each of the six M&A principles in turn. After that, Chapters 7–10 examine further key areas. At the end of each of the first seven chapters, we will spell out the key questions arising for the CEO and CFO.

Here are the topics we will look at chapter by chapter:

1 Clear deal and strategy alignment
- Examining the need to be clear about the objectives of outsourcing, the basis and characteristics of various sourcing decisions, and the role of third-party facilitators.

2 Mitigating risk
- The need to involve all stakeholders, be ready to cope with the unthinkable (including the need to exit), and manage sourcing suppliers to the organization's best advantage.

3 Clear shared value
- Establishing a clearly understood and worthwhile business case for both parties, identifying shared economic value, and stress-testing this value proposition through various scenarios.

4 Value-based negotiation
- Investigating the techniques and dynamics of outsourcing negotiations – both internal and external – while establishing cultural fit and relevant contractual service level agreements.

5 Moving to the new way of thinking
- The mechanics of transition and integration, putting governance, benchmarking and controls in place, and creating a durable framework supporting both the contract and the relationship.

6 Realizing the benefits
- Establishing a skilled, multi-disciplinary post-deal team, using metrics to drive continuous improvement, managing the contract and relationship and ensuring access to innovation.

7 Conclusion: a smarter executive tool
- What an M&A-type approach to outsourcing can deliver to your organization.

8 Are you ready to outsource?
■ A CEO self-test covering twelve areas crucial to success.

9 Five key areas to focus on
■ Five specific areas where rigorous focus is crucial to success – HR, financial engineering, legal, tax and communication.

10 The outsourcing experience
■ Case studies on six major strategic outsourcing initiatives, highlighting what drove success or failure.

By the end of this publication, we hope to have provided you with a primer for successful strategic outsourcing, by bringing together an M&A-style approach with the critical questions to ask at each stage. We will also highlight the areas where outsourcing differs from M&A – not least in its greater power and flexibility as an executive tool. Outsourcing is a journey. Based on our collective experience at the heart of many deals, this book is our personal route map.

1

Clear deal and strategy alignment

Outsourcing just to cut costs is not good for industry – you need profits to grow and provide quality.

Bruce M Caldwell, principal analyst at Gartner, from 'Outward Bound', Chief Executive Officer Magazine

If you look behind the high emotion, union confrontations and lurid headlines often associated with outsourcing, the fact is that the CEOs of most large companies – and their boards – regard outsourcing primarily as a tactical solution to a corporate need for immediate cost reduction. And the cost pressure in question is invariably related to a specific issue, reporting deadline or target that their business is struggling or failing to meet.

In other words, outsourcing comes on to the agenda because of a one-off financial trigger requiring an instant solution. This approach to outsourcing is not merely misguided, but can be positively dangerous in the longer term for the business, its executives – and ultimately its shareholders.

Seeing beyond the trigger

In our experience, the companies with the greatest understanding of what strategic outsourcing is and of what it can achieve are those facing problems much more fundamental than a tactical trigger. The CEOs who most readily grasp the real business enablement power of outsourcing, as opposed to using it as a tool to address a particular issue, are usually at the head of organizations that have found themselves in a deep or potentially fatal financial bind. The deeper the financial hole, the greater the chances that the CEO and other executives will realize that the problem is not in IT or a single business function, but across the whole culture, structure and positioning of the company.

Where a company falls into this type of all-embracing financial mantra it usually reflects a fundamental underlying weakness in the business. This may be anything from gearing, to cashflow, to its traditional cash cow product or service suddenly being blown away by new Korean competitors or an emerging, cheaper technology – or both. New market entrants have little or no historic overheads or embedded bureaucratic practices to slow innovation, and are often able to land-grab market share before traditional companies can react, restructure and recapitalize around new technologies, staffing practices, distribution methods and ability to increase speed to market.

Whatever the cause, the established business realizes it may just have found itself on 'death row'. At this point the CEO starts to ask the real question: 'What can strategic outsourcing achieve for us now?' The M&A parallel applies here, because consolidation with a competitor to remove duplicated costs and gain access to the target company's best-of-breed resources, intellectual tools, customers and experience is the proven management response for decades of 'old-school' executives. Outsourcing, done properly, can give all of these advantages together with a whole lot more – so long as the board philosophically understands and embraces this new executive discipline.

The wider picture

Some businesses grasped this more than a decade ago. As we describe in Case study 7 on pages 207–212, JP Morgan's outsourcing strategy sprang from an inflection point in 1991 when a number of issues were facing the firm. The business had arrived at a point where its annual technology spend exceeded US$1 billion a year, yet the value of that investment remained uncertain. At the same time, even more investment was required because of the business's strategic transformation from a commercial to an investment bank and trading firm. Amid this uncertainty, strategic outsourcing presented a way to exploit economies of scale and make IT budgets stick. The result was a series of ground-breaking outsourcing deals initially masterminded by then Chief Information Officer (CIO) Peter Miller, and still continuing to this day.

The precise circumstances will clearly vary from company to company. But, in every case, asking what strategic outsourcing could achieve now will make the CEO and board colleagues take as a fresh look at a tool they had formerly regarded as a tactical rather than as a strategic weapon. They will start to ask around among their 'club' of business contacts. And they will start to paint pictures and scenarios for what outsourcing might do for their business.

A secret shared

At this point the CEO and whoever else is initiating the ideas around outsourcing – quite probably the CFO, and maybe some other board members – tend to get together and start setting expectations about ways in which outsourcing can help them re-engineer the company, both financially and culturally. These expectations may be either accurate or half-baked, and the board may be divided between those members who are committed to them and those who are half-hearted.

Either way, the next step is that some senior executives go out into the market – often on a relatively informal basis – and start talking to potential candidates whom they think might be able to fulfil their expectations. These candidates will generally include providers from the list of the 'usual suspects' depending on the precise nature of the outsourcing being considered, be it focused on technology, corporate restructuring or particular business functions.

For technology, the board might talk to companies such as IBM or EDS. For corporate structuring, it could be Accenture, or one of the strategy consultancies with which the board may have an existing relationship. Increasingly companies are turning to specialist outsourcing advisers for more objective and independent perspectives and advice. All these discussions should help the company get a better grasp of its potential outsourcing options and begin to understand what executive commitment is needed to embrace and drive fundamental corporate change.

However, our experience suggests you should not look at outsourcing in isolation from everything going on in and around the business. What is needed is a holistic view of the organization and of outsourcing's potential role in it, including understanding how various choices might impact on one another and the rest of the business. A failure to do this can have severe but unforeseen consequences down the line, such as lack of flexibility or the worst possible scenario – that you have chosen the wrong partner or contractual structure for this change. The UK supermarket retailer J. Sainsbury, whose experience is profiled in the case study on pages 193–197, is a case in point. It discovered too late that the use of securitization in its outsourcing deal ultimately had the effect of boxing in its strategic options in the marketplace. For further insights into financial engineering in an outsourcing context, see the specialist section on page 161.

In a cul-de-sac?

It is clearly impossible for the board to cater to every possible eventuality, but J. Sainsbury's story underlines the fact that any decision on outsourcing should take into account all aspects of the corporate risk profile. This includes how quickly and how far the competition will move, the pace of consolidation, how rapidly advancing technology will erode some key cash cows, and how fast the business would be able to respond to all these changes by applying what it already has.

For an example of this all-round view, look at Nokia – a former forestry company that is now a global leader in mobile handsets. Seeing its traditional marketplace under pressure, it invested in a portfolio of technology-driven options. The rest is history. Where a company sees itself entering a cul-de-sac, this can be the point at which the CEO and board grasp the nettle and start to regenerate the business. It is the depth of the despair that can drive answers to the question itself, and reveal ways to exploit strengths and options the business may not even have known it had. As outsourcing has matured in recent years, it has become the primary tool for executing this type of business and cultural transformation.

The message is that what at first sight may appear to be a relatively straight-forward outsourcing decision could actually be the initial step in a complete rethink of the business. However, when their advisers or suppliers give them this radical advice, boards are often a little shell shocked – either because they have not previously considered such fundamental change, or because it broadens the internal agenda and means they will have to start debating with managers a level down, who may be hostile to this change.

The decisiveness to move . . .

Confronting the absolute need for change also brings the CEO face to face with some other uncomfortable facts. One is that the track record of large-scale change projects is actually appalling. The nature of the task that the board is embarking on, together with the advice board members are receiving from consultants, intermediaries and the rest of the supply chain, is forcing them to look in the mirror and make an honest assessment of their own change management record. In most cases the verdict is not good. This in turn raises the question of how capable the board and its senior management are of executing real change – and whether they are prepared to invest in external service providers to drive it forward.

In this context, outsourcing providers have a dual role. Most obviously, they are professional service integrators and innovators. But they are also industrialized tools enabling the board to drive structural and cultural change across the organization. It is when management fully grasp this potential that they either begin to say 'we can do this' or start to pull back because they feel it is a task they will never be able to conclude. For the CEO and board, this is a moment of truth.

. . . plus absolute clarity

Those that go forward need more than guts if they are to succeed. As we pointed out in the introduction to this book, they also need absolute clarity over their objectives, throughout the short, middle and long term. Strategic outsourcing is not a tool for the foolhardy, but the brave.

So the board needs to understand its objectives clearly and unequivocally. The Irish mortgage lender First Active decided that its unique selling proposition would be to achieve an approval decision on every mortgage – whether yes or no – within a maximum one working day of eight hours, compared to the local industry norm of eight days to two weeks. This meant re-engineering its entire technology infrastructure and credit referencing processes, involving accessing multiple sources at multiple levels into the business, to make its operations far better and faster than anyone else's. First Active's CEO, Cormac McCarthy, took the realistic decision that the organization could not – and should not even try to – do this by itself. So he envisioned success via a transformational outsourcing initiative with the single-minded business objective of 'within a single working day' as the rallying call and driver to all parts of the business.

That one ambition defined the business going forward, including differentiating it from the competition and energizing and focusing its staff. As the company explained to its technology and business transformation suppliers, nothing would be taboo in pursuing and bringing about this goal. Certainly, it would mean cutting this process, reinventing that one, losing whole functions, manipulating the risk profile. 'Just do it' was the business enablement message throughout.

Achieving this degree of clarity around a single objective is not easy. And executing it in a way that delivers it fully and rapidly is something else again. It requires both the urgency to drive the change through without affecting the operation of the rest of the business, and also the patience to accept that the full commercial benefits for all this effort and investment will only come two or more years down the road. And it also calls for the board to look beyond that timeframe to consider, at an early stage, how it will exploit its new positioning: new services, expansion into new geographical or product markets? The clarity that drives the initial change must be underpinned by an assumption of success and a faster refresh cycle that shows where the business – and its partners in the transformation – will go next.

To increase the chances of real success, CEOs and boards would do well to engage with dedicated and expert sources of help and advice. With the growing maturity of the outsourcing market in recent years, a community of highly specialized outsourcing intermediaries has sprung up, offering companies impartial, informed and practitioner advice throughout the end-to-end process (see the accompanying box). These third-party consultants now play a key role for many companies around outsourcing-related issues, ranging from clarifying and articulating strategic objectives to gauging the interrelation between various sourcing options and eventualities, and from running bidding processes to negotiating contracts and governance arrangements. Some even underwrite the ultimate envisaged benefit collection, maybe for years into the future.

Specialist intermediaries: objective guidance through the process

One of the most significant changes in the outsourcing landscape in recent years has been the emergence of a number of specialist outsourcing advisers, created to deliver to companies informed, pragmatic and independent advice throughout the whole life cycle of the outsourcing process.

Generally founded by people with extensive experience as both the buyers and the sellers of outsourced services, these intermediaries characterize themselves as being able to offer an independent perspective on issues such as defining the strategy and objectives for successful outsourcing, the scale of the potential benefits, the choice between internal effectiveness and efficiency gains (in-sourcing) and externalizing functions (outsourcing), and the risk factors in out-source-driven transformation projects.

Their positioning as practical and 'no vested or conflicted' interest advisers differentiates these intermediaries both from the outsourcing providers' consultancy arms and also from the strategic consultancies, which tend to provide the theory and set the strategic agenda only to sail gracefully on when the nitty-gritty of the implementation process starts. Continuity is critical to any outsourcing deal, and the best intermediaries will commit themselves to being involved in the negotiation, implementation and ongoing operation and measurement of the outsourcing deal's success going forward.

Aside from advising on these areas, the leading outsourcing intermediaries also provide early analysis and external benchmarking of the existing in-house performance, together with assessments of any embedded business or technology stresses and bottlenecks. Crucially, they do this without a prior assumption that outsourcing is the best solution. As experienced outsourcing practitioners themselves, they also claim to know the 'tricks of the trade' used by suppliers in outsourcing pitches – and are able to head these off or put them into context during the bidding and negotiation phases.

How bold do you want to be?

The progression from a clear initial objective to successful execution is illustrated in Table 1.1 overleaf, complete with examples of those that have made each journey. As the table shows, this journey consists of five stages.

Stage one: Know how bold you need to be

As we have already stressed, the CEO must be very clear about what the company is trying to achieve. This requires the CEO and the board to be honest with themselves about how committed they are to reaching the ultimate destination, and what barriers they are prepared to battle through.

Stage two: Know the art of the possible

No matter how bold the board may feel, it also needs to be realistic. What areas are the senior team prepared to put in scope? What is the appetite among outsourcing providers to join and partner with the management to achieve their objective? And can outsourcing providers really do something better and cheaper than can the business itself?

Stage three: Refine the market proposition

This is where the CEO and board decide what they are actually going to do. This involves engaging the finance and risk community, and thinking about which suppliers the board would prefer to work with. It also involves choosing the corporate vehicle for the vendor partnership, a decision that could open up unforeseen opportunities to increase the value proposition – or leave the organization hamstrung with long-term inflexibilities. Think marriage . . . not passionate weekend.

Table 1.1   **From objective to execution**

1. How bold is your objective?	2. The art of the possible	3. Market proposition	4. Set up for success	5. Make the deal work
Transform the company fundamentally	Market trawl for ideas, solutions and partners	Limited or full market competition – or sole source	Go for win/win deals	Invest in strategic relationships at executive level
Change the company or industry	Define the scope of the initiative	Assess 'value' creation of the deal	Agree what success truly looks like	Judge performance holistically
Collaborate with competitors	Challenge all 'crown jewels'	Determine true and presumed risk, challenge your skills and intellectual property	Get the basics right – solid options and innovations	Drive strategic value iteratively
Increase new skills, speed to market, capacity and services	Commit to demonstrable cultural change	Find real flexibility, options and innovation	Accept the learning curve will be high (for all parties)	Measure business impact – invent metrics to suit
Control/contain costs long term	View offsetting risk to supply chain	Design the vehicle and timeframes	Plan for escalation and mediation	Motivate suppliers at every level
Support M&A and/or disposal activities	Build a view of realizable benefit collection	Reconfirm openly commitment from executive downwards	Expect and encourage a hybrid culture to develop	Retain the original team to manage contractual obligations
Actively influence market analysts/ stakeholders	Establish how to manage all externals – new skills needed	Buy technical excellence without premium. Convey success stories as they occur	Build the future contract team to manage for success	Disclose and plan for iterative strategic change – early

Stage four: Set you and your vendor up for success

During the detailed negotiations, the board needs to stress to the team that the deal must feel like a win/win for both sides – because if the balance of reward is not perceived as 'fair' by each party there will inevitably be stresses in the future. Both sides also need to make sure nothing is traded away that would put the success of the deal in jeopardy; accept there will be a learning curve, and build explicit allowance for this into the timeframes and approaches the management team adopt and will be measured by. There should be agreement that the deal teams on both sides will remain on board long enough to ensure that the transition and first year are in line with expectations. This must not become 'just another deal' that is done, filed away and forgotten about.

Stage five: Making the deal work

Building the learning curve and longer-term relationship into the deal means looking at relationships, governance, benchmarking and management – and especially corporate culture. Outsourcing does not mean abdicating responsibility, but taking on a new and demanding management challenge to ensure business enablement and greater control. So the board should plan to invest time and resources proactively in support of the new partnership, and demonstrate that it believes in judging vendor 'performance' in the broadest sense of the word, leaving the management team to track service, change and cost. The CEO and other executives should focus their efforts on three questions:

1 Is the contract helping to create shareholder value?

2 Is the vendor contributing to furthering the strategic agenda and objectives?

3 Do the governance processes ensure that the corporate reputation will be protected?

If a vendor lets the board down in any of these areas, it should seriously reconsider the relationship.

What is core?

That is the basic path from objective to execution. But what can – and should – be outsourced? Any company considering a journey leading to profound change will have to challenge itself about what the essence of its business really is. As the CEO and the board study the nature and scale of change necessary to achieve their objectives, the question of how to define the core business will inevitably arise.

The debate over the philosophy of core and non-core areas has been well rehearsed over the years. Today, the fact is that very few capabilities can truly be regarded as core to any business, despite the fact that some are commonly seen as sacrosanct. For example, 99 per cent of CEOs would say: 'We can never outsource strategy.' But is that really the case? By applying a simple outsourcing model, a board could quite easily ask two or three strategic consultancies to put their best minds on to the task of devising and presenting a strategy for the business. Then the board, as an informed and experienced management team with closer proximity and intimacy to the business and greater knowledge of its customers, could cherry-pick the best elements of each proposal, blend them together, and delegate the implementation in the normal way. True, it would cost a fair amount of money – but it is clear that a business *could* outsource strategy.

To approach the same issue from an industry viewpoint: what are the core skills and activities of a retail bank? Cheque processing and clearing? Money transfer? Foreign exchange? Clearly not – these can all be, and often are, outsourced. Our case study on Fin-Force on page 185 shows how cross-border transfers can be farmed out to a third party. So is it the customer interface? If this were the case we would not have seen the rush towards automated telephone and Internet banking where differentiated customer contact is replaced by a digitized phone or computer interface. So maybe the core of a retail bank is management of risk, and the ability to assess how much money can be lent against which criteria? Ultimately, the risk loading factors on how a bank lends money determine how much money it makes, so there is a strong argument for saying that risk assessment on lending really is the essence of a retail bank. Note that this capability has little to do with high street branches or incentives to open deposit accounts.

However, even this apparently safe definition of 'core' may be open to exceptions. In a different but related field, Morley Fund Management (MFM – with over US$100 billion of funds) outsourced its investment accounting to JP Morgan in 2003, thereby freeing up resources for front office investment. So here was a fund manager apparently outsourcing a pivotal aspect of the fund management process – raising the question of what its core business really was, and of how it could differentiate itself to customers. In fact, MFM's decision suggests that its core business is risk assessment and the ability to move swiftly to exploit new opportunities and structures; which means tapping into better expertise where it is available – including, in this case, into an outsourcing provider.

Beyond financial services, the management of a range of sourcing options to achieve a given objective is a highly developed skill. Nike is a rather overused example, but still very valid for all that – having evolved into a marketing machine driving consumers' certainty that the best and latest technology will be built into each pair of Nike shoes. Technology, such as the microchip that enables Nike trainers to recognize terrain and pump the sole to the appropriate level of shock absorbency, does not represent the core of Nike. What the company is about is pushing the edge of the product in a marketing sense to maintain its fashion status, by continually pulling in the required components from third parties to do so. The relevance of this is that outsourcing provides the executive team with degrees of flexibility, risk absorption, cost containment and access to new skills and resources. When appropriate, these attributes can then be 'sold' to that most discerning section of the market – the analysts.

A question of emotion

Such examples support our view that there is virtually nothing that is core to today's businesses. For many CEOs and boards, the difference between what is core and non-core comes down to their own mental attitude to what they perceive as the 'crown jewels' of their business.

Not surprisingly, these emotions run deep – right across and through every organization, especially where they affect people's careers and self-esteem. The emotion inevitably triggered by the word 'out' in 'outsourcing' makes it crucial that the concept is presented in the right manner and context to the business units, the technology specialists and whoever else becomes involved in investigating the options. And the right context is that this is not about transferring things 'out', but about creating positive and productive corporate change, and finding the best ways and opportunities for the organization to achieve its objectives – thereby benefiting all its stakeholders, within and beyond the business.

So, where decisions are being considered that may involve outsourcing, it is down to the CEO and the rest of the board to ensure that the communications released from board level are clear, unequivocal and sure-footed, and that they reflect the forward momentum which outsourcing is contributing to the organization. If the messages get garbled or misunderstood the board has nobody to blame but itself.

Driving the deal

While as CEO you know that outsourcing-driven change will ultimately involve removing people from the business, the immediate need at the start of the process is that these same people should come back to you with facts and figures on the performance of internal units. Inevitably, some will feel like turkeys voting for Christmas. To counteract this, the exercise should be portrayed as an investigation requested by the board, and not corporate policy – yet. And it should be stressed that it is a thorough investigation to which all managers are expected to contribute, and that it will investigate all options, including any changes and improvements that the business could implement itself.

Indeed, the internal route is an option that should be seriously considered, and might well be the best choice if the internal departments can generate improvements comparable to those delivered by an outsourcing provider. In this context, the role of specialist third-party outsourcing advisers can be especially valuable, since they do not have a vested interest in any particular option. This means they can take a balanced view of the competing claims of internal business units and external vendors, and ensure that the business does not simply end up buying the best sales story.

Clearly, performance investigations may lead to decisions taken on commercial grounds below board level, if the objectives behind them are purely cost based. The point at which the investigation becomes a matter for the board is where the CEO and other executives have decided there is a fundamental need to reinvigorate the business's position in the market. The overt visibility of the board's commitment helps to make the investigation more fundamental and get it taken more seriously at every level. Generally the clear direction and sponsorship for this initiative is set by a single driving force on the board – usually, but not always, the CEO.

The analogy with M&A is particularly strong here. As with M&A, the board has to provide leadership and refuse to tolerate resistance to decisions. Again as with M&A, the process is extremely sensitive from an internal staff standpoint, while also having major ramifications for external stakeholders and even the share price. So the customary policies and procedures of an M&A deal have to be followed throughout this investigation into the art of the possible.

Talking to the enemy?

However, before they can put the full M&A-style process into effect, many companies looking at outsourcing – especially for the first time – find themselves hitting a 'catch-22'. They want to keep confidential the fact that they are even considering outsourcing. Internally, these discussions are a state secret. The board clearly needs to keep things that way until it has made a decision and chooses to go public with it. But if word does leak out, the viewpoint of many people inside the business will be that the board has gone out unilaterally to talk to the enemy about outsourcing their departments and cutting their jobs.

If such a leak occurs staff morale is damaged – and this will have to be addressed. But surprisingly the best way to examine the options, as far as some board members are concerned, appears to be by talking to a number of vendors! Any CEO who sees this type of situation looming should remember one fact: the moment the board starts to talk to any outsourcing provider, then it has effectively gone out into the market, and sooner or later your people will hear about it. That is why the investigation which may or may not result in outsourcing should be conducted openly, and ideally with a genuine in-house option as part of the mix. The use of suitably qualified intermediaries will add weight to the production of a balanced business case and ensure that internal suppression of key facts and data – usually by middle management – will be spotted and dealt with by the intermediary's proven 'discovery' process and procedures.

The dynamics of the outsourcing industry are central to this need for openness. The outsourcing vendor community consists of a relatively small group of people. Everyone knows everyone else. Many are salespeople, either by origin or profession. Competition is fierce. Inevitably, rumours constantly fly around about who is considering outsourcing what to whom, when, and for how much. Equally inevitably, some of these rumours leak out to the press and to the staff of the companies involved. With M&A deals, the price-sensitive and tightly regulated environment in which advisers and third parties operate means that this sort of information flow would not be tolerated. In outsourcing, it comes with the territory – and customers need to be aware of this.

Here is a true story that illustrates what can happen. A major retail bank was planning to outsource its desktop PCs under a contract worth several hundred million dollars. The deal was all set to be signed, but had not yet been announced. A pre-sales support person in the team that had clinched the deal happened to go for a job interview at a competing outsourcing provider, and was asked about his track record. To illustrate his worth, he mentioned the as-yet-unannounced desktop contract. He did not get the new job – but he did give the rival provider a very useful piece of information. In checking out the chances of making a last-minute counter-bid, the competing vendor allowed word of the deal to leak to staff within the customer organization.

Of course, it reached the unions. The result: union protests, confusion and embarrassment at board level, a corporate denial that an outsourcing deal of this kind was even being contemplated . . . and a dead deal. The message: before vendors are involved, the board needs to make sure of its resolve, and that its internal communications with key stakeholders are up to speed and ready to withstand the 'unforeseen'. The deal cost the bank not just the physical and management costs of an eleven-month negotiation phase, but also the relationship with two powerful unions, bad media coverage and a compelling ROI within a well-prepared business case.

The specialist sourcing intermediaries and consultants that have sprung up in recent years can provide a means of testing out what is possible with less risk than talking direct to vendors. It is more than these consultants' job's are worth to leak what they are doing. Given the importance of potentially sustaining an internal option in the bidding process, these intermediaries can also put the CEO in a better position to compare internal and external solutions in an even-handed and dispassionate way – a fundamental choice that needs to be made before a company can actually proceed to choosing an outsourcing provider.

Internal v. external sourcing

Having decided on its strategic objectives and on which capabilities it is prepared to contemplate externalizing, the board has a wide range of different approaches and structures to choose from, each providing a different balance of shareholder value and risk – as illustrated in the 'alliance framework' in Figure 1.1. While considering these, the board also needs to go through a further process: understanding what will be involved in making the required cultural change at the relevant level – be it within a business unit or across the entire company. In the case of a business unit, it might seem that if the unit were capable of making the required change itself, then it would already have done so. But if time or circumstances permit, the CEO and board owe it to internal units to give them the chance to say what business case and return on investment they could deliver, if they were to undertake some radical self-surgery. As we have already mentioned, this might even turn out to be a better option than outsourcing.

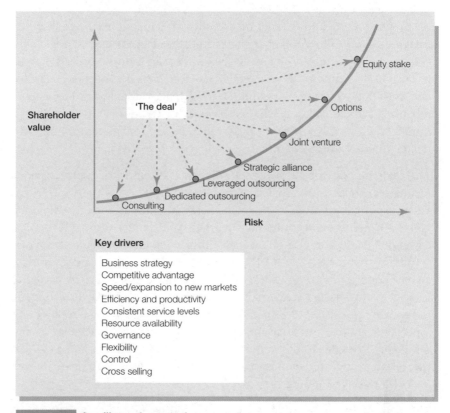

Figure 1.1 An alliance framework

There may be particular circumstances that might strengthen the case for taking the internal route. Can the CEO of a company with a history of acquisitions truthfully say that all the acquired entities have been merged and integrated with the greatest possible discipline and rigour, and with all the fat removed? Probably not. Experience suggests that the more acquisitive an organization, the greater the duplication of hierarchies, systems and people. If this is the case an internal 'night of the long knives' may not only be possible, but overdue. One major international company was advised by its outsourcing consultants that, while it could save 20 per cent of costs through outsourcing, it would save at least 35 per cent through concerted internal action to remove duplication and merge fiefdoms in several areas. It chose the latter option – and the IT component alone of the resulting restructuring ended up delivering savings of 40 per cent.

Benchmarking against external sourcing options was a crucial part of this process, reflecting the valuable role that external sourcing (or the possibility of it) plays in instilling and maintaining discipline in internal units. Imagine a CEO calling together the business unit heads and telling them: 'We are in deep trouble as a business – you've seen it in the press. We need to take 40 per cent out of our costs. If you were me, if you were given free rein as CEO, how would you achieve it? We all know there would have to be job losses, but let me know what you would do. Of course, we will talk to a number of external suppliers at the same time, so they can tell us how they would approach this as well.'

This external discipline is something that all units of today's major businesses should implicitly face on a continuing basis. By the same token, when external options are being considered, the internal teams should be given a genuine opportunity to put their case. In the utility sector it is common practice for internal business units to bid for – and quite often win – sourcing contracts. The key for the board and its third-party sourcing advisers during this type of hybrid bidding process is to ensure that the internal team's business case is not discounted out of hand, and that the team does not understate or overstate any of the parameters affecting aspects such as cost and price changes or required capital investment. At the same time, it is crucial to ensure that external bidders are given access to all the relevant and correct information, and that nothing is held back or distorted through internal pressures.

The overarching imperative is that any bidding process involving both internal and external suppliers must be fair and based on explicit and auditable criteria. In our view it is virtually a prerequisite to have a specialist independent intermediary acting as an 'honest broker' in managing such a process. A company that uses bids from external suppliers as a tool to force better performance from an internal department, with no intention of actually outsourcing the function, is not only acting unethically but also taking a very short-term view. It will find that the external suppliers who have wasted their time on preparing for the bid will not fall for the same trick again.

There are several ways in which the company and its advisers can maintain trust and transparency in a hybrid bidding process. For example, they can state at the outset that if the internal shop comes within 7.5 per cent of the external providers' pricing structure then the function will stay in-house. If the in-house team does win fair and square, then it must be given the same investment and board-level sponsorship that would have been accorded to an external supplier. However, this does not mean that outsourcing will not come back onto the agenda in the future.

Technology v. business process outsourcing

Whatever the structure or business model of an enterprise, it inevitably has some form of front and back office. With more sophisticated and larger companies this has now subdivided further into a front, middle and back office. All of these departments may have had a significant amount of technology investment pumped into them over the years. The level of IT investment tends to vary from sector to sector: a financial institution is likely to have invested far more heavily than a manufacturing business, for example.

When looking at how the front, middle and back office functions are sourced, the first stage is to envisage them not in pure technology terms. Instead, the CEO and board should consider how and where the technology is deployed, what processes it is supporting, and whether the function could be fundamentally re-engineered. Such an investigation often ends up highlighting issues around the in-house back office functions, which have typically been relatively starved of investment for several years. Partly as a result of this, these functions tend to be staffed by people who are – or who certainly consider themselves to be – skilled white-collar employees, but who are also underpaid, undermotivated, and generally underestimated by the rest of the business.

As the CEO's change programme gets under way with the aim of achieving the specific objectives agreed by the board, outsourcing has a special relevance to moribund transactional back office functions. Business process outsourcing (BPO) offers an opportunity in one fell swoop to encompass the back office in the change programme – including the deployment of technology that, if implemented correctly, will improve effectiveness and efficiency by many hundreds of per cent.

However, this improvement will inevitably mean that the bulk of the people formerly employed in the back office will no longer be required by the business. Managing this fallout is a delicate balancing act for the CEO, and the ease with which it can be handled depends on factors including the organizational culture, level of unionization, and the countries the employees are located in. Again, specialist outsourcing intermediaries are well versed in advising on these risks before the business gets to the stage of confronting them.

Whatever the underlying circumstances, the fact is that the outsourcing provider will not want to take all these people on to its payroll. The solutions that vendors put on the table are technology driven and designed to deliver value by minimizing manual input and maximizing accuracy and efficiency. So the vendor's underlying business rationale is about deploying technology rather than retaining people, although it may be willing to take on between 15 per cent and 40 per cent of the in-house staff, depending on the application. Viewed in the round, the combination of lower headcount and greater efficiency can quite easily strip 40–60 per cent out of the costs of a former in-house back office function. The major downside is the need to manage the job losses, and its (probably temporary) effect on corporate reputation.

BPO v. business transformation outsourcing

Once a CEO has decided that savings of this order are viable, either through a 'big bang' approach or in phases, then business transformation outsourcing (BTO) becomes a viable and potentially much more effective option. This involves extending the approach formerly taken with one function to the whole of a division or an entire complex business. With BTO, the CEO takes industrial-strength characteristics and skill sets from suppliers, and swings them into line behind a drive to transform the performance of the division or business by stripping it down and rebuilding it like a car engine. Any component parts that are not suitable or that no longer fit will be thrown away.

The risk of disruption to the ongoing business has to be managed carefully during this process. But, again as with M&A, these needs can be met through basic, familiar executive skills such as paying attention to due diligence, ensuring high-quality management information, working out where this process might lead in the future, and understanding its impact on employees', customers' and suppliers' views of the business itself. One of the biggest impacts is often among investors and analysts, who may well be delighted to see the CEO and board being bold in tackling the generations of inefficiency that have built up within the business and establishing a blueprint for the future. Also, given the discipline needed in this process and the scale of complexity involved, the company will look to place contractual as well as ethical obligations on its suppliers. As with an acquisition or disposal, the outsourcing provider will underwrite the transformation timeframe and savings. These undertakings in turn underpin the board's commitments, targets and vision in discussions with investors and analysts.

However, while the potential benefits are huge, the price of failure is equally high. Offsetting some of the impact of that failure by shifting it to the supplier(s) may not save the reputation or job of the CEO, nor of other senior executives who have been closely involved. However, the reputation of the outsourcing provider, being tied to the ultimate result, will also suffer. So the choice of suppliers, the cultural match between the two organizations, and the level at which they interact are all key board-level issues for both the customer and supplier, since the two will enjoy the benefits or suffer the consequences together.

The rise and rise of business process outsourcing

No company is self-sufficient, and today's enterprises are seeking to focus ever more narrowly on their core activities. So a bank creates credit, an insurance company creates the containment of risk, and an automobile company creates transport – as does an airline, which can also create access to leisure and social activities. Every activity that a company undertakes which is not adding value is essentially an overhead. As overheads, they should be performed at the lowest cost and greatest efficiency, in order to minimize their 'drag' on the company's human and financial resources.

BPO has developed in direct response to this imperative. BPO questions every task or function that an organization carries out, and asks whether it can be conducted at less cost, more flexibility and greater efficiency outside the formal structure of the organization. BPO has evolved far more slowly than Information Communications Technology (ICT) outsourcing, and is bedevilled by a lack of quality information on what constitutes 'best practice', what aspects are measurable, and how the business can derive genuine benefit while retaining full commercial 'flex' on items such as transactional volumes and large-scale business change. For this reason it is perhaps not surprising that BPO is most likely to be taken up by companies, which have already gained confidence in outsourcing their ICT.

➤

Table 1.2	BPO past, present and future – sample services only

Heritage	Current	Future or emerging
Administration	Accounts payable/receivable/etc	4G logistics[1]
Auditing	Asset management	ASP (full service)[2]
Benefits management	ATM management[3] (cash management)	Benefit fraud detection
Catering	Bill processing management	Business development
Courier services	Call centres/customer relationship management/telemarketing	Carbon emissions [compliance and trading]
Custodial services	Cheque processing	Cash-flow management
Document management	Collection/payments	Clinical trials
Education/training	Credit/debit card services	Complex environment aggregated billing
Fleet management	Customer service/fulfilment centres	Digital asset management
Graphics and design	Fund management	Electronic kiosk services
Inventory management	Human resources	Investor relations and management
Payroll	Incident management and claims handling	Library management [commercial enterprises]
Public relations	Internet design, maintenance, content services	Outsourcing contract management
Recruitment	Pension and benefits administration	Policy management & compliance
Reprographics and printing	Real estate management	Procurement auctions/indirect procurement
Security services	Road manufacture and administration	R&D spread betting
Travel/flight reservation and booking	Treasury/international currency risk	Regulatory compliance & reporting
Warehouse and logistics	Web-based fulfilment	Strategy (commercial & corporate)

[1] 4G – Fourth Generation; [2] ASP – Application Service Provider;
[3] ATM – Automatic Teller Machine

> Organizational functions seen as high-growth areas for BPO include HR, Finance and Customer Relationship Management (CRM). New areas for outsourcing come under assessment all the time. Most have been tried at some time in the recent past. Table 1.2 opposite has been compiled using industry opinion and the authors' experience. It outlines the trends in terms of past, present and future business processes that companies may choose to outsource.
>
> A discussion of BPO should carry a word of warning here about the current maturity of the service provider offerings, and the instances of lack of investment in some parts of the industry. Customers should not make assumptions that the size of the provider's brand automatically equates to quality, investment and capability. Whoever the provider may be, the importance of benchmarking and measurement – discussed in Chapter 6 – should not be forgotten.
>
> *Source*: drawn from Morgan Chambers FTSE 100 Study.

A CEO self-test for BTO

Business Transformation Outsourcing (BTO) is a big decision for any CEO – arguably one of the biggest he or she will ever make, on a par with major M&A. Here are eight questions to see if you should consider BTO for your business. If you can answer 'yes' to most of them BTO might well work for you. Even a CEO who is not quite ready to sign up for a BTO deal can take advantage of the trend towards BTO by moving conventional outsourcing relationships to a more collaborative footing.

1 Does your company need a radical change in order to be competitive in its industry?

2 Is speed a critical factor in implementing this radical change?

3 Are you willing to sponsor the initiative personally?

4 Are you willing to accept a difficult transition?

5 Do you lack the people and the skills necessary to drive this major change initiative?

6 Are you willing to work with a partner to achieve radical change, even if it means ceding a significant degree of control to them?

7 Are you willing to share the benefits with your partner?

8 Do you need capital to fund it?

A word of warning here for CEOs. Experience suggests that large outsourcing vendors are not always fully geared up for the type of one-on-one, top-level relationship that the CEO might like. What can often pay dividends for the CEO is to ensure that the contract signing includes a 'glad-handing' photo opportunity, which publicly ties senior executives from both the customer and provider together in the eyes of the media. Both sides know that if their relationship hits serious trouble those photos will reappear in the press. This public commitment on both sides will help to keep the relationship solid and cooperative further down the road, with staff from both sides recognizing the mutual executive commitment to succeed.

Alongside that relationship, what will keep an outsourcing programme on track more than anything else is an ongoing, single-minded focus on the original objectives from the CEO, or from whichever sponsoring executive is driving the programme. This focus will extend to maintaining the momentum for change as well as – crucially – motivating people and encouraging high performance throughout the hybrid business, and ultimately hybrid culture, which the two partners have created. These are critical issues we will return to later in the book.

Key CEO and CFO questions arising from Chapter 1

CEO

- Are you sure that in considering outsourcing it is not a knee-jerk reaction to a 'compelling one-off' event shouting for a solution? Have you really looked in depth into what a strategy of outsourcing can achieve, what your core activities are, and what other areas are 'broken' but could be 'mended' through outsourcing?

- Have you achieved absolute clarity over the objectives for your outsourcing strategy – throughout the short, medium and longer term – as you undoubtedly would with any M&A deal?

- Have you articulated these clear, unambiguous objectives at board level, to provide the scope for a highly confidential and detailed preparation of the business options – does this take into account your company's track record in large-scale change?

- Have you reached a clear understanding of what will be involved in making the required cultural change at the relevant levels – be it at business unit level or across the entire company?

CFO

■ If business process outsourcing is on the table, have you applied your skills and knowledge to ensure that the change is appropriate, that previous investment (or lack of it) is recognized in the shape of the deal, and that critical business knowledge will not be lost at the expense of cost savings?

■ Despite new legislation and reporting requirements, outsourcing still allows for real financial re-engineering and/or flexibility – have you studied how these can be exploited and balanced to benefit the overall business case and support the executive decision-making process?

■ Are you prepared and able to enter financial discussions with potential outsourcing suppliers without revealing internal targets and budgets and commercially sensitive future negotiation data?

Mitigating risk

In addition to controlling costs, we felt that outsourcing would help us to improve control of the business. With outsourcing, not only do we apply our own governance and control structure, but so does the outsourcing company, which applies its own management and control.

Neil Tointon, Operations Director, Abbey Life

Like any other commercial decision, changes in the sourcing of services are fundamentally about balancing risk and benefits. With outsourcing decisions, it is crucial for the CEO to recognize that this momentous change has implications and ramifications far beyond the obvious effect on costs, headcount and processes.

We are not necessarily talking here about the ultimate risk that the deal will fail – although, as we will discuss, that must be allowed for. But even with a successful outsourcing programme it is important to take account of risks such as the possibility of internal tensions and misunderstandings, and the resulting impact on the external corporate image.

The surrounding stakeholder context

The implications of outsourcing range across all the various environmental factors that press in on the business. This in turn means that the board's risk assessment – and its communication of what is being done and why – must be holistic, covering all the organization's stakeholder groups and involving messages specifically tailored to each one. Where there is an immediate and compelling reason to accelerate and or extend externalization – the 'out' in outsourcing – then the speed of the preparations for implementing the decision will inevitably suffer.

But whatever the circumstances it is important that the board fully under-stands the risks that it introduces by speeding up the decision-making process. Specifically, it needs to recognize that the markets, institutional investors and significant shareholders increasingly hold the board respon-sible for any knee-jerk outsourcing actions, in precisely the same way as they would blame it for undertaking a rushed acquisition and failing to carry out sufficient due diligence. For a more in-depth discussion of the communica-tions issues surrounding a major outsourcing programme, turn to the specialist section on communications starting on page 168.

For companies contemplating outsourcing, the need to communicate with regulatory stakeholders is often a key focus, although the extent of this varies by industry. Financial services, a particularly hot area for outsourcing, is also highly regulated (see the box below on the IOSCO principles). While for some businesses outsourcing will require express regulatory and/or governmental permission and – especially if it is offshore – ongoing monitoring, all companies still have to ensure legislative compliance, ranging from employment law to new emissions regulations. Depending on the jurisdictions affected, there will also be a varying degree of need to deal with union issues, workers' councils and staff representative bodies.

Financial services: a sector under scrutiny

In February 2005 the technical committee of the International Organization of Securities Commissions (IOSCO) published its *Principles on Outsourcing of Financial Services for Market Intermediaries*. The document highlighted the perceived regulatory risks raised by outsourcing, together with principles for mitigating them. In the introduction to the document, IOSCO commented:

Outsourcing poses important challenges to the integrity and effectiveness of financial services regulatory systems. First, where outsourcing takes place by regulated entities, a firm's control over the people and processes dealing with the outsourced function may decrease. Nonetheless, regulators require that the outsourcing firm, including its board of directors and senior management, remain fully responsible (towards clients and regulatory authorities) for the out-sourced function, as if the service was being performed in-house. In some jurisdictions . . . regulators impose restrictions on the outsourcing of certain functions where they believe the outsourcing introduces an unacceptable risk or is critical to the function of an intermediary. Second, regulators expect that they will have complete access to books and records concerning an outsourc-ing firm's activities, even if such documents are in the custody of the firm's service provider. Regulators must also take account of possible operational and systemic risks that may exist in the event that multiple regulated entities use a common service provider.

The seven IOSCO principles to mitigate these risks were:

■ Principle 1: A company that is outsourcing should conduct suitable due diligence processes in selecting an appropriate outsourcing provider and in monitoring its ongoing performance.

■ Principle 2: There should be a legally binding written contract between the company that is outsourcing and each outsourcing provider, the nature and detail of which should be appropriate to the materiality of the outsourced activity to the ongoing business of the company.

■ Principle 3: The company should take appropriate measures to determine that:

(a) Procedures are in place to protect the company's proprietary and customer-related information and software; and

(b) Its outsourcing providers establish and maintain emergency procedures and a plan for disaster recovery, with periodic testing of backup facilities.

■ Principle 4: The company should take appropriate steps to require that outsourcing providers protect confidential information regarding its proprietary and other information, as well as the company's clients from intentional or inadvertent disclosure to unauthorized individuals.

■ Principle 5: Regulators should be cognizant of the risks posed where one outsourcing provider provides outsourcing services to multiple regulated entities.

■ Principle 6: Outsourcing with third party service providers should include contractual provisions relating to termination of the contract and appropriate exit strategies.

■ Principle 7: The regulator, the company that is outsourcing activities, and its auditors should have access to the books and records of outsourcing providers relating to those specific activities and the regulator should be able to obtain promptly, upon request, information concerning activities that are relevant to regulatory oversight.

Then there is the wider market audience of analysts and investors. Depending on how the company and its management are currently rated by the markets, this may actually be the most urgent stakeholder group to address – especially since they can regard even the slightest tweak in a declared strategy as either weak or inspirational. To help the analysts keep faith with the company, the CEO might put the message across by degrees, and strive to show that the board is progressively de-risking the future on many levels.

Communicating the nuts and bolts of the deal

This process of winning market buy-in may mean being transparent about the precise contractual obligations that the outsourcing provider is stepping up to, as well as the more obvious information released into the public domain. An equally important element is the joint endorsement of the agreement at CEO level or equivalent in both organizations. This public shouldering and sharing of responsibility for delivering the targeted benefits – and by extension for achieving the corporate strategy – can be especially influential among the investment community, who are pleased to see commitment on the part of a well-regarded outsourcing provider. Obviously such public endorsement does not happen very often, and getting the supplier to take part in it will depend on the size and importance of the deal.

At the same time, the CEO will come under quiet back-room pressure from institutional investors for ongoing, consistent and more detailed communication on the commercial logic, economic case and enablement implications that the relationship should open up over time. This enablement may include extending current products, lines of business and geographies, together with objectives such as shorter product development cycles, and reduced service development or manufacturing risk. An example is EDS's deal with the UK aero-engine maker Rolls-Royce, which is profiled in Chapter 6 on page 110. The timing of the deal quite literally saved the company at a time when competition and demand for aviation innovation was at a peak.

Finally, the press and public relations aspects must be managed to minimize the negative impact on reputation. It is too much to expect that most of the press would actually praise a business for implementing an outsourcing programme and cutting jobs. But a clear rationale will go a long way to make the coverage more positive, especially in the quality business press. You will need to display clear and detailed preparation, simple business objectives, the 'partner' selection logic and rigour, the supplier risk and commitment profile and finally and most importantly, the joint executive commitment.

Throughout all these stakeholder communications the focused thinking on objectives and implications, which we described in Chapter 1, starts to pay off by enabling the CEO to tell a clear and compelling story to each group. The CEO can show that all avenues and impacts have been investigated, demonstrate the single-mindedness with which the company is pursuing its objectives, and describe the operational flexibility afforded by the outsourcing supplier's capabilities, resources, Intellectual Property (IP) and geographic coverage. The stakeholder communications programme also provides a useful two-way channel, helping to build the company's understanding of the specific interests of the various groups whose opinions it needs to carry with the decision, and enabling it to fine-tune its messages accordingly.

Preparing for the exit before the start

A further key element of risk mitigation for the CEO is preparing for the exit before the contract starts. While it may seem a little overblown, the analogy between outsourcing and marriage does have a lot of mileage in it. Like a marriage, an outsourcing agreement is about intent, mutual commitment and respect as well as a shared vision. There is also – in most marriages and all outsourcing arrangements – an express intention and a process designed to produce progeny that are inherently smarter and/or stronger than their parents. So the company and its supplier are passing on their blended genes to the next generation of 'hybrid' company, which will in turn need to be fitter and more adaptable to the rigours of intensifying competitive pressures and advancing globalization.

As with a growing number of marriages, all this is set down in an ante-nuptial agreement which essentially states that if and when the relationship breaks up each party will leave with largely what it came in with, or be financially compensated – but that whatever progeny they have created together will be shared or stay with one or other parent in a predetermined way. For access to children when a marriage ends, read ownership of IP rights in outsourcing. The agreed arrangement on termination may be some form of ongoing joint ownership, or agreement on a price formula that will allow one party to buy the rights from the other.

Many companies are surprised by their suppliers' determination to benefit from the IP developed under their outsourcing partnership. Most businesses' assumption is that when they are paying an employee to develop IP, then all the resulting value belongs to the company – although this concept has been challenged legally in jurisdictions such as Japan and, to a lesser extent, Germany. Whatever the arguments in this regard, the fact is that outsourcing vendors perceive themselves as equal partners rather then employees of their clients, and are ready and willing to argue for their rights over the resulting IP.

Reasons to split

But why would a break-up come about? The varied risk factors surrounding a complex outsourcing deal mean there are various valid reasons why a split might occur either during or at the end of the agreement – not all of them related to performance against the contract.

Most obviously, both parties may be able to foresee a point at which the arrangement would draw to a natural close. This might be through a failure in the relationship, or a decision either to take the outsourced function(s) back into the business or to transfer them to a new partner, because of either shifts in customer requirements or changes on the supplier side. However, you should expect the supplier to feel slighted, as if facing an act of infidelity, and should therefore not be surprised to encounter emotional and irrational behaviour when you choose 'another'. All of these risks should be addressed during the wooing stage of preparation and due diligence, discussed and argued in the negotiations and mitigated in the final contract.

The changes on the supplier side that would trigger a split might involve shortcomings in resourcing, skills or delivery. But they could equally result from a material transfer in ownership of the supplier's business. The rumours that fly around the outsourcing industry frequently include possible exits and consolidation involving one or more major providers. This means a company may find its outsourcing agreement suddenly switches to a supplier with which it does not want to work, or even one that it regards as a competitor. So one of the clauses enabling the customer to extricate itself from the contract should be triggered in the case of a change in beneficial ownership of the provider.

Detailed risk factors: into the schedules

The precise process and formula by which the split will happen should be covered in the contract, together with other issues such as how the associated costs will change as the service grows or shrinks. These factors can be handled as part of managing the contract schedules, which should be renewed on an annual basis. Typically the schedules will define the service and how it will be paid for, and commit the customer to repay unrecovered capital costs in the event of termination – essentially an agreement along the lines of: 'We will pay back the $25 million you have just spent on our network, minus appropriate depreciation.'

A further factor commonly covered in the contract schedules is the issue of manning levels. Imagine a customer whose outsourcing supplier has committed to provide an IT helpdesk with 22 seats. However, the vendor subsequently consolidates its helpdesks to realize economies of scale, so the same facility is now providing a similar service to other clients. The service is satisfactory – but it then emerges that the consolidated helpdesk only has 18 seats, even though the contract still says 22, and what is more it is servicing other clients as well. This type of situation can – and frequently does – result in damaging and largely fruitless circular arguments. The solution is to require the supplier to disclose and verify the manning levels on an annual basis in the schedules to the contract, thereby maintaining transparency and giving grounds for negotiations on pricing.

This formulaic approach using annual updates brings risk mitigation benefits both operationally and financially. It maintains visibility and transparency on how the agreement is actually operating now – not how it was intended to operate when the deal was signed four years ago. It also means that at any point in time it should be possible to estimate the total costs of termination within a margin of plus or minus 10 per cent on either side. Failure to monitor and update your understanding of the running costs, applied resources, capital investment and its associated life cycle and treatment as a deployed asset (dedicated or shared) will cause problems later. There is no excuse for failing to monitor and understand virtually every aspect of your service and potential future liabilities.

Protecting intellectual property

Where a divorce situation looms in an outsourcing relationship – especially when it emerges rapidly or unexpectedly – experience shows that the key element the CEO should watch out for is the ownership of jointly developed applications and other intellectual assets and tools. These are the most common thing to slip through the net, and commercially the most contentious.

The major risk factor lies in the tendency for development people on both sides to get lazy and overly comfortable as an outsourcing contract rolls along. For example, after three years of the agreement they might start to cooperate on something that was never envisaged in the original scope of the agreement – and nobody ever quite gets round to adding it to the terms and conditions. This is despite the fact that the governance arrangements specify that any developments not incorporated into the original contract must be recorded in a detailed formal schedule.

This schedule generally covers eight or ten repetitive but critical facts about the new application under development. The most important is the question of whether it is being developed exclusively for the client company (so the client will own it); whether it is being developed jointly by the provider and client, so it cannot be marketed as a package by either side without the express permission of the other; or whether it is being developed solely by the provider with a view to rolling it out among other clients later on. Failure to nail down these types of detail at the time an application is being developed can cause major problems if a break-up occurs.

Managing multiple suppliers: 'best of breed'

In addition to the risks inherent in managing each individual outsourcing contract and relationship, many companies choose to create a range of niche outsourcing deals with different specialist providers. This adds a further level of complexity and risk that has to be managed and mitigated.

One prevalent approach to managing multiple suppliers is Pareto Optimality, named after the Italian economist Vilfredo Pareto. In simple terms, Pareto Optimality is a measure of efficiency based on the premise that whatever outcome arises, there is no other outcome that will leave every participant at least as well off and at least one player strictly better off. So a Pareto Optimal outcome cannot be improved upon without hurting at least one player. This means it forms a sound basis for managing the interests of multiple suppliers.

While such mathematical constructs may be best left to the CFO and risk management department, what may concern the CEO more immediately is finding the optimal way to deploy a range of 'best of breed' suppliers for various elements of an outsourcing-based solution. These providers, also commonly termed 'suppliers of choice', have a detailed understanding of all aspects of delivering the service for which they are brought in. Recognizing that there are outstanding specialists in some areas or business functions, the CEO and board may choose not to go with a single major supplier, and instead go direct to specialists to achieve greater competitive edge, more accountability (especially in relation to innovation), and encourage some form of competitive spirit between suppliers. This may extend to a 'framework agreement' under which competing suppliers pitch for the right to provide the business units with the same type of service, and then fight it out between them for market share within the enterprise.

A word of caution – best of breed is inherently more expensive to manage, in particular, where too little time is spent ensuring the 'grey' areas of responsibility are clarified. Despite the best of efforts, suppliers will always claim their competitor is liable when problems arise. So it is an absolute necessity for the client to establish strong (though not overly rigid) management, governance and reporting structures. Those that successfully apply these attributes can continue to reap the benefits, despite confrontations between outsourcing suppliers. In the JP Morgan case study on page 207, the company's realization of benefits from its best of breed deals was largely unaffected when one of them (Accenture) launched legal proceedings against another (CSC).

Defining the interconnects

As such experiences show, a best of breed approach brings major implications for how outsourcing is managed – with the main issues often focusing less on the suppliers themselves than on the interconnects and possible gaps between them. Where a company is managing its own best of breed strategy, each supplier must support best practice not only in the service or function it provides, but also in the way it interacts with the others at various junction-points. This means that the 'stove pipe' of who is responsible for what has to be defined very clearly and explicitly to avoid grey areas, misunderstandings or uncertainties.

A classic example of this might occur where the corporate network is outsourced to one supplier and the desktop to another. The network supplier will say that its responsibility ends at the wall, while the desktop supplier's responsibility starts at the desk. That seems clear enough. But between the two there are elements including cables, modems and switching devices, quite probably involving a mixture of different kit built up over the years. What happens when these pieces of equipment malfunction or need to be upgraded because of enhancements elsewhere? The network and desktop providers will point to one other. This might seem an obvious pitfall – but that does not mean it will not happen.

The complexities involved in managing multiple suppliers of choice mean that the ability to write contracts which keep the corporate stove pipe free of blockages or gaps is an important skill (see our specialist section on legal issues on page 164). This is not easy – and it is an area where expert independent advice should pay dividends. Equally importantly, the governance and reporting around the contracts must be capable of giving the CEO an all-round view of overall and individual performance. Where there are four or five providers all striving to prove that an unscheduled outage was someone else's fault, that they are the most innovative of all the company's suppliers, and that they should be allowed to replace a particular piece of proprietary software, the management challenges start to spiral upwards.

The prime contractor route

In projects aimed at transformation of an entire company, the proliferation of interconnections in a supply chain involving multiple suppliers can become more than a management overhead. In the worst cases, turf wars and disconnects between suppliers have actually caused transformation projects to collapse by undermining morale and destroying the crucial relationships between the suppliers, and then between each of the suppliers and the customer.

One way that a company looking to initiate a transformation project can mitigate these risks – or at least shift them down the chain – is by engaging a 'prime contractor' responsible for both delivering the project and managing the third-party relationships needed to do so. In a prime contractor arrangement, the client company engages one major provider, with whom it is then able to discuss and influence which specialist suppliers should come on board to help achieve the targeted objectives. However, while the selection process is consultative, the management of this web of relationships is the sole responsibility of the prime contractor, who should be capable of bringing to bear the resources and understanding necessary to assess and mitigate the risks involved.

This contrasts with a 'single supplier' approach, where decisions to subcontract parts of the project are taken by the supplier with no reference to the client. All that matters in terms of the customer contract is that the project is delivered as agreed, and it is up to the supplier to work out the best way to do this. A 'best of breed' approach is effectively made up of a series of 'single source' supplier arrangements, with each separate relationship managed internally by the company.

The prime contractor's role is akin to that of a service integrator, and it is no coincidence that the same organizations tend to fulfil these two roles. From before the project starts, a prime contractor will be discussing the client's concerns and preferences in terms of specialist best of breed suppliers, and trying to integrate these into the ideal solution. Clearly, this service comes at a price. And where a niche supplier fails to deliver, or gaps appear in the stove pipe, the responsibility is more shared between the customer and prime contractor than would be the case in a single source arrangement (where it would tend to be down to the sole supplier), or in an internally managed best of breed approach (where it would be mainly down to the customer's own contract management). Again, it is hard to overstate the value that informed independent advice can deliver in terms of balancing and managing the inherent risks in all these approaches.

Thinking the unthinkable: coping with meltdown

Even in relatively simple cases, outsourcing involves a mesh of interrelated risks. There is: the assessment and preparation of the internal function; the choice of suppliers; the risk mitigation considerations of multiple providers and influencers, and of the people who are influenced in turn by the decision to outsource. Given all these factors, the CEO has to face up to the unthinkable: the whole initiative could go into meltdown.

While it will probably never happen, it is important to be as prepared as possible to handle this eventuality. It could come about in a number of ways. In a regulated environment, a fraud might be committed in an outsourced function, leaving it unclear whether outsourced or in-house staff were responsible. Either way, the company finds itself the subject of a 'strike team' from the Securities and Exchange Commission (SEC) or the national regulator in the particular jurisdiction – leaving the client (and possibly the outsourcing provider) with a regulatory headache, and a need to repair severe damage to its reputation and share price.

For the CEO, it is important to remember that the outsourcing supplier's good name is also on the line. In such circumstances both parties need to unite behind a common front, bringing the strength and depth of their relationship to the fore. To prepare for this eventuality, meltdown scenarios should be discussed, and general responses laid out, at the start of the agreement – despite the fact that both sides know their deal may well not survive such a crisis.

In a strategic outsourcing agreement, the fact that both parties will win or lose together can serve to strengthen the relationship. This awareness can help to sustain mutual openness, joint cooperation with regulatory bodies, and commitment to a shared disaster policy that will be invoked should the need arise. This may well include the creation of a single point of contact for enquiries and announcements, and the leadership of both companies standing literally shoulder to shoulder to face the press and other stakeholders.

Risk questions for suppliers

To a large extent, risk mitigation for CEOs contemplating outsourcing is a matter of knowing the right questions to ask at the start – before the answers that you never asked for come back to haunt you. A good first step is to sit down with the potential outsourcing providers and ask these questions of each of them up front:

- Do the suppliers have genuine intimacy with and understanding of my industry, the application, operation or service?
- Have they travelled this route before (especially their board members)?
- If they have not, do they have the knowledge and scale to bring in whatever resources and subcontractors are needed to deliver the value?
- Can we check the suppliers' client references personally? Can we conduct executive-on-executive (CEO on CEO, CFO on CFO) referencing, followed by a more operational review (CIO on CIO)?
- Why are some clients not referenced?
- Can we also check at least one client that has discontinued its service from the supplier? This would involve asking about the approach adopted, unresolved issues, unexpected costs, handling of IP ownership, and so on.
- Does the supplier believe and trust the industry benchmark data that is generally available? Does it have reliable and transparent internal cost data? Will it abide by it?
- How will the supplier address the wider environment:
  - regulators
  - unions and staff
  - analysts
  - stakeholder pressures (environmental/ethical lobby, suppliers, clients)?
- How will it manage technology change and provide innovation?
- What would its approach be to a reputational or regulatory meltdown?

These questions can be posed by the CEO directly, or by an intermediary. Either way they will give a good initial feeling for the risk factors likely to be involved in the relationship – and lay down a bedrock for the more detailed due diligence to follow.

Onshore or offshore: risk or economics?

It seems that no debate over risk in outsourcing would be complete without a discussion of offshoring. The move towards locating processing and operations in offshore locations has been one of the most dramatic shifts of recent years, driven – initially at least – by the opportunity to exploit wage arbitrage in countries such as India and thereby reduce costs. Offshoring is now so pervasive that a company looking at outsourcing will almost inevitably find that offshore resources and facilities are put on the table either by its peer group or by prospective suppliers.

One of the most vexed and hotly debated issues in the outsourcing arena is the relationship between risk and going offshore. In our view, this whole area is best approached from the CEO's standpoint by switching the focus from risk to *economics*. By requiring an onshore supplier to apply offshore economics to a certain proportion of the contract irrespective of where it intends to place the workload, a client can shift the risk element on to the provider – thereby ensuring that the entity best positioned and qualified to assess and mitigate the risks of going offshore is the one that does so.

That said, the recent backlash against offshoring, focused especially on criticism of its use in functions interacting directly with the customer, has positioned reputational risk as a balancing factor against the compelling economic case for offshoring. At the same time spasmodic public and political pressures have prompted some companies to state that they will not offshore any functions, while others are seeking to make capital by saying they will not offshore customer contact or call centres. These promises are essentially aimed at generating a marketing edge. But they do reflect deeper issues and risks.

Not a case of all or nothing

The key for a CEO approaching the possibility of offshoring is not to be pressured into believing that this is a black-and-white, all-or-nothing decision – or indeed that it is entirely down to the company. The risks involved in accessing lower-wage locations can be mitigated in two main ways:

1   *Nearshore capabilities*: A number of 'nearshore' centres are now developing rapidly, including – in a European context – the Iberian peninsula (predominantly Spain), and the recent EU accession states in central and eastern Europe. These centres are seeing heavy investment as they seek to compete with established nearshore locations within the EU such as Dublin, and offshore players such as India, China, the Philippines and Malaysia. The emerging EU-based nearshore locations have the advantages of being inherently multilingual and relatively low cost, and of falling within the EU's laws in areas such as data protection.

2   *Imposing a sliding scale of offshore usage*: CEOs and boards should look at the pressure for outsourcing in the context of the overall objectives of the deal rather than making specific decisions on locations. As with decisions on second-tier suppliers in a prime contractor relationship, decisions on locations can be left to the outsourcing provider. To do this, customers should look to sign deals where they dictate to the supplier that a percentage of workload will have 'offshore economics' applied to it, leaving the supplier to decide whether it will actually do it offshore or not. This proportion might typically start at 25 per cent in year one, building up to 50 per cent by year four of a five-year contract. Such an arrangement gives the company exposure to offshore cost benefits in a controlled way, while also defusing the emotions over the offshoring issue.

As the offshore outsourcing industry has grown up, so have two popular misconceptions about offshoring. One is that offshore is inherently more risky in every way than onshore, which is not the case – think, for example, of the likelihood of disruption by labour disputes in India compared to Europe. The other misconception is that offshoring and outsourcing are closely related, when in fact they are two very different concepts that can sometimes be used in combination. Most of the processing industry in India still consists of in-house 'captive' operations owned by the businesses that use them.

Offshore providers' onshore presence

Looking forward, whatever the scale of the current backlash against offshoring, there is little doubt that offshoring itself will continue to grow. Given the caution among North American and European customers, offshore players based in locations such as India have responded by setting up local offices and presences in their key western markets, enabling their clients there to see programming and development going on onshore. They are also keen to stress that certain elements of projects will be handled within the client's own onshore jurisdiction.

At the same time, the major western outsourcing providers such as IBM, EDS and Accenture are building up their operations in India and other offshore centres, from Mauritius to China to the Czech Republic. So despite anti-offshoring sentiment in the west, and rapid wage inflation and high staff attrition rates in places such as India, it looks as though the offshore option will keep expanding. Certainly the expectation in India is for growth of 30 per cent or more to continue for the next three years.

The fact that offshoring is not an all-or-nothing decision, but a strategic refinement of a company's sourcing strategy, is underlined by our case study on GE Capital International Services (GECIS) on page 190. GE initially became one of the first multinational companies to shift its back office processing, data centre and call centre operations to India in 1997 through the creation of GECIS as a captive operation. Seven years later, GE decided that selling off most of GECIS would enable GE to continue to receive the same best of breed services on an outsourced basis, while also releasing valuable funds for investment in other ventures and development, and allowing GECIS to compete successfully in the wider market.

GE's establishment of GECIS, followed by a period of management and ultimately majority divestment, reflects a life cycle that may provide a template for future offshore operations. The GECIS experience contrasts sharply with Shell's approach to its Houston-based processing centre, which it decided to keep in-house as a captive operation.

Key CEO and CFO questions arising from Chapter 2

CEO

■ Are you prepared and able to stand behind your outsourcing strategy with explicit, accountable and highly public personal backing of the deal now and into the future, both reporting on and managing expectations in the face of intense stakeholder interest, keen media and market scrutiny?

■ Have you planned – and made time and resources available for – clear and consistent communications aimed at all internal and external stake-holders on the reasons for and the implications of outsourcing, ranging from unions and staff to regulators, clients, analysts and significant share-holders?

■ While the risks inherent in the outsourcing deal will be mitigated through the assets, resources and experience of the supplier(s), risks will inevitably still exist – so have you identified them, decided how you will exploit and work within the risk buffers that you will acquire?

CFO

■ Have you reduced the financial and investment risk, and thereby aided reporting, by examining and exploiting the potential for fiscal flexibility within the terms of the outsourcing contract to avoid or reduce capital expenditure, contain discretionary spend in absolute terms, dispose of assets, and even securitize some aspects?

■ Have you examined the inherent cost and risk profile of using a single 'holistic' or multiple 'best in breed' supplier option?

■ As with M&A activities, are you ready and able to articulate to share-price-influencing groups the strong benefits and synergies of any out-sourcing agreement versus the risks, and are you committed to continue doing so – potentially in adverse circumstances – for several years to come?

3

Clear shared value

Coming together is a beginning; keeping together is progress; working together is success.

Henry Ford

Having decided that outsourcing offers a way to achieve the company's strategic objectives, there are two ways in which the CEO might approach the deal.

One is to regard outsourcing as a pure procurement play, and to try to use it as a means of *extracting* the maximum value from the market. The other is to use outsourcing as a way of *creating* value in a sustainable way. This involves an implicit acceptance that the outsourcing arrangement will only succeed if it creates value for the outsourcing provider as well, by striking a fair and equitable balance between the benefits achieved on each side.

Each of these approaches has its own pros and cons depending on the precise circumstances, and both are frequently seen in today's outsourcing marketplace. But experience shows that the most successful outsourcing relationships are those where the deal is designed to ensure both parties win. And it is no coincidence that many – though certainly not all – third-party outsourcing advisers apply a philosophy focused on bringing the two parties to a point where they both enjoy a win/win, without a disproportionate amount of value being realized on either side.

A 'free trade' model – or protectionism?

This philosophy is akin to the notion of free trade – which aims to be fair to everybody – as opposed to a protectionist approach under which one side seeks to extract the lion's share of the value on offer. And, as in the international trade arena, while protectionism may appear to deliver short-term benefits there is invariably a price to be paid.

This price is all the higher, in both outsourcing and trade, when you look beyond the one-off deal to consider a longer-term relationship. If a company's approach to outsourcing is to systematically auction off pieces of its business to the highest bidder or the lowest-cost provider, the market will fairly quickly recognize this behaviour and act in the same short-termist manner.

As a result, higher-quality outsourcing providers may decide to drop out of the bidding, since they will have little enthusiasm for entering a process from which they have little prospect of making a reasonable return. And even where bidders do take part in the auction, they will probably incorporate a premium to offset the higher level of risk implicit in the customer's focus on getting the best price.

Achieving a win/win

This underlying clash of philosophies between value extraction and shared value creation is a constant theme of the outsourcing market – and a drive by one side or the other to extract an unreasonable amount of value can be found at the root of most failed outsourcing deals. Table 3.1 illustrates the matrix of outsourcing outcomes in various real-world projects, ranging from a win/win in which both sides realize equitable value, to a lose/lose in which value is actively destroyed for both parties. Also, most of the win/lose (customer wins, outsourcer loses out) and lose/win (customer loses out, outsourcer wins) deals finally end up as lose/lose scenarios – although it may take longer for it to become clear whose shareholders are the bigger victims.

Our experience confirms that if the prospective customer in an outsourcing decides to extract an inequitable proportion of the overall value, and tries to do so via a contract with a high-quality outsourcing provider, then the deal will simply not get done on that basis. This is largely because, between the time when the deal is first struck and finally documented, the supplier's legal and risk management teams will use the contract process to narrow the scope and build in economic or delivery buffers to improve the deal from the provider's side.

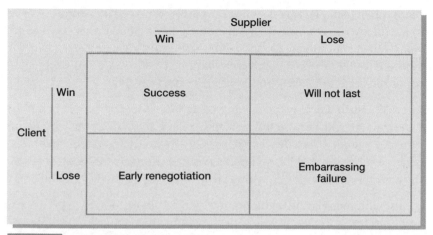

Figure 3.1 **From win/win to lose/lose**

This in turn leads to a drawn-out process in which the negotiations run on for months, soak up a tremendous amount of effort and energy, and all too often end up with no agreement at all to show for it. For the parties to the deal, this is not just a matter of wasted time. Even worse from the customer CEO's viewpoint is the fact that his or her own attempt to force out as much value as possible has resulted in the targeted benefits of outsourcing being pushed back into the future – and possibly never realized at all. However, even this eventuality may be better than the long-term price of entering an unbalanced deal that ultimately collapses because of the strains caused by uneven distribution of benefits between the parties.

Building on trust through shared expectations and objectives

The key to avoiding these pitfalls is for both sides to accept that trusting the other side does not mean being taken for a ride. Again, the analogy of marriage is hard to avoid. What is needed is a clear understanding of the benchmarked value, of how each side is contributing to the relationship for the resulting benefit, and of the fact that if there is a delay or problem the pain will be shared.

What is also needed is a desire to make continuous improvements to the relationship. There should be incentives for the outsourcing provider to deliver services above the contracted level or to achieve an accelerated delivery schedule, accompanied by a genuine commitment from the customer to honour these incentives when they are triggered. This can set the stage for really effective partnering benefiting both sides.

But if it is this simple, why does outsourcing not succeed more often? We are in a world where almost half of outsourcing deals fail to create the targeted value – a recent estimate for the failure rate was 43 per cent. So a win/win agreement that demonstrably works should provide some sort of template for future deals, and a beacon for others to navigate by.

Internally, such a deal will be perceived as success by the people behind it. Externally, it will be a highly referenceable account for the outsourcing provider, a point of excellence that will help to attract and retain talent. This means a successful deal has secondary positive effects that ultimately benefit the customer still further, creating a virtuous circle of shared cause and effect.

For the customer, getting to this point requires a serious long-term perspective and a readiness to look beyond price. A company looking to run a straight auction for an outsourcing deal will end up with what it is willing to pay for – the cheapest option – and will find that the providers most capable of delivering long-term value are the most likely to walk away from such a contest. At the other extreme, the degree of shared interest between the customer and outsourcing provider may be such that they decide to pool their capabilities in a joint venture, and take the value proposition out to market.

One of the most ambitious and high-profile examples of this type of outsourced joint venturing occurred in 2000, when BT and Accenture teamed up to create e-peopleserve, a 50/50 joint venture designed to provide HR services to both joint venture partners and to the wider market (see the case study on page 212). The journey of e-peopleserve from in-house HR operation to joint venture outsourcing provider before finally – following BT's sale of its stake – metamorphosing into Accenture HR Services is a classic outsourcing life cycle. It reflects not only the potential of outsourcing, but also the hiccups and disappointments that can occur along the way, especially when trying to sell a relatively new BPO concept to a cautious corporate marketplace. With BT's renewal of its HR outsourcing contract with Accenture for ten years from 2005, there is a real sense that both sides have ultimately got what they wanted and needed – but that they needed to go through the e-peopleserve life cycle to get there.

The root causes of loss

So e-peopleserve effectively ended up as a win/win. But, in our experience, what factors do we think would tend to drive either customers or suppliers into the 'lose' category? In the case of an IT outsourcing programme, this can go back to the CEO and board's historical perception of their in-house IT organization, and of what long-term value, if any, this organization is delivering to the business as a whole. Depending on the circumstances, the sourcing of IT may be regarded as anything from a core source of competitive advantage to a commoditized procurement play offering little incremental value.

For the CEO, the difference is crystallized by answering one fundamental question: 'What is the underlying stimulus and rationale for outsourcing?' If it is purely economic, you are essentially looking to get the same service at lower cost – in which case it is a price-based procurement play. This is not a problem in itself, but you must be aware of the implications of taking this approach, not the least of which is the risk of creating a misalignment between the outsourced IT organization and the business.

On the other hand, the answer to the question may be that you are looking to use a third party to change your business, and to enable it to do things better and differently, with price being a secondary consideration. This is a transformational play. Experience shows that this is the more likely starting point for a win/win.

Staying in line

A further point to bear in mind is that the risk of severe misalignment resulting from a procurement-type, cost-based outsourcing strategy is currently increasing due to changes in corporate preoccupations. In general, the corporate focus tends to swing between cost reduction and value creation in line with economic cycles. At the time of writing, value creation appears to be in the ascendancy. Recent surveys show that 80 per cent of CEOs are now focused on building incremental value, against 20 per cent still focused predominantly on cutting costs.

The problem is that an outsourcing programme undertaken on a procurement/ cost rationale at a time when the focus is switching towards building revenues can give rise to particular stresses and strains within an organization. The procurement agenda may well result in the business getting the low-cost deal it was seeking. But as soon as a situation arises where incremental revenue is available at some additional cost the result is gridlock, because two different parts of the business find themselves looking in different directions. The outsourcing provider gets stuck between the two agendas, and finds itself getting blamed for not supporting the business's strategic 'direction' as fully as it should.

Avoiding this situation comes down to our starting point for successful outsourcing: an unequivocal statement of objectives up front. 'So let's be clear,' says the chairman or CEO. 'With this outsourcing transaction, are we really trying to cut costs or enable our business? Are we trying to spend less money going forward, or to create a platform to make our business more flexible and more competitive in the long term?' Once the answer is agreed, the board must write it down – and stick to it.

Avoiding 'contract squeeze'

A further characteristic of a procurement play is that it tends to lead to a much more restrictive contract. We are in a fast-changing world, with globalization challenges and pressures intensifying by the day. In such an environment, the authors certainly do not believe that a rigid, contract-driven transaction is the type of deal that businesses – or indeed outsourcing providers – should be looking to do.

The behaviour generated by the resulting construct is that whenever an event or problem occurs, both parties' first reaction is to focus on what the contract says, rather than on establishing what the right course of action is on each side.

Over time this leads to destructive behaviour, with both parties looking for how they can shift blame elsewhere, 'get away' with things, and increase their own margin at the expense of the other side. It becomes all too easy to forget that the greatest value for each party would lie in cooperating proactively, sharing pain and doing what needs to be done straight away.

Understanding success . . .

What this boils down to is a need for both sides to come together to visualize and agree on what success looks like from the start – and then focus jointly on achieving it. Time and again during outsourcing projects, we ask CEOs and boards: 'What *is* it that you want to achieve? Tell me. And if you do tell me, I'll write it down and keep it.' Then, for months or even years after that, this stated vision of success can be presented back to the executive team to anchor their focus on the original objectives, or confirm that those objectives really are shifting.

This is necessary because of a natural drift that exists in any outsourcing transaction. At some point in any deal, even if it delivers value, somebody somewhere – usually, but not always, in the customer organization – is going to try and improve on it. Unless the other party is armed with a clear and agreed definition of the original intent behind the deal, then there will be a drift in the objectives, disagreements will begin to spring up, and trust between the two sides will be damaged.

An approach that is sometimes used to inject this type of discipline is that a senior executive from one side withdraws from the day-to-day negotiations or the operation of the agreement, but keeps a close eye on its alignment with the initial aims. When the objectives start to drift, that individual can then step into the relationship and reaffirm the original objectives by 'slapping wrists' on either side.

. . . and not overselling it

Deal-damaging drift can also occur on the supplier's side. One old trick that is now widely discredited – but that is still attempted by some providers – is where the supplier's sales team goes in and wins agreement in principle by overselling the deal in terms of its costs and benefits. They then leave it to their own negotiating and legal teams to backtrack on those promises and win back concessions.

This is not only an unethical way to conduct any business deal, forming a poor starting point for any long-term relationship based on mutual trust. It is also an approach that will delay the transaction, probably by several months – representing time during which the supplier is not receiving the revenue from the outsourcing programme, and the customer is missing out on the cost and value benefits within its own business. It is an interesting fact that while a three-month delay is actually a massive cost to both sides, nobody is usually held accountable for this lost value.

With this in mind, both sides should resist the temptation to strike postures and slip into negotiating 'roles', since the overall effect will be to prolong the entire process. Instead, a sense of urgency is a commercial imperative, underpinned by a genuine willingness to push the transaction forward and bring the benefits to bear as soon as is reasonably possible.

It is usually quite easy to spot the likely areas where people will drag their feet during the negotiations in an attempt to try and extract value. Typically, where the deal involves a discrete and well-defined service, people will start to adopt bargaining positions and play games around a lot of subsidiary issues and price. Where the price is effectively a given and the service less clearly defined, they will use stalling tactics around the service, hoping to capitalize on the other side's eagerness to do the deal.

Poor service design: the system adjusts

When time wasting and stalling tactics are games being employed by either side around the service scope and design, one factor to be aware of is that the service model ultimately agreed must appear logical and practicable to the user. If value is created by either party for no tangible benefit to the other, or it simply makes life more difficult for the internal customer, then the system within the organization will adjust to negate or bypass that part of the process.

Here is a simple example. An international consultancy told the staff in its New York office that it would end its outsourced car service and get them to take taxis. However, it seems the people taking this decision had never tried to get a cab at 11pm in New York during a downpour. And consultants in the firm not only needed to get cabs for themselves, but also wanted to ensure their secretaries got home safely after working late.

So the system adjusted. Staff began calling the old outsourced car service direct, paying via cash or company card, and charging the fares back to the firm as expenses. Within days the car service was effectively back, but at a far higher cost to the business owing to the lack of the old corporate volume discount. Within two months the outsourcing deal had to be revived.

For another example, think of the many companies that try to make their people travel economy class on flights as part of a travel sourcing policy. The loss of fast-track business-class boarding can mean an executive having to check in an hour earlier to save a few dollars – something which, in practical terms, simply is not going to happen. No matter how tight the time pressure may appear, it is crucial not to agree to processes and restrictions that do not stand up to common sense. These will fail, taking a good deal of internal customer goodwill with them.

Where has that 'A' team gone?

There is also a variation on the overselling tactic that customers should watch out for. This is where the provider uses a hit squad of highly impressive individuals to clinch the deal – and then the customer never sees them again, because they have moved on to the next pitch.

This is how it works. The outsourcing supplier starts by sending in a team of engaging, interesting and hugely able people to discuss the planned outsourcing programme. They talk big value creation and build a relationship – golf, wine, private jets, theatre tickets. Soon they have seen off the competition and clinched an agreement in principle. The customer signs a letter of intent and makes a public announcement. Then the original team suddenly disappears, and the supplier sends in the 'B team' – whose initial negotiating position is: 'You thought we would deliver this service for that price? Sorry, you seem to have misunderstood.'

Surely, you might think, nobody would fall for this. But it can happen. The customer CEO finds him- or herself in a position where the winning supplier's 'A' team – and its competitors – has gone away, and the 'B' team is now there to renegotiate the whole deal painstakingly from scratch. Even worse, the company has announced the agreement and cannot rescind it without losing face.

The CEO feels locked into a deal that he or she feels has been hijacked. The company's lawyers begin to object to clauses in the proposed contract, saying they cannot authorize the client to sign it. At this point, it takes a tremendous amount of courage for the board to scrap the whole deal and start again – but that may actually be the best option at the time.

Getting it in black and white

An even better option is not to get into such a position in the first place. Before a customer announces anything regarding an outsourcing programme, it should ensure it has a solid term sheet with the key principles of the transaction set out in black and white – fully agreed, understood and signed. This should include who the key individuals are, how long they will be on board, and what they will be doing.

This is also good practice for suppliers. Customers are equally adept at shifting the goalposts after a deal has been announced by throwing new risks on to the table. This is before you get to discussing the detail of the workflow, where honestly different interpretations can arise. In either case, prior agreement on the key principles will be a valuable asset.

However, the primary cause of major disconnects in outsourcing deals is still the break-point where the baton is passed from the sales team to the negotiation team. If there is no single, consistent team in charge from sales through negotiation to delivery, an environment will be created in which the same issues are discussed time and again, making it virtually inevitable that some points will be renegotiated. This repeated revisiting of issues that appeared to have been closed will fundamentally affect the relationship.

The value of consistency

Ultimately it is down to the customer to ensure that this problem is avoided, by looking ahead and getting an explicit agreement that the supplier's team will remain in place to do and execute the deal. Historically, customers have applied surprisingly little sophistication to the issue of why people behave in a particular way during the sales and negotiation process. Basic behavioural traits – such as the B team's consistent backtracking on the A team's pledges – tend to get masked by the complexity of the whole exercise. And it can be further complicated by the presence of subcontractors, who in turn play negotiating games between themselves and with the prime contractor.

The complexities of contractor/subcontractor relationships also have ramifications for suppliers. On some deals there have been lawsuits flying around between the subcontractors and prime contractor – a development that inevitably has the effect of hurting the client. Imagine, as an outsourcing customer, coming to work one day and finding that your two main outsourcing contractors are suing one another. This has happened before, and will probably do so again.

It is impossible for customers to guard completely against this type of eventuality. But a good first step is for the customer to demand that the same individuals stay engaged with the project throughout. This will give stability and real shared ownership that the solution sold, the solution contracted and the solution delivered will all be the same, and will involve – for at least the whole of the first year – the same people.

Given this sort of stability the whole hybrid team can sit down together and write on a single sheet of paper what 'success' would look like a year from now. Then they can each sign it at the bottom. For one member, it may be that the customer and provider are enjoying a good working relationship. For another, it may be that both teams are proud of what they have achieved. For others, it may be cost savings or revenue gains. What the exercise will do is build in a basis of consistency of objectives, and ensure that any drift is explicit and clear to everyone.

Procurement v. relationship building

As the two parties seek a way to create shared value on this basis, they face a constant tension between immediate procurement pressures and the longer-term development of the relationship. Crucially, they should avoid making (or agreeing to) the type of excessive procurement demands that will doom the contract.

In this context, one technique that buyers often try to use is to run an auction among their suppliers. This may be appropriate where the outsourcing programme is focused on extremely well-defined, standardized and processing-intensive areas such as payroll. But where wider transformational change or customer-facing processes are on the agenda the risks are several magnitudes greater, and running an auction is nothing short of crazy.

An individual needing an operation – be it a nose job or heart surgery – would hardly run an auction among the available surgeons to see who got the job. Yet companies continue to seek the best price for critical surgery to their business. It is genuinely astounding how often companies will take these decisions without paying close attention and scrutiny to the relevant track records of the providers.

The underlying reason for this is that the process is often driven by procurement people with a costs-focused mindset and a weakness for 'buying a story' from the supplier on the basis of a slick PowerPoint deck. Pitches based on statements such as 'It's do-able . . . sure, we can do that . . . we have seen it done' should simply not be taken at face value. The customer CEO's immediate response should be: 'When, where and how have you done this before, and can we talk to the client?'

Third-party coaching: extracting value – or destroying it?

Coaching by third-party advisers can also affect the value basis of a deal. Specialist intermediaries face a fundamental question about their role. Are they focused on extracting value, always looking to secure an outsourcing agreement for the client for the best possible price? Or are they genuine 'sourcing' advisers, looking across the range of options – in-house, outsourced, joint venture, insourced – to find the best unique solution for that particular client, and then advising on the best long-term way of achieving it?

The answer to this question can have a major impact on the quest for shared, equitable value in deals where third-party advisers are involved. And the approach to sharing value varies from intermediary to intermediary.

Some operate on a template-based model focused narrowly on organizing and running outsourcing auctions, and on screwing suppliers down on price – sometimes by using detailed multi-contract information from other bids in which they have been involved. Others take a genuinely independent approach, advising customers openly on all the options and then – where outsourcing is appropriate – using industry benchmarks to help both sides reach a fair and sustainable division of value.

In some cases we have seen, intermediaries focused purely on extracting value can actually damage their client's long-term interests, and effectively undermine the whole deal, by coaching the buyer to make unreasonable demands on the outsourcing suppliers. Sometimes deals get done on this basis, and they are invariably bad deals as a result. So this is not only a problem that suppliers need to watch out for, but customers too.

Pre-negotiation workshops

The way to avoid this type of issue is to choose intermediaries carefully on their track record of successful (rather than low-cost) projects, and make sure that the two sides – plus any advisers – have a clear view on a 'surface' of fair and executable outcomes.

To lay down this groundwork, a workshop of senior executives from all sides should be held early on in the process. The key is to develop a value platform to build on – a construct that is not quite contractual but that is 95 per cent of the way there. Crucially, this platform should be sufficiently well defined that the CEO could present it to the board at that point as an explanation of the deal, how it would work, what the risks are, and where and by whom value would be realized.

For example, in an infrastructure outsourcing programme, this agreement would deal with issues such as whether the supplier will buy the customer's assets, who will pay for redundancies, and how VAT will be handled. While the finer details may change, the basic model is agreed. Other elements that will be agreed at this stage – reflecting the need we have already stressed for consistency of personnel – include who is going to stay on the project and for how long; how disputes will be resolved; the governance model; and the degree of oversight and reporting to the CEO and board.

Creating this common understanding between buyer and seller is an area where genuinely independent third-party advisers can play an especially valuable role, by facilitating the workshop, ensuring all the key issues are addressed, and giving their client guidance on what is reasonable and sustainable in practice. Some issues may be 'parked' – but at least everyone knows they have been parked. Having all the important framework elements agreed *before* final negotiations begin helps to maintain the deal's momentum and avoid time-consuming disagreements at a later stage. And if the workshop cannot reach agreement then at least everyone has found out the deal is a non-starter before the costs really start to mount and before any public announcements are made.

Evaluating the business case through M&A principles

As well as establishing the common ground with the other party, each side must also evaluate the resulting business case to ensure it not only represents a fair and sustainable arrangement but is worthwhile commercially for its own business. This means balancing short- and long-term targets, risks and value creation, and taking a view on the potential for sharing of future gains from innovation. At the same time, the CFO should construct an off-balance business case – essentially calculating the price of doing nothing. Often the price would be commercial oblivion, or even the company becoming an M&A target for a key competitor.

This crucial assessment of all the options is clearly an issue to be tackled at the level of the CEO and board, and raises once again the skills and perspectives that underpin successful M&A. A useful approach for the customer is to return to a checklist of what makes M&A deals successful from the acquirer's viewpoint. This might typically include:

- clarity of strategic rationale
- buy-in from key stakeholders
- commercial and operational synergies
- complementary capabilities
- cultural compatibility
- sustainability
- logistical considerations
- ease of integration
- whether there are 'hidden' or unrecognized assets to exploit
- creation of value for stakeholders.

All of these can be applied to the business case for an outsourcing. But the clinching consideration is the last one – value to stakeholders. Given the right approach to the identification of (and agreement on) shared economic value, the deal will have a good chance of joining the 50–60 per cent of agreements that actually succeed in creating value.

Stress-testing the value proposition

Given a positive assessment of the business case, the CEO should then oversee a further process often applied to M&A situations: stress-testing the value proposition through various 'What-if?' scenarios. This means looking at what can go wrong, who can go wrong – and what will happen if either of these eventualities comes about.

From the CEO and board's perspective, this involves a warts-and-all evaluation of the risks inherent in moving ahead with the deal. 'We are where we are today,' runs the board's thinking. 'The deal is embedded in that position. What if we acquire another business? What if we sell a division? What if there are union problems after the deal? What if we enter a new country? What if the ownership of our outsourcing provider changes? What if VAT rates change?'

This stress-testing will not only focus the board's thinking around risks, objectives and ongoing operation. It will also help the firm to articulate a clear value proposition from day one, and ensure the CEO enters the deal with eyes wide open to the risks and opportunities.

Moving forward

So, you have achieved clarity on shared economic value in the planned deal. You are 95 per cent of the way to a contractible agreement. You have ensured that expectations and objectives are clear on both sides. It is time to press ahead.

But to do so you also need something else: checks and balances in place to ensure that the alignment and clarity you have worked so hard to achieve is maintained throughout the process. These effectively form the governance structure for the negotiation, and again they should be agreed explicitly by both sides.

One crucial shared element is a clear term sheet, setting out the underlying principles hammered out in the senior-level workshop. Another is agreement on the roles of the outside advisers. The CEO of the customer should also put in place – and then follow – a fixed schedule of board presentations and updates to keep the board up to speed on progress, or lack of it.

As the negotiation phase begins, one question should be uppermost: 'Are we still in line with the original value proposition?' That is the touchstone which will guide the business to a successful agreement – and hopefully a fruitful long-term relationship.

Key CEO and CFO questions arising from Chapter 3

CEO

■ Are you prepared to articulate the underlying rationale for outsourcing and remain focused on building incremental value, while also allowing for mutual value creation by recognizing and accepting the right of the supplier(s) to a reasonable return?

■ Given the fact that continuity is critical to mutual success, are you ready to commit in writing – before progressing to detailed negotiations – that your own 'A-team' members will remain in place after the transition, in return for a parallel commitment from the supplier?

■ Rather than merely 'buying' the marque, have you instituted and validated early, deep, detailed and thorough due diligence on all possible suppliers' track record and capabilities, including speaking to clients whose deals with the particular supplier failed?

■ If using an intermediary, have you engaged one that is prepared to pursue a 'reasonable' balance, and establish mutual upside for all innovative, proactive and sustainable supplier achievements – thus avoiding purely extracting value, and making unreasonable and/or potentially self-defeating demands?

CFO

■ Have you reached a clear decision on how you will balance cost reduction versus contracting for cost stability, offset by strong effectiveness and efficiency gains?

■ To establish an auditable and explicit basis for supplier negotiations, have you constructed an off-balance business case – i.e. what is the price of doing nothing?

■ Have you also identified any hidden value that may benefit the supplier, such as the opportunity to create a pilot reference site for a new service,

➤

or IP assets, which the supplier can deploy effectively elsewhere? How do you want to reflect this 'advantage' within the negotiations and ultimate contract – value now, sharing the upside, offsetting costs at a moment of your choosing?

Value-based negotiation

A truly global company will be one that uses the intellect and resources of every corner of the world.

Jack Welch, CEO of General Electric

Imagine you are the CEO of a business contemplating an M&A deal. Would you engage with a potential target without first being clear about the possible synergies, which parts you will keep and which you will divest, what your plans are for the workforce, and what your overall objectives are?

Of course not. But many CEOs, even today, still try to start negotiations about outsourcing without first determining exactly what it is that they are trying to achieve through the transaction. In cases where the negotiation process goes wrong or becomes overly drawn out the root cause is invariably a lack of clear professional clarity – on one or even both sides – about the relative importance of a vast array of possible objectives.

Procurement – or partnership?

To a large extent this problem comes down to the fact that the bulk of outsourcing decisions has historically been driven by the CIO, head of logistics or a business unit head, charged with trying to resolve short-term cost pressures. The resulting decision making has all too often been reactive, embodying a focus on quick fix procurement rather than partnership. This is also the root cause of a continuing and widespread confusion between sourcing, which is essentially a broad procurement exercise, and outsourcing, which – as we have pointed out repeatedly in this book – is a tool more akin to M&A.

Assuming the CEO and board are seeking to achieve not just a one-off cost benefit but permanent, structural improvements in costs and processes, they have one crucial decision to make. Are they going to approach the deal as a 'pure' cost play – or as a transformational exercise, with all the implications that this brings? In short, what are they really trying to do?

In too many cases this question is not answered before the negotiations start, storing up problems from day one. The tensions created by this lack of clarity on objectives are all the greater in circumstances where the market pressures are focused more on achieving revenue growth than cost cutting. In these conditions the transformational aspects of outsourcing have the greatest potential to take over from short-term cost reduction.

Creating a clear two-way view of strategy

So the ranking of objectives needs to be established and agreed internally by the customer before it starts to be applied externally. The only person who can really drive this is the CEO, with the backing of the board. So it is critical that the CEO draws up and imposes a clear list of prioritized goals before the start of negotiations.

The same process has to be undertaken on the supplier's side, where it can be made even more complicated by the sales process. Suppliers' sales people have quotas to meet and targets to achieve – and, understandably, they do not really care whether they sell a one-off deal that is quicker and easier to structure or a transformational solution that takes longer both to sell and implement, and which requires a far more expensive structure. This means they have little incentive to press for clear objectives, as in doing so they may delay or reduce their commission on the sale.

A further supply-side factor which can inhibit clarity on projects is that many suppliers tend to have a step-by-step vetting process. Under this approach, increasing levels of focus and sophistication are applied progressively to a potential deal, rather than tackling the question up front of whether an opportunity is essentially a sourcing/outsourcing or transformational exercise. In each case this step-wise approach is focused on determining whether the supplier has a real competitive chance of winning, rather than what the shape of the resulting structure will look like. So the project's objectives are subordinated to the commercial drive to clinch the deal.

Unasked questions

The result of these pressures on both sides can be that nobody actually addresses these issues. Deals do get done where the most important questions are never even raised, let alone answered. It is akin to a dance where neither partner has a clue why they came to the ball in the first place.

Even more worrying, this lack of clear objectives against which to establish a governance structure does not necessarily prevent the partners at the dance from getting engaged to be married. Instead, its usual effect is to postpone these critical decisions to the stage either where the expensive legal drafting of the agreement is under way, or where the transaction has been done and is actually being implemented. The result – again as with a marriage carried out without any mutual communication – is a tremendous degree of pain and frustration on one or both sides, as issues that should have been dealt with much earlier are finally worked through.

Obviously there will be give and take during any negotiation. But our experience confirms that – as in M&A – the set-up for an outsourcing negotiation must be very ordered and methodical, and that both sides must have line of sight on all aspects; which means asking the questions that matter *before* the talks kick off. What do we want out of this? Can we achieve it? Who needs to be on board when? What will success look like?

Lining up the goalposts

In cases where these questions are not asked, the underlying cause is a lack of focus. Time and again we have found that the client organization can be made to home in on its real objectives by asking its CEO one simple question: 'What are you trying to achieve through this transaction with regard to the products and services you deliver to your own customers?'

This opening can then be used to drill down and establish the prioritized aims of the deal from the client's viewpoint around the three key issues of cost, quality and risk. If a major satellite television broadcaster were outsourcing its customer call centres, we would ask the CEO: 'Are you trying to improve the level of service to your customers through this outsourcing programme? Or are you trying to cut – or make more variable – the cost required to achieve the same level of service as you do now? Or are you seeking to improve your risk management, for example thorough a more structured approach to compliance with sales practices?'

Different individuals on the client's board may give different answers to these questions. This may mean that there are fault lines that need to be addressed. However, if this is the case, it is far better to find out early – certainly before the negotiations start. Exposing such rifts where they exist is a vital part of the discovery process to ensure that the business is ready to come to the table.

In cases where clarity of objectives has not been established, or where there are significant differences between the objectives expressed by different members of the senior management, then we would strongly urge the company to bring in an independent third-party sourcing intermediary to help it structure the various facts and opinions into an actionable game plan. This applies whether the firm is considering a private transaction with a chosen supplier or arrives at the negotiating table through an open auction. Either way, the customer needs to start negotiations armed with clear and agreed objectives.

Discovery: beware nasty surprises

So, as CEO of a potential client outsourcing agreement, you have established your objectives. The board is fully behind you. You are ready to start talking to one or more suppliers. What else do you need to know? The answer is: everything about your own operation. Discovery of the real facts – as opposed to commonly held management assumptions – about your own business is one key element that seems obvious, but often gets overlooked.

Picture the scene. An IT outsourcing deal focused on achieving cost savings is on the table. The two sides have reached a clear handshake to a reasonable degree of certainty on the overall costs, so they set about getting more detail on the critical aspects. The discovery process then shows that the client company had not got a firm grasp on the number of servers in its business. In fact, the client has 30 per cent more servers than it thought it had when it entered negotiations.

Is this a problem? You bet. The two sides have shaken hands over a general level of costs that will provide savings of about 20 per cent per unit to the client. The discovery of 30 per cent more servers not only leaves the supplier facing more work than it had assumed, but opens the way to an outsourcing contract that actually increases the agreed costs to the client rather than reducing them.

The results can be severe – as well as very public and potentially embarrassing. In 2003 EDS found that the UK Prison Service's estimate of 12,500 PCs under an outsourcing contract should have been 18,500. It took more than a year for the scale of miscounting to become clear. Rather than the number of PCs, the greater problem was the extra volume of work for EDS – and EDS's fee had to be renegotiated as a result. And back in 1995, in another case involving a US-based outsourcing supplier and UK-based client, front-page press reports said CSC was asking British Aerospace for up to £30 million in compensation as a result of 'potential liabilities' arising from a huge £900 million outsourcing deal negotiated the previous year. The alleged liabilities were believed to include hardware leases, software licences, extra telephone lines and pension costs – all because of the failure of the initial discovery process.

A similar situation we have seen many times is where the activities covered by a given level of service, as listed by the supplier in the contract, do not exactly match the totality of the service currently provided internally by the client. These gaps should be leapt on by the client team and closed through negotiation. As in the cases described above, the worst case is that the holes in the service provision may not emerge until the agreement is up and running – forcing both sides back to the negotiating table, but hopefully avoiding the glare of the media.

Understanding assumptions and motivations

Where disconnects such as these exist sharp detailed questioning by experienced, specialist and – by definition – external lawyers during the drafting stage will bring them into the open. If this questioning is left too late the result will be tensions between the parties, and the reopening of commercial issues that had been perceived as effectively closed under the terms of the 'handshake' deal.

The need to avoid this eventuality – and the resulting delays or even collapse of the deal – means two further perspectives are crucial when entering negotiations. One is to document key aspects of the transaction in a term sheet, so that both parties understand each other's assumptions and can see how the plan will be turned into reality. The other is to be aware of the inherent tension in the role played by lawyers and other consultants.

On the one hand, these external advisers have a vested interest in the completion of the deal. On the other, they are usually paid – and therefore incentivized – on a time and materials basis. It would be going too far to suggest that advisers charging an hourly rate actually want to draw out the process. But the fact is that extending the time they spend on the deal is actually to their economic advantage. Trying to negotiate flat fees or caps in advance with advisers is one approach that some clients try to take. But the better lawyers will usually reject this, and other advisers may simply hit their agreed cap and then attempt to walk away – potentially leaving the client with a worrying void in its team.

Regular project updates – as with M&A

Instead of trying to fix advisers' fees in advance, we recommend that clients treat the transaction negotiations and management of advisers in the same way as with a major M&A deal. This means creating a fixed schedule under which the most senior executive involved – a solid and experienced project owner trusted by the board – and/or the board as a whole, receives updates on a fixed (and at least a monthly) basis covering the current progress with the disclosure process, areas of contention and the route to resolution for any outstanding issues, along with the current time costs of all the advisers.

This means the executive management always have a clear view of the timetable to the actual start of transition of service and/or staff. Failure to do this can create a situation where the board announces a deal and is awaiting completion, only to find that the agreement suddenly collapses from under it, apparently without warning. In fact the warning signs were there, but were either never seen or not heeded. The recriminations and damage in such circumstances are not pleasant.

A further key attribute to help maintain this line of sight throughout the negotiations is strong project leadership, including first-class programme management skills. This will enable the client to build a degree of clarity around the internal accountability that will both improve the quality of decision making inside the company, and also force the supplier to be far more professional and controlled through all aspects of the transaction, including negotiation and drafting of the final agreement.

Rigorous project leadership has one further positive effect: it can dramatically improve the quality of communication within the client organization. Gaining and delivering clarity on what is actually happening is the best possible way to reduce the fear, uncertainty and doubt – 'FUD' – that can surround negotiations of this type and have a demoralizing and destabilizing effect on the individuals affected by the deal. There is more information on this issue in the specialist section on communications on page 168 and on HR on page **176**.

Can you work with these people?

As well as being the route to the final agreement, the negotiation phase is the period where a client and supplier really get to know one another. So it is here that the cultural fit between them is really tested, sometimes to breaking point.

In this book we have used many analogies related to personal relationships – courtship, engagement, marriage, nurturing offspring. Don't get us wrong: outsourcing is not about love. But it is about positive relationships between people. We would strongly advise any CEO and board not even to consider outsourcing their activities to a supplier with whom they did not feel they could have a close personal relationship on a day-to-day basis, as if those people were working within the business itself.

As a client CEO, try asking yourself some questions about your own feelings. If you were recruiting, would you hire your supplier's project leaders? Do you trust its sales people to tell you the truth and not oversell? Are you comfortable dealing with difficult issues with the supplier's senior management? How well do you know these people? Do you know people who know them, and who can give you an objective view? Have you conducted basic due diligence in the market about how these people behave when things turn difficult? And, critically, would you see their executive representative as an equal within your own board?

The human factor

All of these questions are relevant. At the end of the day the outsourcing agreement will be about people delivering services to other people. Our experience shows that if there is a fracture in the personal relationships between the parties, and it is not addressed early, frankly and openly, then it will eventually emerge with a vengeance. Unless the two sides actually get on with each other, and the supplier's senior management show real and sustained commitment both to delivering the agreed quality of service and to aligning their own extraction of value to that of the client, then any hiccup will result in both sides resorting to the letter of the contract rather than its spirit. And what you will then have is a marriage made in hell.

Given this risk, once a client finds a team of individuals in the supplier side with which it can work, it should make sure they stay around, at least until the agreement is fully bedded in. The same applies the other way, from the supplier's perspective. So we would recommend that the buyer and the seller explicitly demand that the sales and the buying teams remain in place throughout the negotiation – and become the delivery teams for at least 12–18 months after the signing of the deal.

Where this is achieved it has a markedly positive effect on communication between the two sides. It enables people to get used to dealing with one another's ambiguities and uniqueness, and to build trust on that bedrock. Even in a successful outsourcing programme there are difficult decisions and periods of pain, especially during the transition and transformation. At these times deep personal relationships will make the difference between a true sense of partnering and the type of 'us and them' attitude that may lead to failure.

Our case study on US-based Nextel Communications' outsourcing agreements with EDS and IBM (see page 204) is a good example of cultural considerations being taken successfully into account. Faced with headlong growth in its customer base, pressure on its IT infrastructure, rising costs and high customer churn rates, Nextel set out to develop an efficient information environment that would stem costs, maintain revenue growth and improve its standards of customer care. Its outsourcing agreements – underpinned by appropriate Service Level Agreements (SLAs) – provided the route to achieve all these benefits. Nextel stresses that its choice of outsourcing partners was driven by relationship considerations alongside cost and technical capability – and it is significant that Nextel's partnership with EDS is continuing to deliver value to both parties in new ways that were unforeseen at the start.

Internal SLAs: a step in the right direction

Alongside these people issues, moving to an outsourcing model involves more than a change in the way a service is delivered. For the client, it involves a shift towards a more industrialized set of conventions – with wide-ranging implications for both culture and operational processes.

Where companies have created internal service levels and shared service 'factories', this has enabled them to codify activities more clearly. In doing so they have tackled difficulties very similar to those they would encounter in trying to outsource an activity without the benefit of existing SLAs to use as benchmarks. The difference is that with outsourcing the pain is inflicted by a third party, as opposed to being an internally imposed discipline.

For the client going into an outsourcing negotiation, having existing SLAs in place for the services in question – even if these SLAs are by no means perfect – is definitely a step in the right direction, because it allows an apples-to-apples comparison with the service levels that might be provided by a third party. However, suppliers are alive to the fact that internal SLAs presented by the client might simply be a construct to trip up the service provider and extort higher levels of provision, rather than being real measures of existing performance.

Controllable, not autonomous

Whether internal or external, the two key attributes of SLAs is that they should be controllable and that they should continue to reflect real business needs, rather than becoming a business activity in their own right.

This is not an easy balance to strike. Many clients confuse technical measurement with actual service levels. Instead we would argue that measurements – from basic system uptime all the way up to Six Sigma practices* – are the *basis* for solid service levels. But they do not constitute service levels in themselves. At the same time it is very difficult to detach SLAs completely from the individual components (i.e. granularity) of the service they are measuring without making them irrelevant.

With this in mind we believe that the most appropriate approach to SLAs is to focus on the service's impact on the end customer. For example, the service level of an Internet-based service should be measured on the availability of all aspects of the service to the end customer, not just on server uptime. Similarly, it is irrelevant to say that the machines in an ATM (automated teller machine) network are always operational if there is sometimes no cash in them. Actual availability is key.

---

* Six Sigma is a quality management program to achieve 'Six Sigma' levels of quality. It was pioneered by Motorola in the mid-1980s and has since spread to many other manufacturing companies. The aim is to reduce the total number of failures in quality or customer satisfaction to below the sixth Sigma of likelihood in a normal distribution of customers. Sigma stands for a step of one standard deviation. Thus designing processes with tolerances of at least six standard deviations will, on reasonable assumptions, yield fewer than 3.4 defects in one million.

From the customer's viewpoint

Looking across all a client's existing SLAs in this way, from the outside in, can dramatically reduce the number of individual SLAs tracked, and shift the focus towards solid and granular measurement practices aligned with the end customer's experience and perception of service quality at the point of delivery. This perception should be the guiding light for both the client and the outsourcing provider.

But even if this focus is achieved with SLAs, complications can arise in cases where multiple contracts have outcomes that affect each other. A few years ago a situation arose on a major city's underground rail network involving three separate companies – one contractor responsible for cleaning the track, another contractor responsible for cleaning the platform, and the transport operator itself responsible for pasting posters up on the walls. All were working overnight to minimize disruption to passengers.

During the night, after the tracks had been cleaned, some glue from the posters dripped on to the rails. Dust raised by the platform cleaning stuck to the glue on the tracks. And when the trains started to run in the morning the glue and dust heated up, giving off smoke that triggered a fire alert and service suspension. The result: a major section of one of the network's busiest lines was closed for two hours during the morning rush hour. Of course, the various providers pointed to one another. Each had done its job individually, but the ultimate SLA – availability to the customer – had suffered.

As this experience suggests, the approach to SLAs needs not only to be relevant to the customer but holistic. Increasingly, services to one client company are provided by a variety of suppliers, and it is important to establish a single point of view and accountability across the totality of the service, as seen from the customer's standpoint. This means looking across all the services and the related SLAs to pick out and address the interactions and interdependencies between them.

Avoiding legalese

When approaching the issue of SLAs, one point to bear in mind is that while they are pivotal to the legal construct of the contract, they should not be in legalese. Rather than being exercises in the most perfect yet impenetrable legal drafting, they should be applicable and understandable by both the recipient and provider of the service. Our specialist section on page 164 provides further insight into the legal issues that arise in outsourcing.

During the negotiations the question often arises of who should be in charge of SLAs. The lawyers? The procurement people? The answer is neither. The people who are directly responsible for providing and receiving the service should be jointly responsible for the way service levels are tracked, and should be able to explain to senior management what is being measured, and why. Senior executives should test out these explanations by asking fundamental and basic questions, such as: 'What happens if there is a breakdown in the service and parts are no longer delivered to our assembly plants? Walk me through it.'

Outsourcing suppliers are increasingly sophisticated in their management of SLAs. Some now provide information systems enabling their clients to track service levels directly, automatically and in real time. Where this type of information is available, the client company should roll it into the company's senior management dashboards to give a constant all-round view of the organization's central nervous system, across both internal and external services. This helps to put the management in full control of the company's integrated operations, however they are sourced.

The recent steps in this direction have been encouraged by the advent of the US Sarbanes–Oxley legislation, especially through its impact on internal controls. In this context, moves towards real-time monitoring of service levels are a positive development, since they encourage executives and administrators to assume a greater degree of hands-on control and governance over corporate operations, rather than leaving them to a hierarchy of reporting processes that can obscure or even hide certain issues.

Revisiting the value case . . .

Even if the outsourcing plan looks to be on track, irrespective of the effects of discovery, negotiation and commercial give and take, there is still a further danger to watch out for. This is the risk that the project will assume a life of its own.

A typical situation – one which we have seen arise in a number of projects – is where changes in market pressures mean that the effects of the pure cost-cutting exercises envisaged in the original objectives start to run counter to the client company's interests. For example, with the economic environment improving and competitors starting to invest in their offering, the CEO's focus is likely to shift from cost management to revenue management and protecting market share. But unless they are directed otherwise the negotiating teams will continue to follow the old cost agenda

– and will end up agreeing something completely unsuitable for the new environment.

To prevent this from happening the CEO and board need to revisit the project on a regular basis, and compare the original intention and the status of the project negotiations to the organization's current objectives in the wider environment. Each time, they should make a decision over whether the current direction is in the best interests of the company itself, or whether both sides have now got to a negotiating position where they are simply focusing on doing a deal. Fundamental to this review is the quality of the documentation of the original aims of the project.

. . . even to breaking point

This is a further reason why regular senior management or even board-level review of the progress of outsourcing negotiations is every bit as critical in outsourcing as in an M&A deal. A company making an acquisition must keep its eye out for market changes that affect the deal – especially if they have the effect of undermining the original rationale. As with a good M&A deal, a sound outsourcing agreement can rapidly lose its value case because of developments beyond the control of anyone involved. So the client has to be prepared to test and retest the value proposition, even to deal-breaking point if necessary.

Short of calling the deal off, fluctuating external changes may require the client or supplier to push for greater flexibility to be built into the contract to enable it to adapt to new conditions if necessary. Taking a typical project span of six to nine months, if changes in the market during that period cannot be absorbed or catered for by the services provided under the proposed contract, there is virtually no hope that they will be robust and flexible enough to do so over a five-year project term. If this is the case the CEO or supplier must blow the whistle and revisit some of the basic assumptions.

Picture the mindset of a mortgage provider during a mortgage refinance boom. Heady with their recent run of success, both the client and outsourcing supplier are looking forward to ongoing exponential growth in the home loans business – even as the central bank starts to edge interest rates upwards. The project develops a life of its own, and is signed even as the board's unvoiced fears start to become reality. The result: the mortgage company's business collapses below the levels envisaged in even the worst-case scenario in the contract, causing massive pain on both sides. Instead of building in more capacity, the two parties should actually have been taking a more realistic forward view, thinking strategically and looking at how to scale the business down.

It is unfair – and rather pointless – for the CEO and board in such a situation to blame their project negotiating team for getting it wrong. The project teams are there to get the deal completed in line with their instructions. If a major strategic 'blind spot' subsequently emerges in an outsourcing agreement, such as the way in which Sainsbury's acquisition aspirations were effectively blocked by its use of securitization (see the case study on page 194), then it is ultimately down to the board and no one else.

Homeopathy or surgery?

So the CEO and board overseeing the negotiations for a major outsourcing agreement have to undertake a fine balancing act. On the one hand they need to keep an eye continually on the original objectives, and revisit and retest them for alignment to the current prevailing conditions, to the business's shifting needs in the light of those conditions and to the status and direction of the project negotiations themselves. On the other hand they need to recognize the need for shifts in those objectives, while ensuring that the project has not taken on a life of its own. They must also understand and track the motivation of the various parties involved – ranging from suppliers to unions to their own advisers.

The ability to recalibrate and fine-tune an outsourcing deal as negotiations proceed is a further reflection of its power as a corporate tool. In comparison, M&A – in which there is a sense of finality when the deal is done – is a much blunter instrument, with a far greater sense of finality. If M&A is a surgical operation, outsourcing is homeopathic. And while it can be difficult to reverse an outsourcing deal the fact is that it *can* be done, even after several years in operation – unlike unscrambling an M&A deal, which is generally a totally different story.

Outsourcing also presents an industrialized way of spreading risk – akin to spread betting – through the value chain, rather than leaving risk focused in one place. If consumers buy fewer cars, the impact ripples all the way down the value chain of (frequently outsourced) suppliers, eventually reaching the aggregate companies producing sand to make the windscreens. Flexibility and interdependence are built in all the way through the chain. And the risk is shared, rather than being concentrated in the car manufacturer that assembles the final product. Even as we write this book, value chains of the type pioneered by Nike, Dell and Toyota are slowly but steadily permeating whole industries, including government services in more advanced countries such as the UK and Canada.

Review – and review again

While outsourcing can be a highly flexible and powerful tool, its effectiveness in practice clearly depends on the skill and rigour with which the CEO and board apply it. As in other areas of business, the key to effective management of the process lies in information – and in information that is not just made available, but that is used, absorbed and acted upon.

This is why we believe that the board of a client company should establish a clear set of ongoing checks and balances to be applied during the planning and negotiation of big deals. These should be used to review the project on a regular basis, with each review being approached with the same level of rigour, thoroughness and healthy scepticism that a divisional manager might bring to the idea of acquiring a business which is to be integrated into his or her own business unit.

Again as with M&A, this review should include revisiting the motivations behind the deal. With M&A the question might be: 'Are we looking to acquire growth because we can't grow our own?' With outsourcing, the board might ask: 'Are we outsourcing because we don't have the management discipline to cut costs by ourselves?'

Third-party facilitators can play a valuable role in this questioning process. However, the CEO and board must ensure they have a clear view from the start of what these intermediaries have been brought in to achieve. Are they there primarily to provide market insight into what may be achievable in the contract for a given cost? Or to advise on a fair balance of value? And is the board sure that the intermediaries' underlying motivation is not simply to 'get their own back' on the outsourcing supplier that is now across the table from them, and which used to employ them as sales people?

Alignment for a win/win

As so often in outsourcing, the key to success in the use of third-party intermediaries lies in finding a way to achieve alignment of interests between the various parties involved – thereby creating a win/win.

With this in mind we would recommend that for very large outsourcing transactions the board should retain its own specialist outsourcing adviser, to help it retain control, oversight and governance over many of the most important aspects of the transaction. In very much the same way, companies are already starting to employ more than one M&A adviser for big deals. The aim is also the same: to retain a balanced and holistic view of the deal. When achieving alignment between different and disparate elements is critical to success, two experienced heads are likely to be better than one.

This approach, based on achieving alignment prior to a transaction, and then applying checks and balances throughout the negotiation phase, is a vital element of successful outsourcing. The same approach can also continue once the agreement is in place. For example, committing an independent third-party adviser to review the success or otherwise of the agreement every six months should be a central input to the ultimate renewal or reallocation of the contract. But it should also ensure that the CEO and board are able to grow their own expertise in this fast-changing area, thereby ensuring that each outsourcing deal they put together is better structured than the one before.

Again the parallel is clear with the way many boards review acquisitions or divestitures on a 'morning-after' basis, so their knowledge and insight grow continually into what makes M&A deals work and where the problems might arise. With outsourcing, the opportunities for ongoing improvement are far greater and more frequent – and the board's increasing expertise can be put to more immediate and constant effect through management and fine-tuning of the contract. For CEOs, an ability to manage these relationships in a manner that is sure handed, responsive and aligned with the strategic needs of the business is an increasingly important skill in the drive to ensure the business becomes, or remains, a first-class enterprise.

Key CEO and CFO questions arising from Chapter 4

CEO

■ Have you drawn up and prioritized a clear list of goals related to your business's products and services – lower/more variable costs, higher quality, better risk management – and gained explicit, unanimous, board-level agreement and backing for both the objectives themselves and the order of priority?

■ Are you looking to let the procurement function lead the negotiation, fundamentally making it a cost play, or are you willing to go for business/process transformation, accepting the higher risk and commitment but also the much bigger strategic upside that this entails?

■ Are you entering the negotiations with a clear understanding of your own costs and capabilities, of the possible synergies with potential suppliers, of how the relationship with your business fits into *their* business strategy? Do you know which parts of your organization you will keep in-house? And how clear are your plans for the workforce, and any related fallout?

■ Have you laid down a fixed schedule of regular reports and communications to keep the board fully up to date with progress and costs – together with a process through which the business case for the outsourcing agreement is continually reviewed against subsequent changes in either the business or the economic and market environment?

■ If you have not yet engaged a specialist outsourcing intermediary, have you examined the possible contribution and benefits that a third-party adviser might bring to your business and its ability to negotiate and collect envisaged benefits?

CFO

■ Are you ready and willing to look beyond a short- and medium-term financial boost from the proposed outsourcing, and engage with the rest of the board, business units and potential suppliers on quality, innovation, continuous improvement programmes – and ultimately business transformation?

■ Are you ready to help develop and implement SLAs that focus on business enablement as well as end-user perceptions of service quality rather than just on financial performance against targets?

■ Are you building longer-term financial and economic projections into your forecasting and planning of the financial benefits from the deal?

5

Moving to the new way of thinking

Key finding: Some CEOs now view outsourcing as a fast, targeted, and relatively inexpensive method for acquiring expertise and fostering corporate change. In contrast, they view M&A as an expensive blunt instrument – with difficult internal political challenges – for entering a new market.

Institute of Management and Administration (IOMA) Research, June 2003

Our experience has confirmed time and again that the three most important watchwords in managing the transition to an outsourcing arrangement are: communication, communication and communication.

This may seem self-evident. But it may not be when you are in the thick of doing the deal. During the run-up to an outsourcing transaction and transition, many CEOs and boards actually feel pressure the other way – with the urge to stop information leaking out seeming more urgent than the need to release it. Fearful of the response from the workforce and unions on one side, and facing penetrating questioning from investors on the other, they feel it is safer to clam up rather than open up.

Openness or secrecy?

The competing claims of secrecy and openness result in outsourcing clients becoming polarized between two distinct and fundamentally divergent approaches to the transition phase. At one extreme there is the board that creates a specialist team in complete secrecy to manage the change, pursues the project as a covert operation, and tries to prevent information leaking out both internally and externally. At the other extreme, some boards look to proceed with a high degree of openness via an approach based on early and coordinated communication throughout the process.

CEOs and boards may find the first of these approaches superficially attractive for a number of reasons. Opting for secrecy means that the senior management, when facing up to and getting their heads round this major transaction, should be able to come to an agreed and educated view about the opportunity without having created significant – and probably far-reaching – waves among shareholders, employees, unions, suppliers and other stakeholders.

What is the problem? Basically, that people are not stupid – and if they feel they are being kept in the dark, they will assume the worst possible outcome is being planned. The practical reality in most businesses is that it is impossible to collect all the relevant facts *and* keep the whole exercise completely quiet. This puts the board between a rock and a hard place. The risk on the one hand is that decisions will be taken on the basis of incomplete or wrong information, resulting in huge problems and embarrassment at a later stage; or, on the other, that information will leak out piecemeal though rumour and hearsay, causing widespread disruption, loss of morale and potentially union problems. In practice, a company could fall into both pitfalls at once.

Setting the pattern of communication

To circumvent these traps, what management need as they enter and move through the transition is a controlled and tightly managed pattern and process of good, clear communication, of the type outlined in our specialist section on communications on page 168. The initial communications should show that the outsourcing option – as with the M&A option – is just one possible tool among many, and is being entertained and considered as part of the normal, everyday management process. So any examination of the possibility of outsourcing is really just one element of business as usual.

By positioning outsourcing in this way, and ensuring there are no hidden agendas at play, the CEO and board can create the context for a truly constructive two-way dialogue with employees, unions, and governmental and regulatory authorities. This in turn will enable better decision making, and ensure that there are no nasty surprises for the stakeholders or any resulting knee-jerk reactions.

So, when should you start to communicate? The plain answer is: as early as you honestly can. The first communication might run something like this. 'As a business that is always striving to remain competitive, we constantly evaluate and re-evaluate the options for various parts of our business, in the light of the best interests of the organization as a whole. These options may include selling the entire company, selling some operations, implementing internal restructuring, or agreeing to outsource one or more processes to a third party. It is our duty, and our culture as a management team, to optimize everything our business does – and in evaluating these options we are seeking the most effective way to do that.'

The message is both clear and inclusive. The fact that outsourcing is being looked at does not mean it will necessarily happen. No decision has yet been taken. Any choices that are made will be based on the facts and reviewed rigorously at the highest levels. There is no conspiracy of silence. Management are simply trying to manage the business as well, as honestly and as openly as they can. The rights and expectations of all stakeholders will be taken into account – and they are welcome to become involved in this process, since it affects us all.

A coherent story

When management set out their stall in this way it can lead to the kind of mature, balanced dialogue that the most successful outsourcing clients manage to create with their stakeholders. It is no coincidence that the businesses which do this are generally those that are already well managed and well organized, and have an established culture of management openness.

By the same token, the secretive way in which dysfunctional, opaque organizations approach outsourcing means that outsourcing will not generally improve their standing with either internal or external stakeholders. Instead it tends to create an additional level of complexity and tension that makes the overall governance of the business even more difficult.

So when advisers ask the board to 'communicate, communicate, communicate', this involves much more than picking up a loudspeaker and broadcasting noise throughout the organization. Content and timing are every bit as important as reach. It is absolutely critical that careful planning by trained, experienced professionals is applied not just to the mechanics of the transition, but to the issues of what is communicated, when it is communicated, and how it is communicated.

At the same time, all communications must be vetted by both the HR and legal teams – to ensure not only that they comply with the relevant local laws and regulations, but also that the organization responds in a consistent and coherent way to legitimate questions about the process from staff, suppliers and other stakeholders, including the press.

The role of FAQs

In formulating and delivering these messages to all stakeholders, well-prepared answers to a list of frequently asked questions (FAQs) developed jointly between the firm and its actual or potential suppliers are very effective tools for ensuring that a given question always receives the appropriate reply. The response should be both the same answer and the right answer, irrespective of who is asking the question and of the forum or channel through which it comes about. So the responses given in an informal face-to-face chat over the water-cooler, on the corporate website and in an off-the-cuff email should all be identical in content, if not in tone or detail.

This is not easy to achieve. One tool that can help to build this consistency is a series of internal staff workshops, which become increasingly important as the transition draws nearer. The two-way communication at these events enables the board to ensure that the various emotional waves that the affected employees are going through are not just acknowledged, but are managed through the message that the chosen course of action is both fair and in the best interests of the business. Staff may still not welcome what is happening at the time, but they can accept the commercial logic behind it, and can be shown that their future may be all the brighter for it.

Change + uncertainty = pain

Not that managing the people side of outsourcing is purely a matter of getting the message across. What is really required is an acknowledgement and recognition within the business that change brings pain, at all levels of the organization. During our fifty years' collective experience in corporate restructuring across many cultures we have never come across a business that was totally comfortable in the face of dramatic change. Change invariably creates ambiguity and uncertainty, which many people instinctively hate. But tried and tested psychological tools, applied professionally to both individual and group communication, can help to increase the level of certainty and thereby reduce the pain.

Recently one of the authors was speaking at a staff meeting in an organi-zation considering a major outsourcing. The employees were told there was a possibility that their employment might be transferred to the third party. Immediately one employee raised the question of whether the subsidized mortgages available under the current in-house employment terms would be honoured by an outsourcing supplier. This issue quickly threatened to hijack the entire meeting.

The author headed off the situation by speaking with complete honesty, stressing that no agreement had yet been made, and certainly nothing as specific as employment terms and benefits. Then he pointed out that the current employer had been cutting 10 per cent of the workforce a year to reduce costs. In contrast, an outsourcing supplier would regard any trans-ferred employees not as a cost, but as a source of revenue. And all the issues surrounding the employment contract would be discussed on that basis, at the appropriate time.

This response made the staff realize that leaping straight to the question of subsidized mortgages was to look at the situation from the wrong end. The emotional pitch of the meeting calmed down immediately. Months and even years later, the author encountered people he did not know coming up to him and thanking him for his honesty and frankness at that meeting.

In this type of joint staff/supplier workshop or Q&A session, a further useful tip is to bring in people who have actually been through a transition process before, and who can talk honestly and calmly both about the experience itself and about life on the other side of the transition. The staff at the meeting may be facing up to their worst fears, but here is someone who has done exactly the same and not only lived to tell the tale, but thrived after-wards. This again helps to underline the fact that outsourcing – as is M&A – is an aspect of business as usual, and part of the career experience of millions of people around the world.

Governance and controls: be holistic – and rigorous

While management of emotional and behavioural factors is critical, it will only succeed within a sound framework of clear reporting lines and respon-sibilities, and in the context of rigorous project management.

Evaluating the possibility of outsourcing is part of business as usual, but the transition is not. In its scale and complexity it is like sending a man to the moon. Every activity must be listed and scheduled, along with who is in charge and where all the links and interdependencies occur. Myriad elements need to be aligned between the two sets of assets, and everything must be painstakingly cross-checked. So it is crucial to have people with solid project management skills, able not only to run the process but also to spot embedded risks, danger signs and potential pitfalls before their impact actually emerges.

A key element of managing the transition successfully lies in monitoring and measuring what is happening on the employee side during the transition. Employees' responses and perceptions need to be captured and taken into account. Their positioning and direction on the 'FUD' curve is an important input to decisions on whether to accelerate or delay certain activities, or to launch new communication initiatives.

At the same time management must take a holistic view of the project's wider environment, including keeping track of apparently unrelated factors that might affect it. Imagine a company that tells its staff it is considering outsourcing, but which just happens to be running a periodic audit of its real estate assets at the same time. There is no link between the two projects. But the employees who then see people in hard hats going round their office premises with measuring tape will put two and two together – and their reaction when they come up with five could conceivably kill a deal before it even gets off the ground.

Documenting the start and end state

Given this broad spread of risks, the key attributes of governance and controls for the transition come down to quality of execution, the level of professional care overall, and the degree of attention to detail at all levels. All these attributes will be needed – and each will be severely tested during the process.

On top of this, it is important to know exactly where the transition is starting from, and where you intend to end up. Our experience shows that the most successful transitions begin with a clearly documented picture of three things: the current mode of operation, the future mode of operation, and the path from A to B. This is the route map around which the project plan is built. It means progress can be measured and assessed continually, and that any gaps that emerge between the plan and the reality can be identified and dealt with professionally and immediately – without emotions being raised on either side.

In contrast, a situation in which ad hoc steps are invented on a daily basis can, and generally will, lead to a dysfunctional outcome. This will in turn affect service levels and damage the interests of internal customers and both businesses. Similarly, the outsourcing will fall short of expectations in cases where the client organization does not have firm control and clarity on issues such as its existing costs, headcount and employee benefits. As in a disposal, if a business does not know what assets it actually has in a particular area, then it can hardly expect to outsource that area successfully.

Contract v. relationship

As well as shifting the operation from its current mode to a future mode, the transition has to achieve something else: lay down a robust and resilient framework for the long-term relationship.

As we pointed out in Chapter 3 on shared economic value, there are two ways of approaching outsourcing – or indeed any other commercial deal. One is to seek to extract greater value by screwing down the value derived by the other party. The other is to share value equitably and fairly to try and create a win/win.

Where the second of these approaches succeeds its effect is to align the interests of the parties. When one side wins the other wins too, and risks and benefits are shared. In outsourcing, this arrangement is the most durable basis for a long-term relationship. By the same token, where interests are not aligned in this way, then both parties are in for trouble.

Why? Because, where there is a lack of alignment, the immediate response of each side to the first sign of a problem will be to go back to the wording of the contract, rather than to use the day-to-day relationship to identify and initiate a joint response.

Avoiding winners and losers

The risk that partners will start to resort to the contract is especially pronounced in transformational outsourcing deals, where decisions are being taken that affect the long-term operation of the business – meaning those decisions are especially exposed to changing market conditions.

A good example of the targeting, crystallization and realization of benefits amid change in the wider market occurred in the deal under which the Dutch insurer Aegon bought Axa's UK life and pensions business, branded

Guardian Royal Exchange (GRE), in 1999 (see the case study on page 197). Faced with integrating this new purchase as quickly and smoothly as possible in order to run it down and absorb its products and client base, Aegon decided to go 'straight to outsourcing' for the whole of GRE's IT and telecoms infrastructure, through contracts with BT for telecoms, Computa-center for desktop systems, and Fujitsu for mainframes. The result was an object lesson in using outsourcing to facilitate fast and successful M&A integration, while also avoiding the need to retrain and reskill significant numbers of in-house personnel.

In this case, all parties understood what they wanted, and got it. But unless a transformational deal is underpinned by a contract that is perceived by both sides as fair, caters for changing circumstances, and includes a gover-nance deal based on partnership rather than an 'us-and-them' culture, situa-tions will arise where there is a clear winner and loser. This imbalance may not be clear immediately, but it will inevitably become apparent over time. Where that loser is the client, then the client will start to seek out ways to redress the balance – potentially by going so far as to cancel and exit the contract.

The risk of this happening is usually at its greatest in the early phase of the contract. This is typically the stage where the outsourcing supplier is investing heavily in transition and transformation, but this investment is not yet especially highly valued by the client, which regards it more as a cost of doing business. At this point it is very important to use joint workshops and open communication to ensure both sides have a clear view of where value lies and where it is being created, for both themselves and the other party.

Crystallizing the benefits

This awareness of shared and mutual value is the basis of the 'win/win' – and it does not just spring up on its own. A few clear instances where there is common gain in the early stages will help to crystallize the benefits of the partnership, and build trust between the parties. This trust will then carry them forward, and help them to apply a sense of give and take to specific situations where the gains may appear skewed to one side or another. Where the relationship is especially robust and mature this give and take will shape the way negotiations are conducted.

For example, the client and supplier might agree the SLAs and price for a particular service – with the client saying it is prepared to pay, say, £100 a month per desktop for maintenance to an agreed standard. With this broad agreement in place the two parties could then go on to have a separate discussion about the best choice of entity to own the asset. The supplier might point out that, since procuring PCs is hardly the client's core business, it should consider outsourcing their ownership and upgrade cycles as well. The decision may even come down to which party can get the better discounts from Dell or Apple. The key is that the decision is based on mutual trust, a common understanding of the objectives and an awareness of shared value.

This give and take enables the partners to split apart the pluses and minuses of any particular initiative, evaluate the value and risks, and draw the border between them in the most appropriate place. Depending on the specific circumstances, this will shift from element to element. Where the relationship is especially mature the two sides may even agree to take turns getting the lion's share of the benefit on an initiative-by-initiative basis.

The supplier's revenge

We have already talked about the risk that the client will walk away, especially if things turn sour early in the contract during the supplier's investment in the transition. But suppliers also have their way of getting even if they feel the contract is tilted against them.

The totality of an outsourcing contract is made up of a hugely complex network of interrelated factors. Aside from the obvious sourcing, service quality and technical issues, there are asset ownership aspects, tax, compliance, and a whole raft of other elements. This means that if a supplier wants to redress the balance in some way it has myriad opportunities to do so, quite possibly without the client even realizing it is happening.

A supplier that figures out that it has been 'had' somewhere along the line will always have the scope to make a few adjustments here and there to edge its margin up slightly and/or shift a little more risk back to the client. This approach is actually a natural element of a fractured commercial relationship in which the concept of a win/win has been abandoned and the letter of the contract – what each side can 'get away with' – is the only arbiter of appropriate business practice. The supplier's attitude might well be: 'If the deal blows up, so what? We're losing money on it anyway.'

Maintaining the balance of value – and pain

As we have said before, the best solution to this type of situation is not to go there in the first place. Rather than both descending into a confrontational dynamic where every discussion represents an opportunity for position bargaining, both parties should strive to stay in territory where the mutual benefit in the partnership is very clear, and the split of ownership and responsibilities is geared to maximizing it.

This culture should be supported under the contract by regular fixed reviews, perhaps quarterly as part of a senior management governance model. Ideally these reviews should ensure that the mutual benefits are still in focus, and that any areas of excessive value or pain on one side or the other are discussed early and addressed before they start to cause undue tension within the relationship.

Clearly there has to be give and take. From the customer's viewpoint there is nothing more frustrating than asking the outsourcing supplier for help in an area and finding that the supplier's first reaction is to look at the contract and say 'Sorry, it's not covered.' For an outsourcing relationship to work the underlying attitude and expectation on both sides has to be that the supplier will first and foremost serve the client. Of course, activities that are clearly above and beyond the contract should be priced and billed for. But the supplier should bill for these in a fair, open and responsive manner – not rack up the price on the basis that the client is a captive audience that cannot go elsewhere.

We are not saying that 'relationship is all', or that the best outsourcing contract is one that is signed and never looked at again. In today's heavily regulated, post-Sarbanes–Oxley world the reality is the contract and the parties' adherence to it will have to be reviewed periodically. But the acid test lies in the way the contract is put into operation. This is where the governance model becomes critical, because it should provide a process and forum for interpretation and continual dialogue between the parties.

What gets left behind?

Central to this dialogue is the size, focus and structure of the organization retained by the client to manage the outsourcing relationship. We have not seen – yet – any significant outsourcing transaction in which the totality of the functional organization has transitioned to the supplier. In every case the client has retained some subject matter expertise by way of a 'leave-behind' organization that remains within its own business.

However, the nature and scale of that leave-behind organization varies widely from deal to deal. At one extreme, the client firm retains only a stripped-down core competency in the form of a senior manager. This person – often just a sole individual – receives very little organizational support, and essentially operates as a relationship manager overseeing the execution of the outsourcing contract and the performance of the supplier. Under this type of arrangement the supplier typically handles all the processes related to the outsourced service, leaving the client with responsibilities around planning and contractual auditing.

At the other extreme is an approach we have encountered in a number of situations – especially with large client businesses outsourcing major elements of their activities for the first time. This approach involves maintaining a substantial leave-behind organization in-house, effectively acting as an insurance policy against poor operational performance from the supplier. The CEO and board's thinking in this case is that retaining a unit of this type and size within the business will make it easier to unwind the outsourcing transaction. At the same time, either consciously or subconsciously, they may also want to create a relationship 'buffer' between the internal demand and external supply – thus preventing the supplier from having a direct interface with its actual end users in the business.

Leaving dysfunction behind

In our experience this second approach usually proves to be a big mistake. When the leave-behind organization is too large it creates dysfunctions that could ultimately destroy the deal. Put simply, this approach indicates that the board has lost its nerve or is not fully committed, and has therefore tried to go for a compromise solution that is neither in-house nor outsourced. The resulting dysfunction means client business is likely to pay a heavy price.

The first area of dysfunction resulting from too large a leave-behind organization is that it tends to create a tremendous amount of finger-pointing, by making it far too easy for the retained organization to blame the supplier for unpopular decisions. This, together with the organizational split between the in-house and outsourced entities, positions the outsourcing supplier as a foreign body imposing new and unnecessary rules and constraints on what everyone suddenly decides was actually a perfectly good process in the first place. In such circumstances selective memory is amazingly quick to kick in.

The second area of dysfunction springs from the leave-behind organization's role as a buffer between supplier and end user. In practice, it starts to act as a shield preventing change from flowing into the client business in a timely and effective manner, and also blocking the free flow of clear information and feedback the other way. Over time the resulting series of time lags and errors in translation in both directions generates growing rifts between the supplier and the actual end user in the business.

So arguments begin to escalate between the suppler, leave-behind unit and end-user organizations. All too often the client CEO and board that have created this situation will accept the word and judgement of the leave-behind organization over that of the outsource supplier – despite the fact that the leave-behind organization may have a vested interest in making the supplier look bad. In a few cases the board understands this dynamic and will question and evaluate the competing claims of the two entities on their own merits. Either way the rumbling disputes between the supplier and the retained client function will hardly foster a positive long-term relationship.

The third dysfunctional effect is that rapid advances in technology and the continuing evolution of outsourcing models create a growing distance between the end user in the client business and the supplier. An outsourcing supplier thrives on real and direct contact with the actual user of the services it provides. The talent in the supplier will not grow or develop fully without touching the end client. And because of the opaque leave-behind shield that has been put in place between the supplier and user, the supplier starts to find it difficult to attract and retain high-quality people with the right skill sets. At the same time, talented people working in the supplier's other outsourcing relationships will not want to move to one that is increasingly awkward and uncomfortable on both sides.

The result: the relationship becomes impoverished, service delivery suffers, the in-house leave-behind organization claims its criticism of the supplier has been vindicated – and a vicious circle of declining performance, quality and talent sets in. Yet it is the barrier created by the leave-behind organization that has helped to create the problem in the first place. So this is a problem that is entirely – and repeatedly – self-fulfilling.

Reasonable retention – not too much

This vicious circle can be seen in action in many outsourcing relationships – you can probably think of some instances from your own experience. Our recommendation is that the client should retain a reasonable level of leave-behind organization, and ensure that rather than acting as a barrier it plays a role as the facilitator and creator of a flow of information and personnel between the user organization, the leave-behind entity and the supplier.

The ongoing flow and exchange of expertise and experience along this supply chain will progressively increase the hands-on knowledge and expertise contained within the client business. In time the company will be able to nurture, build up and deploy a strong pool of outsourcing-savvy individuals, opening the way for more sophisticated and successful outsourcing models in the future.

Imagine the enhanced value and insight of an employee who returns to the client organization after spending a couple of years working within the outsourcing supplier's business. Or of that same person after they have spent a further two years in the leave-behind organization, and then two more working with the users of the outsourced service. This six years of experience would be akin to a university education and probably also a Master's in outsourcing theory and practice – creating an individual who could then put the same learning into effect in many other parts of the client's business.

Defining and monitoring roles

These are some of the ways in which the benefits of successful outsourcing can roll on through the client business over many years, and the ability to reap these rewards to the full will be largely determined by the approach to the transition. A crucial first step is to create a clear and unambiguous definition of all roles and responsibilities on both sides in both the previous mode of operation and the future mode of operation, as well as during the transition phase that shapes the journey between the two.

As well as roles and responsibilities, this definition also needs to include the milestones and triggers that will – for example – permit the retained organization to shrink, expand or change in nature as the outsourcing contract matures over time. It is also vital that the definition is comprehensive, covering all the relevant activities and processes.

A recent encouraging trend in this regard has been the growing use of senior management dashboards and various quality of service information systems that can enable the right level and rigour of monitoring, without resorting to the use of a large contract 'police force' to track and enforce compliance once the contract has been signed.

An industrial parallel can be found in Toyota's use of a production system predicated on the fact that suppliers will consistently deliver just-in-time, Six-Sigma-optimized, total-quality parts. Adherence to the service level requirement is assumed, and is verified though polling techniques rather than systematic testing of every single rivet. Quality of outsourced services can be monitored in the same way, at far lower costs than constantly testing the quality of every element.

Making alignment resilient

Alongside this rigorous but realistic monitoring it is vital to ensure that the shared alignment to the project's objectives – and the construct put in place to deliver those objectives – will stand the test of time.

Our experience suggests that this can only be achieved if both parties' alignment with their shared goals and conflict resolution processes are not only monitored, but progressively nurtured and improved over time. This enables the one-time alignment achieved at the time of the contract to be expanded into an ongoing and embedded culture of give and take. This culture will be a huge asset as the project matures and develops, and will facilitate the renewal and extension of the contract when the time comes.

As we have mentioned before, a prerequisite for success lies in avoiding the development of 'us-and-them' behaviour. The governance process should provide the right setting to capture, analyze and resolve situations where this type of divisive behaviour starts to arise, helping senior management to keep the original spirit of the 'win/win' relationship on track.

Linkage with users' interests

This ongoing alignment needs to extend to the interests of users. In tandem with compliance with the agreed SLAs, it is crucial for end users to be polled at regular intervals to ensure that their perception of the service is still in line with their expectations and requirements. This polling process is especially vital since users' expectations may change over time. And it will act as an early-warning system in cases where some SLAs may be losing their relevance and will have to be adjusted for all or part of the user organization.

Imagine a situation where changing market conditions create a demand bubble. For example, a large and rapid influx of money into a mutual fund means that workstations for processing applications need to be set up at an increasingly rapid pace. SLAs agreed during quieter and more 'normal' times may have set the agreed time span for installing, configuring and supporting a new employee workstation at, say, three weeks.

But changing conditions now mean this will no longer do. The user department needs each workstation to be set up in two working days, or its processing backlog will grow even longer. Capturing the real demand signals early at the user end will enable the leave-behind and supplier organizations to put their heads together and develop a solution that will ultimately benefit them both, and enhance the perception of the outsourced service in the eyes of the users. Over time, this type of alignment with users will help to make the outsourcing contract a perceived success for both parties.

There are many examples where outsourcing might have helped companies to manage dramatic surges in business. In 1998, Egg – an Internet-based bank launched by the UK insurer Prudential – was forced to take out full-page newspaper adverts asking potential clients to stop sending in applications and deposits. The huge response to its launch meant its own IT and back office had proved unable to cope with demand. Outsourcing might well have helped it avoid this problem, because the ability to handle the step up and step down in volumes is one of the major reasons for outsourcing.

Getting this right in the contract clearly requires a fine balance between compliance and readiness to change. Too rigorous and unquestioning an adherence to the SLAs, blindness to the underlying and changing needs of users, and allowing the leave-behind organization to act as a barrier and delaying factor will all damage the interests of both parties. But most of all, these errors in approach will hurt the users – on whom the success of the deal ultimately depends.

User perception *is* reality

In this book we have focused primarily on the outsourcing of services – and services have a high content perception. Over the years it has been our observation that unless the value delivered is communicated regularly and clearly, time will tend to erase this value and gradually diminish the perception that the outsourcing transaction was a good move. This can happen even in cases where the quantifiable cost and quality targets are met and exceeded.

This risk makes it extremely important for both parties to invest in internal and sometimes external communication that articulates and reinforces the value that has been delivered as a result of the transaction. The need for these exercises reflects the extent to which the perception of success contributes to the actual success of an outsourcing arrangement.

Activities such as shared innovation, joint initiatives and celebratory events held to mark project milestones can all help to create and sustain an atmosphere of success and mutual momentum. This in turn prepares the ground for stretched targets and higher benchmarks that will not only increase the value delivered, but also help to motivate and energize the individuals providing and receiving the service every working day.

Using intermediaries for early benchmarking

While perception is a useful tool, as a CEO or board member you are ultimately interested in results – both in absolute terms and relative to those achieved elsewhere. In quantifying these, third-party advisers often have a pivotal role to play.

One of the most important elements of a third-party adviser's value is the expectation that he or she has been exposed at detailed level to a wide variety of transactions, and is therefore able to provide sound and practicable benchmarking of what is available and achievable in terms of service levels, pricing and governance. This means the adviser's input can dramatically reduce the level of external and market discovery that the client needs to undertake ahead of the transaction.

However, the pivotal nature of this role brings some clear risks. One is that the third-party adviser has seen too narrow a slice of the market, and therefore tends to fall into a single pattern of behaviour and perspective that may not provide the real best-of-breed solution which the client is expecting and anticipating. The other risk is that the third-party adviser may actually be looking to fulfil a role more akin to an auctioneer, with the objective of having the client extract as much value as possible from the supplier.

For clients, it is important to remember that smart outsourcing is not auctioning. Some commoditized services can probably be auctioned – we highlighted payroll as a possible example earlier in this book – but before entering an auction process one has to be really sure that the services in question really *are* commodities, and that there is very little requirement for customization.

In our view, client companies should use third-party advisers as a guide, to help them achieve a better understanding of the market forces at play in outsourcing, of what can really be achieved in terms of cost/benefits, and of the trade-offs between various types of deal and supplier. All this advice will help the client to act smarter at every stage of the process. This means putting trust in your advisers – but also keeping checks and balances in place to ensure they are not pushing you down the wrong road, especially if it is towards a commoditized auction.

External industrial metrics

Outsourcing is an industry that we believe is moving into a more industrial age. This means that while we are encouraging – and indeed advocating – notions of trust and partnership, it is critical that elements of the contract are subject to stringent measurement and regular benchmarking. This ensures that the customer continues to receive an acceptably market-competitive service in terms of quality, costs and benefits.

Establishing the right external benchmarking against other contracts is very difficult, because of the inherent problems in comparing one contract or service with another. What is needed is some form of apples to apples comparison, and it is not always obvious where this can be found. However, this is an important ongoing activity, and some third-party advisers are both adept and experienced at identifying meaningful external benchmarks and conducting useful comparisons.

After the inception of the transaction, a third-party adviser involved in it will have a good knowledge of its dynamics and perceived benefits, and is therefore in a good position to re-evaluate these at regular intervals – probably every two to three years. A fair review of the contract performance in this timeframe relative to similar contracts in the market, conducted by an objective and independent third party, is a clear advantage to both supplier and client, and a further supporting pillar for their ongoing relationship and alignment.

Key CEO and CFO questions arising from Chapter 5

CEO

- As in any M&A activity, coherent communications are critical. Have you identified all the key influencers/stakeholders and created an effective, well-planned and holistic internal and external communications strategy? Does it reflect the decisive impact of communications on maintaining staff morale? Will it avoid potential legal challenges, help manage regulatory risk and is it designed to support share price stability?

- Will you stand publicly shoulder to shoulder with your outsource supplier to announce and promote the deal, and remain ready to do the same in the future to proclaim successes and manage crises?

- Are you sure that your middle management in the retained contract management team are incentivized and empowered to assess and monitor all supplier's suggestions on possible innovations, and that they will pass them on to the relevant business heads for debate and auditable decision making?

- Have you instituted a governance model that enables both the retained team and front-end delivery organization to present any successes and complaints to the relationship's senior governing body?

CFO

- Do you have a clear picture of the expected end state, the financial and business impact of the benefits? Will you ensure that any 'value' statements are understated and not overplayed to ensure some leeway in the event of unforeseen issues arising in the future?

- Do you have the personal time and commitment to take the outsourcing deal to the investment community and portray it as a major benefit for the long-term financial well-being of the business, its flexibility, profitability and thereby ultimately its share price?

- Is the leave behind organization, structure and governance capable of feeding back early warnings of issues and potential failure points to ensure you retain the ability to foresee any investment community 'impact'?

- Do you trust the supplier sufficiently to negotiate with it on areas such as who should own the relevant assets, and to take the resulting decision based on the best way to promote mutual shared value?

- Are you prepared to continue supporting the necessary investment in communications, capabilities and initiatives around the outsourcing transaction throughout the life of the deal and beyond?

6

Realizing the benefits

With cost savings of around 39 per cent, there is enormous pressure on companies to move some operations offshore. Financial services companies are
way ahead of everyone else and are the pioneers. Banks such as Citibank
were among the first to turn to outsourcing and have put other financial institutions in the marketplace at a disadvantage.

Chris Gentle, Deloitte & Touche

Having successfully managed the transition to the new outsourcing
arrangement, you now expect to start reaping the anticipated benefits. But
this will only happen if you have already planned meticulously how you
will realize them. Once again, a useful orientation point for the CEO and
board at this stage can be found in the parallel with M&A.

As a client CEO, would you conclude an acquisition *without* planning how
you were going to realize the targeted benefits – however you have defined
them? Would you decide to do the deal *without* a top table team with overt
collective sponsorship? And without a very clear mission on cost synergies,
people reduction, product synergies and removal of duplication – all to be
achieved within a tight timeframe?

Of course not. But in outsourcing this does happen. The difference is that in
M&A stakeholders, public or private shareholders and – for a listed company
– market analysts have clear expectations of the deal being done, and apply
explicit yardsticks to it. This means that planning and stating the benefits at
a detailed level, and putting sponsorship in place to deliver them, is normal
in M&A. There is good reason to regard these prerequisites as every bit as
normal in outsourcing.

Thinking ahead?

But research and our own experience show that this is not yet happening in most cases. Over 80 per cent of all clients going into outsourcing contracts fail until the last moment to think about the leave-behind organization – the retained team – that will manage all this complexity. Very few have the necessary overt sponsorship at the top level to ensure success on what will be a hugely challenging agenda.

The result is that the retained team is brought in at the last moment, usually from the periphery of the supplier selection and negotiation process, or worse still from an unconnected activity. Critically this means that its members are seldom aware of the business imperatives that have led to the outsourcing decision.

What they *are* aware of is the need for cost reduction, the target SLAs and the estimated timeframes for the exploitation of synergies. These are there in black and white in the contract, so they can read them easily enough. But the fact that these individuals have come in at such a late stage means they are probably not qualified to know how these outcomes can be brought about – which is a big problem not just for the client, but for the supplier as well.

Defining the role of the retained team

So, as a client looking to realize the benefits that you have signed the outsourcing contract to achieve, you need to start early in planning how it will be managed post-deal, by whom, and what resources and budgets will be put at the team's disposal.

In putting together this team you should remember that one of the differences from M&A is that in outsourcing you are buying not assets but bandwidth – access to expertise and even experience on demand from the supplier. Therefore outsourcing is fundamentally different in one aspect of benefits realization: the contract has defined the minimum. If you have a good-quality leave-behind team in place, and have picked the right supplier, you should actually be expecting to achieve more. Much more.

Sadly, in only about 10 per cent of outsourcing transactions does the client really plan well ahead to put the right people in place with the right top-level backing, allocate clearly defined responsibilities and create proper, purpose-built governance, reporting and escalation structures underpinned by clear criteria for measuring progress against business objective. It is no coincidence that these 'sponsored' deals tend to succeed. Crucially, the client has prepared the retained team early, taken on the best people within a formal structure, given them a meaningful implementation and operational budget that is sufficiently large (albeit probably tiny compared to M&A), and allowed them active access to – and overt sponsorship by – top management, visible to both the business and the supplier.

Staying in command

The key to making this work lies in retaining command of both demand management, which means handling the business's requirements as they change and evolve, and supply management, involving understanding exactly what the supplier is doing and why, where its priorities lie, and possibly redrawing timelines and requirements in line with changes in the business and statutory requirements. This role is illustrated in Figure 6.1.

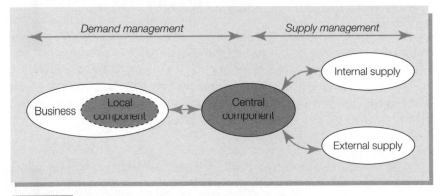

Figure 6.1 The components of the retained organization

In almost every case the demand side requires a more formal approach than was previously in place before the outsourcing arrangement. Specifically, the business needs to be more exact about what it wants – and more explicit about how much it is willing to pay for it.

This degree of command and control is not easy to establish. Time and again we find that the client business continues to treat the supplier as though it were an internal shop, still looking for the old 'grace and favour'-type arrangements and not expecting to be billed. This cuts across the basic tenet that an outsourcing supplier should – quite rightly – charge in some way for whatever it provides. The costs of these ad hoc changes and piloting were there before the outsourcing, but were not explicit. The difference now is that these costs must be met overtly rather than disappearing into some central corporate pot, meaning that commercial cost–benefit disciplines now have to be applied to any enhancements requested by the business. Functional change requirements, in particular, can mean a lot more work and cost for the outsourcing supplier.

To instil the necessary discipline in the business, the retained team should require that any requests that lie outside the scope of the contract should be evaluated as projects, complete with costings, timeframes and risk profile from the supplier's viewpoint. This will give an accurate valuation of the true costs – always bearing in mind that 5 per cent extra functionality could involve 40 per cent extra cost.

Ten key competencies – correctly positioned

We have already pointed out that the retained organization should be made up of the best available people, to handle its complex and pivotal role in benefits realization. But what competencies will it need?

Our experience of major deals has enabled us to identify nine crucial competencies, split between three interrelated domains controlled by one key overarching competency: sourcing strategy. These ten retained competencies are illustrated in the context of an IT organization in Figure 6.2 but they apply equally to other functional outsourcing agreements.

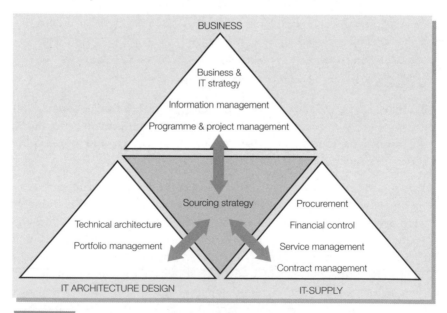

Figure 6.2 The ten competencies within the retained organization

In the *supply* domain, the team needs competencies in:

■ procurement

■ financial control

■ service management

■ contract management.

In the *architecture design* domain, it needs competencies in:

■ technical architecture

■ portfolio management.

In the *business* domain, it needs competencies in:

■ business and strategy

■ information management

■ programme and project management.

At the focal point of these domains is the sourcing strategy, which defines and shapes the organization's approach to both internal and external sources.

For the team to fulfil its role effectively, these competencies then need to be positioned correctly within the organization (see Figure 6.3), in relation to the matrix of six key organizational elements – functional, application and

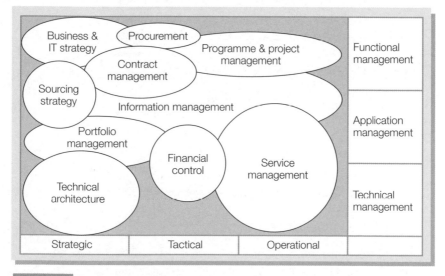

Figure 6.3 Positioning the ten competencies within the retained (IT) organization

technical management on the one axis and strategic, tactical and operational on the other.

Clear responsibilities in a shifting environment

Having identified the competencies and capability positioning of the retained organization, the next step is to define its responsibilities – the most important of which are set out in the accompanying box. As we have already pointed out, the retained team needs to be composed, at an early stage, of the very best available people, to make realization of the benefits as certain as possible. It also needs the budget, career structure and board-level backing to manage the supplier relationship effectively. And it must benefit from the skills, empowerment and experience necessary to oversee commercial, training and cultural issues.

Clearly defining the responsibilities of the retained team

Effective supply management

Establishment of the contract/supply interface

- the best available staff recruited early in the process
- large-scale budget both initially and ongoing
- formal structure and good career prospects
- regular executive access and overt sponsorship.

Commercial structure

- output-related criteria/pricing
- business-relevant performance measures.

Training commitment

- both demand-side maturation and education and . . .
- . . . supply-side motivation, controls and safeguards.

Cultural development

- commitment to develop a hybrid demand/supply culture
- exchange knowledge and achieve mutual benefits.

A key consideration in defining and allocating these responsibilities is the dynamic environment in which the retained organization will be operating – against the background of a complex mix of shifting competitive forces, emerging priorities and regulatory change. All of these elements will play a role in dictating the degree of success the business can achieve in realizing the benefits of the outsourcing programme.

Imagine a deal in which cost reduction is the primary driver. Suddenly, a major market competitor leaps forward with an innovation that threatens to undermine a key product line. The organization has to move quickly and decisively to counter the challenge. The pursuit of the predicted cost savings from the outsourcing programme is pushed down the agenda. Market share is at stake, and must be defended – or the business could end up dead in the water.

The result is an array of new pressures on functions from IT to production. The outsourcing supplier disrupts and redirects investment and resources towards what the board has said is the new priority. But, once the crisis is dealt with, bringing the agenda back to the original objectives may not be easy. For one thing, if the event was especially compelling, a complete return hardly ever happens. For another, while both sides know the event has resulted in considerable one-off costs or the exhaustion of discretionary project spend, it is now very difficult to come to an agreement on what its precise impact will actually be on the original cost reduction agenda – and, equally importantly, on the timeframe allocated for achievement.

Building maturity . . .

In such a situation, both sides need to take a mature approach that transcends the immediate circumstances. A knee-jerk response will not help. Even without a cataclysmic event, the client CEO and board must have the discipline to describe at least annually how their business strategy is unfolding and evolving.

So it is vital that changes to strategy, as they affect the outsourced services, are communicated to the supplier as early as is prudent. This enables the outsourcing provider to plan ahead in support of the strategy. If the board says it wants to move to innovations such as billing and CRM over the Internet, it should expect the outsource provider to come back with vital information such as which areas can be transformed to an 'e-'basis fairly easily, which will be more difficult, and how much of the change would fall within and outside the existing contract.

This in turn enables the board to reach better decisions, in the overarching knowledge that the crucial cost elements are known and accounted for – and with an awareness of where the dividing line will be between discretionary project spend and ongoing payments to the outsourcing supplier. So long as the parties have signed the right sort of flexible contract underpinned by a shared culture and trust, they may also be able to agree to downgrade some of the less crucial service levels and key performance indicators (KPIs) to create savings that will help pay for the initiative.

Throughout such discussions it is important to remember that a perceived lack of benefits realization is the main reason for disappointment among outsourcing clients. So it is vital that the client's board has early and advance notice of the impact and realignment resulting from changes in strategy. It needs to be involved in decisions on targets and cost control, and to be confident that the retained team is geared up to implement these decisions. This enables new benefit realization targets to be fully understood and expectations to be reset in the light of the new situation.

. . . aided by continuity

The board also needs one more thing from the multi-disciplinary retained team: continuity. It is critical that the retained future organization has people who: understand where the services were before the outsourcing programme; have experienced the journey of discovery; and know why the supplier was selected. People who know how priorities may have to change and sacrifices made to achieve them.

These people need to be kept on board in the retained organization, and incentivized to stay. If they leave, the resulting lack of continuity will seriously impair benefits collection and realization from the board's perspective. This is especially true if there is also a diversionary event that requires objectives and expectations to be reset.

In contrast, continuity in the retained team means that the board can rely on people who understand how and why criticism of the outsourcing agreement emerges from the business, and how to support or disarm it. Continuity of personnel helps the retained team play its full role as the first buffer against fractures in the relationship caused by ignorance or lack of sympathy in the business.

Metrics for improvement

Continuity also assists in benchmarking the success of the deal – or lack of it. The key is to start from the basics and understand whether the original in-house organization had challenging metrics. The odds are it did not.

A lot of companies – even major global organizations – that have not outsourced still operate with either very rudimentary or non-existent SLAs. This results largely from the fact that functions are seen as having their own discrete budgets, or from the use of a centralized funding mechanism that absorbs expenses without recharging them to the unit responsible. So it is only when recharging or cross-charging is introduced that questions arise – typically resulting in exchanges such as: 'Why are we paying for three people when we hardly use them?' Response: 'Because a three-person team is what you asked for.'

Even where in-house metrics and SLAs do exist in an organization which has never outsourced, it is unlikely that they will challenge even a mediocre outsourcing supplier, let alone a world-class one. If a client decides to strike an outsourcing deal for a function without ever finding out what world-class service levels would look like, it is highly unlikely that the chosen provider would volunteer this information. Instead, it would – quite understandably – keep its powder dry, and use the gap between the client's expectation and the reality delivered to delight the client over time, without even stretching itself.

However, assuming the client does understand the difference between mediocre and excellent service levels, this information is invaluable. Accepting that tuning up the measurement and risk carrying has cost implications, there is great scope for using specialist market advice to help step up the quality, consistency and resilience of the service over time.

Becoming a well-oiled machine?

The generally accepted way for an outsourcing supplier to take a client business from 'sleepy hollow' to well-oiled machine is via continuous improvement programmes (CIPs). These are about balancing cost with improvements in efficiency and effectiveness. We believe that for most clients a sensible approach is to view cost containment as the top ongoing priority, but demand ever-increasing levels of effectiveness and efficiency as supporting themes.

Within CIPs, fads and fashions tend to come and go. Six Sigma, made famous by Jack Welch at GE, and Capability Maturity Model (CMM) Level 5, the highest standard for application development and support, are currently in vogue. However, any CEO looking to adopt these standards must recognize the hidden costs.

For example, many companies now send application development offshore to India, where it is carried out to CMM Level 5 standards. But they frequently fail to realize that the reciprocal measuring and monitoring of the amendments must also be carried out by people qualified at CMM Level 5, or the standards are not met. And most companies are currently happy with CMM Level 2 for in-house personnel. So a balance has to be struck in the pursuit of continuous improvement. Clients need to take an educated decision on whether to go for that extra layer of complexity and cost, as well as investing in skills that may well be poached by headhunters the moment word gets out.

Benchmarking BPO: a do-it-yourself approach

In the context of CIPs, a further word of caution is in order about BPO deals. Because outsourcing of large areas of the back, middle and front office is so new, there are as yet no formal benchmarks commonly available. True, there are indicators – so an insurance company will understand the industry's average cost of maintaining a policy, or an airline will know the capacity and relative cost base of its competitors. But these are broad indicators, not true outsourcing benchmarks.

There are no Gartner or Compass benchmarks for BPO as there are for 'pure' technology outsourcing – nor indeed are there recognized standards yet. The whole BPO arena is too new and too broad for specialists to have emerged in all but a few vertical business applications. Client CEOs basically have to accept that, for the next few years at least, a BPO deal effectively becomes its own benchmark.

This is not something to be afraid of. There will be few if any clearly comparable competitors to measure against. So the client and its outsourcing partner must constantly challenge themselves over the way the process is delivered, the amount of duplication in the supply chain, the lack of automation, historic under-investment and the impact of power users' demands in order to reduce manpower and apply technological solutions to reduce cost and increase efficiency.

If a BPO relationship is becoming more effective and efficient over time it should – in the short term at least – be regarded as a success. This is despite the fact that you are realizing the benefit without using detailed bench-marking of the type that would be available with an IT outsourcing agreement. However, the BPO measurement provision must be flexible enough to include market data as and when such comparators become generally available.

SLAs: meaningful outputs

Whatever the availability of benchmarks, service levels and measurement should focus on factors with real business impact. Earlier in this book we described the experience of the Ireland-based mortgage lender First Active, which set out with a clear objective of delivering each mortgage decision within one working day.

It is not often that a client company can identify a single objective as clearly as this. As a simple, overarching, agreed and clearly articulated business target that can drive transformation all the way though to the setting of KPIs and SLAs, First Active's objective represents something of an ideal. This is partly because it is a benchmark that looks not at what goes into the process, but at what comes out.

Business-impactful measurement is about gauging enablement. For this reason, it should measure *outputs* – as did First Active. These outputs should be identified as common denominators that matter to the business, be it reducing the number of average debtor days or improving the share price performance.

Towards metric-based gain sharing

Whatever the objectives, it is crucial that the measures to be used and pursued are understood right from day one. They will drive the selection of the supplier, since potential providers that have demonstrably performed well against similar metrics elsewhere, and which can bring this experience to bear, will offer a greater likelihood of achieving the client's goals. This is especially the case where the output measure can be pursued via some form of risk-sharing partnership.

An example of a successful measure of this kind was the outsourcing deal some years ago between EDS and the UK-based aero-engine maker Rolls-Royce. The client, engaged in a dynamic and fiercely competitive market, wanted to lift its position from fifth to third in the global marketplace. To do this it needed to ramp up its investment in sophisticated technology to test engine designs through computer simulations, enabling it to achieve greater speed both up to design and from design to market, and to reduce its reliance on physical wind-tunnel-type testing. EDS already had acknowledged expertise in electronic simulation and prototyping technology, having worked in this area for other clients.

To facilitate the necessary investment, the deal struck between the two companies created a very real and demonstrable gain-sharing partnership. A key metric-based innovation in the contract was that a percentage of the fees EDS would receive as the fixed and day-to-day running costs of the outsourcing would be linked to the performance of the Rolls-Royce share price. This close alignment worked for both parties – with Rolls-Royce able to capitalize faster and more effectively on market opportunities, and EDS therefore benefiting from the resulting rise in its share price. Rolls-Royce redesigned and prototyped engines for the now booming aviation sector, and gained vital market share while rising up the industry league stakes. EDS achieved high margins reflecting the client's success, and Rolls-Royce ensured its survival as an independent aerospace company and centre of technical excellence.

There have been many similar deals since then, although few are in the public domain. Interestingly, in some deals the focus now is on increasing speed to revenue rather than speed to market (see the box below) – an arrangement that gives the outsourcing partner a vested interest in the market success of the client's product or service.

From speed to market to speed to revenue: the world flattens

Outsourcing is frequently portrayed as a route to achieving greater speed to market in product development. But this focus is increasingly being replaced by speed to revenue, as the old relationships and assumptions between and about global business break down. Such close alignment underlines once again how the borders between outsourcing, joint venturing and M&A are becoming increasingly blurred.

In his recent book *The World is Flat*, Thomas L. Friedman* describes what he terms 'the flattening of the world: the fact that we are now in the process of connecting all the knowledge pools in the world together'. He adds: 'We are on the cusp of an incredible new era of innovation . . . . When the world is flat, you can innovate without having to emigrate. This is going to get interesting. We are about to see creative destruction on steroids.'

Offshoring is pivotal to this process. Friedman writes of how, during the 1990s, the opening up of the economies and political systems of countries such as China, India and Russia resulted in 3 billion people entering the global market for business processes and IT services. 'Be advised,' he says. 'The Indians and Chinese are not racing us to the bottom. They are racing us to the top. What China's leaders really want is that the next generation of underwear and airplane wings not just be "made in China" but also be "designed in China".'

And he goes on to quote Craig Barrett, the CEO of Intel: 'You don't bring 3 billion people into the world economy overnight without huge consequences, especially from three societies' – such as India, China and Russia – 'with rich educational heritages.'

A hierarchy of measurement

When approaching the issue of metrics it is helpful to apply a three-level hierarchy – with measurement able to roll up from one level to the next. The three layers are:

1 *Top:* **Balanced scorecard**: Most people think of balanced scorecard as being about relationships and technical delivery. In fact, it can mean exactly what you want it to mean. It is about business impacts in the most general sense – which is why a vast array of outputs, from the influence on share price to directly shortening product development and deployment to reinventing business competitiveness, can be incorporated. They are all business impacts, and nothing is ruled out or in. It can be cerebral or arbitrary, simple or interpretative. But whatever it is, you can get service providers to sign up to it.

2 *Middle:* **Key performance indicators**: These track immediate business benefits. While balanced scorecard is about big-ticket impacts, KPIs are more granular and focus on benefits predicted and delivered on a day-to-day basis.

3 *Bottom:* **Service level agreement**: SLAs are technical performance and – crucially – service availability and delivery standards agreed between

---

*   Thomas L. Friedman, *The World is Flat: A Brief History of the Twenty-First Century*, Allen Lane, 2005.

the client and supplier. An SLA is a contractual agreement that defines both the terms of the supplier's responsibility to the customer in terms of service quality, and the financial implications and actions if those levels are not achieved.

The client CEO and board need to think through how they will use these three levels of measurement. Balanced scorecard is often the best place for aspirational and demanding measures. For example, transitional milestones are often seen as arbitrary, meaning the business is reluctant to sign up to them at a lower level until there is a concrete and realistic reason for believing they can be achieved.

A further factor affecting metrics is the changes in expectations among end users in the business. As client staff become more educated their expectations increase – and they tend to forget the journey they have come along, and how low their expectations were when they embarked on it. As a result they become more critical and demanding, which is a natural by-product of rising quality and expectation.

Relationship and contract management: the role of governance

We have already stressed the need for openness in the relationship, underpinned by a mutual readiness to communicate when issues arise rather than to go straight to the contract. The fact is that the quality of communication is directly related to the level of trust in the relationship (see the box opposite).

But full and effective communication can only take place in the right context. And the context comes down to one quality: governance. Contract management divides fundamentally into two parts. On the one hand, it is commercial – which absolutely involves more than just price. On the other, it is service – which is absolutely bigger and better than KPIs and SLAs.

The four categories of governance that apply to the management of an outsourcing deal are illustrated in Figure 6.4. Each category – purpose, people, processes and procedures, and performance – includes a range of specific governance items that should be covered. In the 'risk' column on the right, we have applied a warning system to show which items generally require the most urgent attention. For example, ignore people skills and resources – and you are dead, or soon will be.

Maintaining full and effective communications

The ability to achieve full communication depends on the level of trust between the partners (Table 6.1).

This trust sets the basis for effective communication, which:

- is proactive
- is continuous
- tackles difficult issues early and directly
- acknowledges and deals with perceptions as well as realities
- gives more focus to positive messages than negative messages
- personalizes successes, generalizes failures, and shares the learning available from both.

Ineffective communication throws all these positive dynamics into reverse – and will inevitably lead to a failure to realize the expected benefits of the relationship, and even to its collapse.

Table 6.1

Trusting partners	Non-trusting partners
Trusting partners communicate *continuously*	Non-trusting partners communicate *transactionally*
Trusting partners demand *open communication at every level*	Non-trusting partners *channel communication hierarchically*

The inputs to the governance of both outsourcing and M&A are drawn from a comprehensive exercise to capture the business environment (see Figure 6.5 overleaf). In this chart, the upper bars are more relevant both to outsourcing and M&A, while those lower down become increasingly applicable to M&A alone rather than to outsourcing deals.

	Governance item	Risk
Purpose	Corporate objectives & priorities	Low
	Partnership strategy	High
	Business strategy	Medium
	IT strategy	High
	Programme	Medium
	Service definitions & planning	Medium
People	Retained IT & account organizations	Medium
	Defined interfaces	Medium
	Defined roles & responsibilities	Medium
	People skills & resources	High
	Relationship management	High
	Meeting & reporting structure	Medium
Processes & procedures	Legal framework	Low
	Policies standards & guidance	High
	Procedures & processes	Medium
	Service management	Medium
	Change management	Low
	Finance management	High
Performance	KPIs/Critical Success Factors/SLAs	Medium
	Customer satisfaction	Medium
	Savings & benefits tracking	High
	Effectiveness scorecard	High
	Continuous improvement programme	Medium

Figure 6.4 Four categories of governance

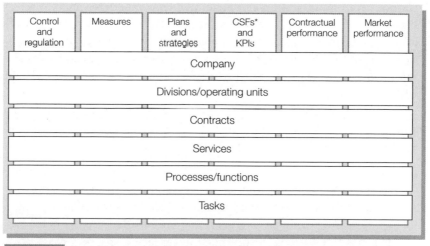

Control and regulation	Measures	Plans and strategies	CSFs* and KPIs	Contractual performance	Market performance
Company					
Divisions/operating units					
Contracts					
Services					
Processes/functions					
Tasks					

Figure 6.5 Capturing the business environment for outsourcing and M&A

Service beyond KPIs: the willingness to flex

When we pointed out above that service in an outsourcing deal means much more than adherence to KPIs, we were underlining the complex inter-relation and close interreliance between management of the contract and the development of the relationship.

In service, the key is for the supplier to be able to flex and to apply a spirit of give and take. For example, in the early days of the contract it may become increasingly apparent to the client that one particular aspect of the service does not really suit the supplier. If the relationship is sufficiently open and robust, the client will be able to say to the supplier: 'This may cost you some revenue, but would it be OK if we approached a specialist subcontractor to take over that part of the service?'

Usually the supplier is already aware of the problems in this area, and may well feel it is stretching its capabilities, IP or systems beyond its own area of strength. The odds are that it will agree to the request, since it is worth a small loss in revenue to maintain and strengthen the wider long-term relationship.

A return to 'grace and favour' projects?

Another aspect of governance around service is that informal arrangements may become possible. We have already pointed out that the in-house

* Critical Success Factors

culture of unmonitored and unaccounted 'grace and favour' projects is swept away by outsourcing. However, if the relationship works well and the client is allowing the provider to make a decent margin from the service tower, then a fresh culture can develop that allows a comparable level of informality, with the creation of unbilled and undocumented elements which may never be formalized into the contract, or only when they are fully or widely implemented after a pilot project or trial period. This kind of arrangement could cover initiatives such as prototyping a new service element, or trying out a new mode of operation to see if it works.

However, there are strict limits to this relationship-based type of service development. In particular, neither party should start to abuse the process – and the most likely culprit is the client, mistaking the supplier's cooperation for weakness and pushing too hard for free add-ons. The capability to retain this balance without taking too much advantage is a crucial part of the retained organization's role, and a key skill for it to develop. It is also a true test of its discipline and neutrality.

Brand damage: consequential losses – by another name?

A parallel and far more formal trend in terms of outsourcing contracts is the growing acceptance by suppliers of the need to accept liability for damage they could cause to the client's brand. This is hardly the type of clause that brings supplier and client closer together. But it can provide protection for clients who find their key intangible asset is damaged through no fault of their own.

The background to this development is that suppliers have never been willing to accept liability for 'consequential losses' that result from their failure to fulfil their side of the bargain. However, suppliers and their third-party advisers have recently made headway with the argument that where these failings result in brand damage – measured, for example, through negative column inches in the national or international press – they should be willing to compensate the client. Of course, if someone sues the client's business as a result, then the damages would be escalated to a higher category.

Imagine an airline whose outsourced engine maintenance provider fails to keep its service turnaround levels, leaving passengers without scheduled plane services, and that suffers a storm of media criticism as a result. Or consider the way the UK railway infrastructure operator Railtrack was arguably forced out of business (and ultimately out of existence) by the bad publicity surrounding its maintenance contractors. Or the major retailer which found one Monday morning that all its EPOS terminals had been put out of action by an automatic software download from its outsourcing supplier the day before. Where brands are at stake, so are share prices and long-term value – and for outsourcing suppliers to be true partners they must accept their share of this responsibility.

Ongoing access to innovation

As we mentioned earlier, one of the biggest and most frequent complaints levelled by outsourcing clients at their suppliers is a perceived lack of innovation delivered. They believe that ongoing and ready access to innovative thinking and service delivery is part and parcel of the outsourcing deal.

The reality is that this was usually an undocumented expectation when the deal was negotiated, because the client was so focused on cost reduction. And cost reduction and innovation do not make easy bedfellows. So trying to force the two together once the deal has been agreed is difficult, to say the least.

When we carry out audits on relationships that break down, we find that an 80/20 rule applies. Generally, the client CEO and board, believing that there has been no innovation, will ask for mediation of the contract. About 80 per cent of the time we find that the supplier *did* supply that innovation regularly and consistently. However, the retained organization believed that its primary role was as a gatekeeper charged with keeping costs down. So it has actively prevented the supplier from 'selling' service changes or modifications to the business by effectively vetoing the innovation without ever highlighting it to the business, end users or the board for their comments or approval.

In most cases the retained organization genuinely believes it is doing the right thing. It may even turn down innovation because it would only result in a 1 per cent reduction in costs. But even a modest reduction of that order not only is worth having but can open up debate about other inter-departmental efficiencies that may end up saving much more.

Where it happens, this type of innovation blockage is clearly very bad news for long-term benefits realization. The retained team is stifling the flow of innovation from the supplier, and deciding not to escalate it to the business for perceived 'cost containment' reasons. The immediate need is to restart the flow of innovation, and make sure it is transparent to both sides. The question is: how?

The power to escalate

In fact, you can and should contract for demonstrable future innovation in an outsourcing deal. It works like this. The supplier must deliver its proposals for innovation in writing to the retained organization, with a basic business case and costs justification. If the retained organization likes the idea, it will escalate it for further consideration. But where the supplier feels it has been unfairly rebuffed, or that the innovation has not been sufficiently tested within the business, then it can escalate it for review itself, at least to the level of the business unit heads.

Alternatively, if the innovation is so sweeping and ground-breaking that it would enable a step-change in the business, there should be an automatic right under predetermined criteria for the supplier to escalate it straight to the CEO and main board for consideration. Crucially, this arrangement also benefits the retained organization, by restoring clarity about its role as an enabler, facilitator and manager of the relationship – and not as a gatekeeper.

A further key aspect of the flow of innovation from the supplier is that it need not be confined to the areas covered by the contract. In delivering their contracted services, outsourcing suppliers often become aware of inefficiencies and duplication located elsewhere in the business. As a result they can – and ideally should – be prepared to make suggestions to help the client outside their own particular scope. Whether this results in extension of that scope is irrelevant; the innovation still counts towards their quota of innovation delivered.

In technology outsourcing, a 70/30 model is often applied under which the supplier is expected to deliver 70 per cent technology innovation and 30 per cent streamlining or automation of manual systems, which may or may not move into the technology scope as a result. An example of one innovation of this type that is currently going strong in many outsourcing relationships is electronic revenue billing, in which the client's customers agree to be sent an automatically generated invoice as soon as their electronic order is received.

This apparently small change, frequently proposed by outsourcing suppliers, brings major benefits. There is little or no manual processing. Billing errors are reduced from an average of 10 per cent with manual systems to virtually zero, increasing customer satisfaction. And cashflow is improved by virtue of getting invoices out more quickly and free of errors.

Managing future risks through flexibility

Alongside access to innovation, a further aspect of long-term benefits realization is ongoing and robust risk management – including the ability in the contract to allow for events such as peaks in business and integration issues, before edging back down to a more 'normal' focus and level of activity.

One of the most obvious provisions to include is what happens in the event of M&A and disposals – covering aspects ranging from the top-level approach to systems integration or disintegration, down to fairly detailed principles of the costings to be applied. This kind of agreement can be underwritten contractually, and potentially publicly, to ensure that the analysts understand that the enterprise is being rigorous in offsetting its risks. It can be invoked as a foreseen but not necessarily imminent benefit that can be realized in the future and directly affects the business's ability and scope to flex and execute its strategy.

One area that our research has highlighted as a major failing in many M&A deals is that the internal focus and operational sluggishness of the acquiring enterprise can hamper its efforts to re-energize and refocus the acquired business and capitalize on continuing revenue generation. A well-constructed outsourcing agreement will have much of this disruptive effect already catered for in advance and will be a clear enabler for M&A to take place.

This kind of benefit in terms of future risk profile is not something for which clients should expect to pay a premium. Suppliers today are increasingly comfortable about making future regulatory compliance a standard element of their contracts, meaning the supplier will ensure the client stays in line with regulatory standards as they evolve. If there are additional costs involved these should be passed on in a transparent and formulaic rather than arbitrary way. There should also be big savings for clients as compared to managing compliance in-house – the logic being that the outsourcing provider is managing compliance for multiple clients, and will therefore spread the resulting costs among them.

A further aspect of flexibility to bear in mind is strategic flexibility – with the objective being to structure the outsourcing deal in such a way that it enhances the company's ability to exploit future market opportunities. In some cases, outsourcing has the reverse effect. An example of this can be found in our case study on the UK retailer J. Sainsbury on page 193, where the outsourcing deal included using securitization – effectively borrowing against its future revenue stream – to fund a whole range of transformational change. At first this seemed a neat solution, but reducing liabilities and removing leverageable debt made Sainsbury's unleverageable in an M&A context. This effectively created a financial straitjacket that prevented Sainsbury's from making a move when a market-redefining M&A opportunity emerged.

Mutual executive openness for mutual benefit

With the outsourcing agreement up and running, and both sides consulting one another on strategy and receiving a fair and equitable proportion of the value, the scene is set for a transparent long-term relationship.

This brings into play two key factors. The one we have already discussed – the outsourcing equivalent of motherhood and apple pie – is the building of trust between the parties at every level. The other factor, still emerging and far more controversial, is the maturity of the supplier's executive leadership, and its readiness to get close to client CEOs and boards on a personal level. Global supplier executives in particular do not yet have the maturity to see themselves as personally accountable or engaged with the post-deal client relationship. This may cost them dearly in the future when regional and local competitors erode their market share with more visible and demonstrable personal commitment.

As both client and supplier strive for transparency in their relationship, the issue of how to achieve and sustain trust is uppermost for both parties. The answer seems simple: the basis for trust is disclosure and audit. Right? Not quite. In fact, the basis for trust in an outsourcing relationship is *bilateral* disclosure and audit – which can be quite a different matter.

If those elements represent the basis, the enablers for a trusting relationship are openness and honesty. Finding these comes down to the selection criteria, with clients seeking out a provider that is culturally compatible with their own organization. There also has to be a mature acceptance of significant, ongoing and unplanned change, and of one another's economic realities. And the mechanism underpinning all these elements consists of audit and measurement. When the parties reach the stage of an 'open book' relationship they are optimizing truly significant and ongoing trust.

The role of 'trust brokers'

However, even after trust has been established, there is always the possibility that various events might blow it off course. In cases where relationships do falter, third-party intermediaries can play a key role by acting as 'trust brokers'. This involves reinforcing and reiterating the value and contribution of both parties, set in the context of the historic achievements to date, the current contract and the future enablement.

As well as aiding the smooth operation of the contract, trust also delivers benefits in more direct ways. Clients will often do 'favours' for existing trusted suppliers by allowing them to prototype new ideas and concepts.

The benefits also flow in the other direction. With global IT outsourcing suppliers currently scrambling to get into BPO in functional areas outside their traditional core skills base, they are eager to set up sample client sites where they can develop and demonstrate their new-found expertise. The teething phase is best done in a friendly environment – which will generally mean it is done with a trusted customer to create a solid, credible and cooperative reference site for business development.

The key enablers, constraints (Table 6.2) and prerequisites for trust are summarized in the accompanying box. As this shows, an integral part of trust is being realistic in the way responsibilities are defined. In a fast-moving and evolving environment, responsibilities can only be defined in general terms. They generally become more of an issue in the context of failures – while a trust-based relationship allows the parties to have a looser definition of roles and less reliance on functional job descriptions. It also means that when problems emerge the immediate focus is not on who was responsible but on how to respond and, in the longer term, how to ensure it does not recur. Realization of benefits must always remain the mutual key goal.

This in turn comes back to the role of the retained team and the selection of the right people, recruited for their business and technical knowledge, track record and understanding of the pressures that drive and shape the shared culture. It is crucial that the team is backed by wholehearted commitment and mandate from the executive team, and that the team members are mature enough to know how far they can take the trust with the supplier without starting to take advantage. And when this happens on either side, a key aspect of the hybrid culture is that the side which feels imposed upon can voice its concerns to the other – and effectively draw a line that neither will cross.

Building trusting relationships in outsourcing: a primer

Table 6.2

Trust relationship **enablers**	Trust relationship **constraints**
Clearly defined objectives	Lack of preparation
Carefully planned relationship	Poor cultural fit
Well-designed processes	Differing objectives
Encouragement of teamwork and sharing of outcomes	Inappropriate governance environment
Effective reporting and communications at every level	Cost versus profit pressures

The prerequisites for trust are:

- honesty and openness
- cultural compatibility
- acceptance of significant ongoing change
- acceptance of each other's economic realities
- the mechanism to audit and measure.

Maintaining trust:

- involves optimizing *'open book' relationships*
- employing trust brokers – third parties can assess, reaffirm and share the parties' value and contribution throughout the life of the relationship
- makes defining responsibilities less of an issue:
  - less definition is required in a trust-based relationship
  - responsibilities usually become an issue in the context of failures rather than successes
  - trust enables a shared focus on defining how failures will be managed and how repetition will be prevented.

Suppliers' executive team: the need for maturity and vision

There is one pivotal area of the relationship between clients and outsourcing suppliers where trust is still in an embryonic state – and where we believe most larger providers must rethink their approach to avoid being challenged by more agile players. This is in instigating and nurturing close and personal contact between suppliers' senior executives – up to and including the CEO – and their counterparts in the client businesses.

When an outsourcing deal is on the table, a client CEO expects to be challenged by the supplier on the business's strategy and goals. But clients currently do not then expect to do the same in reverse to the supplier's executive team. Well, the client should – and the supplier's executive team should encourage the client to do so.

Why? Because if the members of the client board are really convinced that the outsourcing deal represents a fundamental and permanent shift in their ability to achieve business goals, then they should make sure they understand how they fit into the supplier's own strategy. What are the supplier's long-term objectives? Is it pursuing this deal primarily for revenue or for wider purposes? Does it provide similar services to clients in the same sector? Will it use the project as a reference site to market its BPO or industry offering? Will it use it to test innovation?

These questions are simply not being asked by client CEOs. The reasons for this one-way information blockage lie with executives on both sides. The key challenges facing each of them are listed in Figure 6.6 overleaf. However, the key to breaking the dialogue of the deaf between supplier and client lies with the supplier's executives. And to do this, many of them need to radically change their perspective and behaviour. Success here will truly drive a new generation of mutual benefit realization.

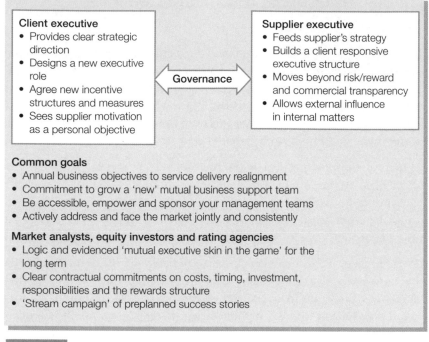

Client executive
- Provides clear strategic direction
- Designs a new executive role
- Agree new incentive structures and measures
- Sees supplier motivation as a personal objective

Governance

Supplier executive
- Feeds supplier's strategy
- Builds a client responsive executive structure
- Moves beyond risk/reward and commercial transparency
- Allows external influence in internal matters

Common goals
- Annual business objectives to service delivery realignment
- Commitment to grow a 'new' mutual business support team
- Be accessible, empower and sponsor your management teams
- Actively address and face the market jointly and consistently

Market analysts, equity investors and rating agencies
- Logic and evidenced 'mutual executive skin in the game' for the long term
- Clear contractual commitments on costs, timing, investment, responsibilities and the rewards structure
- 'Stream campaign' of preplanned success stories

Figure 6.6 Strategic executive challenges on both sides

Towards a joint approach

We have already pointed out that the basis for trust in an outsourcing relationship is bilateral disclosure and audit. Similarly, the basis for successful strategic outsourcing itself is visible and continuous executive sponsorship. But again, this must be bilateral rather than just one way. The supplier's team, understanding the 'interest' of its own executives, will strive harder to achieve mutual benefits and objectives. Excuses will be harder to sustain under mutual executive scrutiny and disclosure. A-team traits will be the only standard in town.

While suppliers are now beginning to recognize that their executives must take on what is akin to a 'super sales management' role for their top 50 or so clients, progress has been painfully slow. However, this dialogue is key not only to suppliers' sales efforts, but to the realization of benefits for such key clients over a prolonged period of time. The supplier CEO and other senior executives should articulate their reciprocal business objectives and how the client fits in. This is especially important where the supplier is on an acquisition trail, with the prospect of new capabilities being brought to bear for mutual advantage.

Given this approach, the creation of a series of truly common goals not only is possible, but will in future effectively become mandatory in outsourcing deals, as competition for prime accounts grows increasingly intense. And the common goal, on which it will be especially important to establish alignment, is *the active management of the pressures exerted by market analysts, institutional investors and rating agencies.*

Managing the investment markets

What does this mean? In short, that the two CEOs should stand shoulder to shoulder behind the deal to provide visible evidence that both have a lot of 'skin in the game'.

However, this not only underlines and cements the supplier's full commitment to the success of the client's business. It also influences the share price of the client for the longer term by illustrating containment of the company that outsources and spreading risk through the use of expert, world-class providers.

At the same time, clients should not underestimate the supportive effect that the linkage with their own brand and company mark has on the *supplier's standing* in the global investment markets and ultimately its share price. Extensions of scope, illustrations of innovation and demonstrable mutual successes reflect equally on the panoply of estimates that market analysts produce, thereby benefiting both parties – and building unprece-dented trust at the highest levels in both companies. Careful and continuous communication of these co-joined objectives and the successes along the way positively bolster both parties' market standing.

A key factor in influencing the investment markets is appreciating the diversity and frequent superficiality of views and priorities that they apply. Research shows that outsourcing clients with high-profile CEOs tend to gain a more favourable response to the outsourcing announcement than those with more low-key or nondescript CEOs and boards. This may be irrational, but it underlines the emotional importance that the markets attach to the belief that a prominent individual has put his or her reputation at risk through the deal, and is taking a clear strategic position on it. In fact, there is more behind this belief than just emotion. Research published in 2001 by

Morgan Chambers and CW360 (the Computer Weekly information portal), entitled 'Outsourcing in the FTSE 100: The Definitive Study'* showed that the 21 companies in the UK's FTSE 100 with a clear and demonstrable strategic sourcing policy achieved shareholder returns 5.3 per cent better than the FTSE 100 average, and 4.9 per cent better than their sector.

That said, managing market perceptions remains a huge challenge. Figure 6.7 illustrates the complexity of the task by tabulating the priorities applied by three groups – CEOs, analysts and institutional investors – to corporate performance. To pick just one anomaly, earnings ranks first for institutions, fifth for analysts and eighth for CEOs. Effective management of market opinion in an outsourcing deal involves understanding and exploiting these differences.

To date, supplier executives have been too heavily occupied with the operational side of their business and with maintaining revenues to pay much

The reporting companies	The market analysts	The institutional investors
1. Strategic direction	1. Market growth	1. Earnings
2. Cash flow	2. Strategic direction	2. Cash flow
3. Market growth	3. Competitive landscape	3. Quality/experience of management team
4. Gross margins	4. Quality/experience of management team	4. Competitive landscape
5. Quality/experience of management team	5. Earnings	5. Market growth
6. Market size	6. Market size	6. Strategic direction
7. Competitive landscape	7. Gross margins	7. Gross margins
8. Earnings	8. Market share	8. Earnings
9. Speed to market (first to market)	9. Cash flow	9. Speed to market (first to market)
10. Market share	10. Speed to market (first to market)	10. Market size

Figure 6.7 Contrasting priorities for companies and investment stakeholders

Source: PwC

* See URL: http://www.morgan-chambers.com/studyftse.htm

attention to their ability to influence the investment markets. But they can do this today by highlighting shared strategy and innovation, thereby benefiting both themselves and their clients. We believe they should start *now*.

Imagine a client that goes out bullishly, backed publicly by a world-class supplier, to trumpet the strategic benefits of a major outsourcing initiative to both parties. In the past, analysts might have focused on the company's debt and marked its shares down. But research shows that going out to the markets with an outsourcing announcement on the front foot with a positive message can boost a client's share price by a sustained 5 per cent. That is a huge benefit for a client to realize from a deal – even before the operational benefits kick in.

Executive challenges for suppliers

We believe that the suppliers which move fastest to create and build this virtuous circle will be the winners in the outsourcing market of tomorrow, clearly differentiated by their proven ability to realize benefits for clients. Achieving this involves a sharp rise in openness and face-to-face communication at board level. In turn, it raises five key challenges for the CEO and executives of suppliers:

1 **New executive structures:** These are needed to underpin commitments to strategic sourcing, share the client vision and mandate the direction being taken by both parties. For global suppliers, this will require greater 'in-region' autonomy from head office. All too often delays and politics are caused by the need to escalate major deals to head office, especially those involving substantial financing. This results in regional teams submitting risk-averse proposals stifled of innovation in order to attain approval at group level, thereby resulting in lost contracts and damaging opportunities and relationships into the future.

2 **Ramping up investment in BPO:** IT outsourcing suppliers need to develop new models for BPO and employ 'industry-intimate' people. They should look at *shared service centre economics* – not try for *single client deal* economics. A large part of BPO is about achieving volume economics. To sell clients the idea of BPO, they also need to actively originate metrics and business-relevant measures. Service providers will in future face a choice between investing to create factory entities or going to market and acquiring industry utilities through M&A. Some

clients may benefit by selling a business function and buying back the service under a conventional sourcing (not outsourcing) contract.

3 **Deciding on positioning towards the SME sector:** The small and medium-sized enterprise (SME) market presents major opportunities – but its economics mean that suppliers' existing sales and delivery mechanisms are not economically viable. Factories or utilities will be the route to capture a share of this vast market. Commoditization of these services will mean less personalization and little in terms of relationship for these clients – reflecting the fact that what they are likely to want is a low-cost, reliable commodity service rather than a relationship.

4 **Actively influencing the markets:** The perceptions of analysts, rating agencies, investors and regulators all need to be actively managed, most crucially by standing shoulder to shoulder in a public sense with clients, and reaffirming the shared vision and strategy. This is the most critical investment decision for the industry, suppliers' *own* shareholders and clients' shareholders. Suppliers need to marshal other powerful influencers to their cause, while also cooperating with clients to develop the persuasive models and arguments that will win round the analyst community.

5 **Ascending to new levels of underwriting client risk:** Prospective M&A integration should be covered in client contracts, while regulatory developments such as Basel II, International Accounting Standards (IAS) or Sarbanes-Oxley (SOX) bring huge opportunities for taking on and offsetting the risk of regulatory change. Closer involvement by suppliers' senior executives will help to build the perception and reality of greater shared risk carrying.

We have said that we believe outsourcing is a more powerful and smarter executive tool than M&A, and looked at how and where the benefits can be realized. But in the future, the benefits will go far beyond operational savings, efficiencies and innovation. Sourcing strategy will also become a key element in companies' management of market perception. To exploit this opportunity, suppliers and clients need to open a two-way dialogue. It is in both their interests to start it as soon as possible.

Key CEO and CFO questions arising from Chapter 6

CEO

■ Are you applying the same rigour as you would with an M&A deal to the tasks of planning and stating the benefits to a detailed level, and putting accountable ownership and sponsorship in place to deliver them?

■ Have you put together a retained team that consists of highly able people with clearly defined responsibilities and an awareness of the underlying objectives of the deal – or a loose collection of historical underperformers charged with keeping the ongoing costs as low as possible?

■ Does the retained team have the consistency of personnel, organizational muscle and competencies needed to manage the ongoing relationship flexibly and effectively in a changing environment, while also approving and managing discrete innovation-focused projects with potential for mutual value creation?

■ Have you benchmarked your SLAs against your own previous service delivery outputs and – where available – global best practice, as a basis for continuous performance improvement?

■ Have you asked your suppliers' executives to articulate how your business fits into their organizations' strategic thrust – and did you receive a sufficiently open and committed answer to suggest that a truly collaborative approach to communication with the investment community may be possible?

CFO

■ Are you expecting to receive the minimum service defined in the contract for the stated price, or hoping to see outperformance against the contract terms and ongoing innovation flowing through to the business on a continuing basis?

■ Will the board get early and advance notice of the impact on the financial performance of the outsourcing agreement resulting from changes in the company's strategy – including the effect on targets, costs and benefits realization?

■ Will your supplier relationship be sufficiently close and robust to support informal arrangements in which potential innovations can be trialled and prototyped outside the financial constraints of the contract, before being shifted to a formal basis?

■ Is your supplier now looking at servicing your business on the basis of *shared service centre economics* rather than single client *deal* economics? If not, can such economics be expected as any shared services come on stream?

7

Conclusion: The ultimate executive tool

The difference between what we do and what we are capable of doing would suffice to solve most of the world's problems.

Mahatma Gandhi

The major cycles of change throughout history have all opened up new possibilities that sweep away the status quo – not just in their immediate area of influence, but in other apparently unconnected sectors.

Take the Industrial Revolution. It not only created the means – and the demand – for the mass production of low-cost, high-quality manufactured goods. It also marked a watershed in society, transforming our cities and destroying cottage industries that could no longer compete. These developments, together with the resulting need for new means of mass distribution, triggered a vast swathe of change in areas ranging from transport to social structures.

Less well known than the Industrial Revolution is the Agricultural Revolution, driven in parallel by the need to feed the exploding urban workforce amid widespread depopulation of rural villages. By the early nineteenth century British farmers were using a rotation system that meant no land would remain fallow, thereby intensifying the farming process and setting the scene for the modern agrochemical industry.

The sourcing revolution?

So revolutions in one sphere trigger change cycles in others. Opinions vary over the precise starting point of the Information Revolution, whose ripples are still spreading – and whose implications are now playing themselves out across the world every day, from Baltimore to Bangalore. Cycles of change are always easier to identify and isolate with hindsight, and the overlapping nature of the current rapid evolution in technology and communications means we have a feeling of several cycles happening at once.

History will judge whether this is the case. But one of the most powerful legacies of the Infocom Revolution could well be how it has impacted on the way companies source their services and capabilities. High-capacity communications coupled with commoditized processing power and rapid globalization have opened up new vistas of sourcing opportunity, and made geographical location virtually irrelevant for many activities and services.

This opportunity is now reaching fulfilment, with flexible and eclectic sourcing developing from a concept to a philosophy, and ultimately to a discipline. As we enter this sourcing revolution a store of best practice thinking and experience is building up, but is not yet being collected or communicated with enough speed or accuracy to prevent CEOs and their colleagues making serious – and sometimes extremely costly – mistakes. The primary stimulus behind our decision to write this book is the dearth of informed, independent sources of information on this pivotal discipline.

At the frontier

However, the experience of past revolutions shows that mistakes at the frontier are part of the learning process. And there can be no doubt that sourcing is now the major frontier of business, as it strives to come to terms with the pervasive impact of globalization.

So, what is globalization doing to us all? Look at your own business and you will see its effects. Globalization is establishing and enforcing conformity and regulation. It is creating an ever-increasing focus on the best price. And it is driving workloads to be relocated to those places where they can be done more cheaply and/or effectively.

These changes are being driven by economic forces that are virtually irresistible. True, national governments can – and do – try to protect the workload handled within their own jurisdictions by setting up enterprise zones and offering tax breaks to those who invest onshore rather than moving their assets overseas. Perhaps the most striking example of targeted government intervention in recent years came in 2004, when the French government agreed to give massive tax breaks to the French media and communications group Vivendi Universal in return for creating jobs in France – but not even within its own business. Under the deal, Vivendi agreed to create 2,100 jobs among its suppliers in France, and was therefore allowed to unlock tax credits worth up to €3.8 billion (US$4.6 billion) over the following five to seven years. Reports said that none of the 2,100 employees would work directly for the company. The tax deal with the government, which followed eight months of discussions, came as finance minister Nicolas Sarkozy prepared to announce measures to encourage companies to keep jobs in France rather than offshoring them.

Governments may also intervene – as the Irish government did in the 1990s – with a view to not only protecting what they have but attracting new companies and workloads from other locations. Such a strategy of aligning national political measures with the prevailing global economic tides can reap spectacular successes, as demonstrated by Ireland's resulting 'Celtic tiger' growth rates and transformed infrastructure, skills base and education (not to mention house prices). However, the use of tax breaks and other inducements often proves to be a double-edged sword. Companies that choose a location for cost reasons alone are precisely those which will choose to go elsewhere when a more favourable option emerges.

Societies in competition

As such social impacts demonstrate, the effects of sourcing decisions go far beyond their direct effect on the businesses that do it and their onshore workforces. For high-cost western societies, a clear question emerges: how can we possibly compete with third-world nations offering such massive wage arbitrage opportunities? Our economies and societies are simply not geared up for this.

The model response of western politicians can be summed up as 'manufacturing bad, services good'. A natural corollary of 'services good' is to become more efficient and innovative in those services. The ability to do this is driven by technology and by the speed at which sustainable change can be achieved.

We would argue that what western countries should *not* aim to do is emulate Ireland's experiment in the 1990s. For a time, Ireland turned itself into the

CRM centre of Europe, if not the world. Call centres from the UK and Benelux gravitated there, drawn by attractions ranging from tax rates to a lilting, tuneful accent. Now those call centre operations are drifting elsewhere – albeit with some layers left behind in Ireland. If you look at today's global costs league Ireland is now floating somewhere near the top, and global companies are actively seeking out lower-cost locations where they can site operations until the cycle of wage and asset inflation in those countries prompts them to move on yet again.

It is our belief that it is *sourcing* in its many forms and facets – rather than *out*sourcing, which is just one part of this spectrum – that will provide the way for the western world to keep its head above water without suffering a dramatic fall in the living standards to which its citizens have grown accustomed. This means buying better and more cheaply, manufacturing outside the country, and importing finished goods, or sometimes components and semi-finished goods for skilled onshore assembly.

The philosophy of sourcing

Sourcing decisions are all the more powerful as a solution to business issues because sourcing is a process with no end point – a discipline that never achieves an ultimate conclusion. Adopting the philosophy of sourcing means looking constantly across existing and potential suppliers and locations, and seeking out the right balance amongst quality, economics, flexibility and innovation. It also means adopting the new mindset shown in Figure 7.1 – one on which the balance shifts away from attributes such as the scale and size of the organization itself, to focus more on the skills it can bring to bear and the resulting outputs such as speed of execution.

The discipline of moving or switching sources in a planned and responsive manner – 'Spanish wage rates have risen? Fine, we'll move to Portugal' – is now so well defined that it has been formalized as an MBA course in several European universities and management schools. The core of this discipline is knowing how to buy correctly while fully taking account of your responsibilities as a buyer, both to the stakeholders in your organization and to the particular market you are buying from. Purchasing pure services, as opposed to products, demands more sophisticated and open-minded approaches, governance, and the management and motivation of the supplier. This in turn drives quicker, better business enablement into the core of your business and ultimately through to your increasingly discerning client base. Value is more than a buzzword – it is an achievable differentiating sales tool.

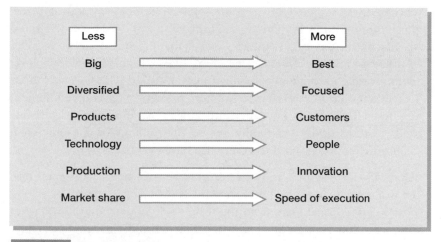

Less		More
Big		Best
Diversified		Focused
Products		Customers
Technology		People
Production		Innovation
Market share		Speed of execution

Figure 7.1   The new mindset

Given the irreversible change wrought by technology and globalization, strategic outsourcing is clearly not just a passing fad. As we have already said, it is just one slice of the sourcing spectrum. Used correctly it represents today's ultimate business enablement tool. Without the necessity of heavy up-front investment, it enables a business to experiment at the frontiers of areas that may or may not be supplanted by new technology or new ideas, by cheaper delivery mechanisms, or by some other as yet unthought-of intervention.

Whether it's outsourced, in-sourced, co-sourced or joint ventured makes little difference. These all involve exploiting the investment, specialization, resources, assets and intellect of third parties to further enable a business and change its clients' perception of value. This approach is already enabling a new generation of enlightened executives to achieve more, cheaper, faster and better than any previous generation. This is the true goal of the philosophy and emerging executive discipline of sourcing.

The supplier of the future . . .

This change process is not just taking place on the buyer's side of the deal. Already there are specialists out there that companies can contract with to exploit those suppliers' previous and ongoing investment and resources – in people, IP, physical assets, geographic stretch, financial flexibility, and ability to flip production lines from one part of the world to another.

Who are these suppliers of the future? Take Celestica – a Canadian-listed spin-off from IBM in 1998, now established as a world leader in electronics manufacturing services. Celestica's global manufacturing network covers Asia, Europe and the Americas, handling highly sophisticated outsourced manufacturing for original equipment manufacturers (OEMs) across industries from mobile phones to PCs, and from printers to telecoms equipment. As a result Celestica is now the third largest manufacturer of electronic goods in the world – yet hardly any of the millions of consumers and businesses that use its products every day have ever heard of it.

Celestica has made itself an exact mirror image of what its customers need in a world where fast, responsive sourcing is the key to competitive edge. It combines traditional manufacturing scale – warehouses full of production lines, some 200 feet long and consisting of five complex assembly machines – with the flexibility to switch each line from making mobile phones to PC servers. And then the ability to make that switch, including all the retooling and recalibration, within just six hours.

Picture the scene. UK-based mobile networks start giving away 3G handsets free, as an introductory offer to get customers hooked on seeing football highlights on their mobiles. Demand surges – and any handset vendors that miss out on the boom will take years to recoup the lost market share. However, not only are the handsets scarce, but they are being manufactured in Asia and would have to be shipped at huge expense. So what does the handset 'manufacturer' do? Call in the outsourced manufacturer. By that evening, Celestica is stamping out handsets in Italy, ready for the short freight hop to the UK.

. . . and the sourcing 'web'

The result: the handset vendors get the product they need in the place they need it, faster than they could get it there themselves. And they are freed up to focus on their core differentiated capabilities of design innovation, marketing, brand building and relationship management. True, they will pay a premium for a premium manufacturing service. But they have not had to make the massive up-front investment needed to build and own the whole chain themselves – an investment that would have left them weighed down with a barrel-load of gradually depreciating and increasingly obsolescent fixed assets. So they have mitigated their exposure if demand never materializes or evaporates overnight. The ROI business case is easy to justify, whichever way you view it.

However, this sourcing story does not begin and end with the relationship between the OEM and Celestica. Like its customers, Celestica wants to focus on its core business. So the sourcing chain is actually a web that goes through and beyond Celestica. And when Celestica decided that it wanted to outsource some of the technology that supports its production runs, it hit a problem.

Why? Because flexibility on that scale means it is almost impossible to pinpoint an aggregate level of risk. A technology outage at any stage in a production run will result in the destruction of up to a mile of sophisticated components. One morning, these might consist of printer components worth a few tens of thousands of dollars. That afternoon, it might be US$2 million worth of catalytic converters for car exhausts. Asking, say, an IT outsourcing provider to take responsibility for underwriting a risk factor that swings so alarmingly from one hour to the next is never going to be easy.

As Celestica demonstrates, it is not just data and services but also manufacturing capacity that can now be flipped round the world on a day-to-day basis, in response to changes in key target markets, natural disasters affecting the production facility or any other relevant occurrence. The key benefit throughout these sourcing choices is that a company can gain massive flexibility and enablement at lower risk and without the huge capital investment that would have been required in the old world.

Creating complementary flexibility . . .

So, how does the board manage all this? As part and parcel of this business enablement philosophy, you as a board member – and your direct reports – must accept that your own interests and those of your outsourcing providers will be closely linked, meaning in turn that effective motivation of suppliers has to be one of your company's core skills. This motivation has to start at the top because any change in your strategy will affect the capabilities you source, the way they are delivered and the costs they involve.

Outsourcing agreements need to be written in the full knowledge that the customer's business may hit a downturn or perform below expectations. Equally, its business may take off. Within these two extremes it is accepted as inevitable that volumes will rise and fall to some extent. So suppliers are generally expected to absorb 'knocks' equivalent to a 30 per cent fall or rise in the workload without changing the price or quality commitments. The outsourcing provider should not use a 30 per cent jump in volume to excuse a rise in the failure rate.

For outsourcing providers, this is a strong argument for developing a spread of relationships in a broad portfolio of industries to provide a degree of hedging of this risk. When the air industry is suffering, the motor or retailing industries may be doing well. When retailers are in a trough, banks may be thriving. These differences between industry cycles may also help to provide outsourcing suppliers with the flexibility to reallocate and recruit the people needed to support their customers in strongly performing sectors. Again, this flexibility comes at a price to the client. But this price should be offset against the fact that the customer would find it impossible to achieve the same agility in-house. The redundancies in a downturn would cost too much. The recruitment campaign in an upturn could not be stepped up quickly enough.

. . . through the new generation of suppliers

Realizing similar flexibility across your business means appreciating the benefits of outsourcing, and embracing it as a means to execute strategy and achieve both your immediate performance objectives and wider strategy. The more you use external sourcing as an underpinning of your development as an organization, the more you will find yourself creating – and encouraging – strategic alignment between yourself and your suppliers.

This raises one of the major inhibitors to successful long-term outsourcing relationships. We have already pointed out that the customer's CEO needs to recognize outsourcing's potential to deliver benefits way beyond mere cost cutting – and that too few do so. But there is also a major blockage at the same level on the other side. All too often the CEOs of outsourcing providers do not see their reciprocal responsibility for running their business in a new way: one that involves absorbing the impact of the customer's flexibility, becoming specific and intimate with the customer's industry, and freeing their middle and senior management to make decisions without slowing the whole process down through constant escalation back to the suppliers corporate/group management.

The next generation of outsourcing suppliers – and they are now starting to emerge – will recognize the limitations of running their business in a philosophically old-fashioned way. This may seem ironic, as the outsourcing offering is widely seen as an invitation for customers to join the future. But what is now needed is a new wave of executives in outsourcing providers who appreciate that it is part of their role and responsibility to include the client needs and objectives as an integral part of their own strategic thinking, planning and investment in existing and new services or geographies.

Making strategy cut both ways

What does this mean in practice? Well, every outsourcing supplier will ask you, the client CEO, about your business's strategy. This involves posing questions such as: 'Where are you going as a business? What are your objectives and aspirations? What new markets are you looking at? How active are your competitors? How can we fit in, in order to help you achieve your strategic aims?'

But few client CEOs ask similar questions and expect detailed answers the other way. 'What is your strategy as a provider? What industries are you focusing on? How important is our industry – and our business – to your strategic direction? What new functions, industries, capabilities or locations are you considering investing in? How strong is your innovation capability in my vertical business speciality? How do *we* fit into your client portfolio – and into your view of your business's future?'

Even today, outsourcing customers tend not to ask these questions at senior executive level. But they have an absolute right – and, shareholders might argue, a responsibility – to do so. If, and not when, the next generation of informed institutional shareholders comes to ask why a particular supplier was chosen, and whether better commitment, risk management or innovation might not have been found elsewhere, both the CEO and any other executive will find it is very useful not only to have asked those questions ahead of time but also to have current information throughout the contract's lifetime.

Hybrid culture – not bastardized culture

A further issue for customer CEOs to face is the deep cultural impact of using outsourcing on a wide-scale basis. It is a brave board that recognizes, encourages and monitors the blending – some might term it 'bastardization' – of its cherished corporate culture into a hybrid culture with the outsource provider.

But if the relationship is to realize the full benefits, that is what must happen. Otherwise there will be a cultural polarization between the business and the outsourced delivery function – irrespective of whether that function is delivering enterprise-wide technology or a specific business process. This cultural fusion is the single most critical determinant of long-term success, which is why the sponsorship and motivating leadership from the executive teams on both sides must be constant and consistent.

Barbara Cassani, who established a low-cost airline in the United Kingdom, summed up her attitude to cultural fusion by stating:

'I believe you do have to make outsourced staff feel part of your team. For example, we had a MAD (Make A Difference) award, where staff nominate colleagues they feel have performed above and beyond. Many of those nominated work for suppliers, and we gave them the same prize and recognition as we give our own staff. It's important to remember that, fundamentally, people want to do a good job. We have a bear-hug approach, embracing individuals who deliver service on our behalf. However, although this works well for the outsourced staff, it can be far more prickly with their own management. Bear hugs may not be part of their corporate culture! That's where outsourcer selection is so important – you need to choose companies which are like-minded to your own.'*

As Cassani's comments demonstrate, the buy-in and visibility on both sides must be demonstrated in day-to-day behaviour at all levels, ranging from the involvement of board-level executives in decision making to the holding of joint Christmas parties for staff. This behaviour is crucial to preventing the type of internal xenophobia that can fatally undermine an outsourcing relationship. The executive team must visibly lead from the front in illustrating the need and acceptability of a growing hybrid culture.

From cost, to quality . . .

Equally important is the need to remain focused on the envisaged and specifically targeted benefits and objectives. For the customer enterprise, outsourcing is about enablement and speed. As we have already discussed, a key determinant of how readily it will embrace the right type of behaviour lies in the severity of the situation that causes it to contemplate outsourcing in the first place. The absolute need to address this situation will take it through the generally straightforward cost comparators that make up the initial business case.

* 'Outsourcing in the FTSE 100: The Definitive Study', Morgan Chambers and CW360, 2001 (http://www.morgan-chambers.com/studyftse.htm).

Moving beyond that early cost focus, the customer will then start to examine what more it can get for its investment. This will involve asking itself some fundamental questions. Is higher quality the priority? Or is it effectiveness and efficiency on an ongoing basis? The choices at this stage may reflect the overarching day-to-day pressures and preoccupations keeping the CEO awake at night.

But whatever the immediate pressures may be, soon after the outsourcing project comes into effect the customer CEO and board will invariably start to accept that – from a technology standpoint – quality is the biggest plus point. The business now has reliable, robust systems, and costs are under control. Having initiated the outsourcing deal with a focus on costs, the almost subconscious next step is to seek higher quality.

. . . to innovation

Turning the focus from cost to quality is a significant shift in the customer's mindset and objectives – and it is important that it takes its outsourcing supplier with it during this transition. In practical terms this change involves revisiting the costs agenda and finding the right balance between cost and quality, since it is unreasonable for the customer to expect the highest possible quality at the lowest possible cost.

However, many customers – especially those who are outsourcing for the first time – move unilaterally to a quality focus without involving their outsourcing provider. Where this happens the relationship is set for severe strain, since the customer will start to criticize the supplier for a lack of quality-boosting innovation in terms of service delivery.

A far more productive approach is for the customer CEO and board to recognize that the business may have entered the relationship for tactical cost-focused reasons – a perfectly reasonable rationale so long as it is within a strategic context. But once costs have been contained, and the business is positioned to climb out of the 'hole' that prompted the decision to outsource, the CEO needs to recognize when the time is right to push the button for a greater focus on quality. And the route to quality is through innovation, above and beyond the original innovation used to deliver the costs agenda.

A structure for improving quality

If innovation has not initially been built into the agreement on a formal basis, the time to do so will inevitably come if the relationship succeeds. The most fruitful basis for long-term innovation is for both parties to come together in a regular, planned and structured way to discuss possible innovative initiatives. The output from these meetings must be reported upwards to senior management and, where change is far-reaching, potentially even to the board. For example, 'power users' such as commodity traders or underwriters command respect and priority support systems and specialist technology. They tend to abhor change, but by their 'special case' nature they incur disproportionate costs. Changing or innovating work practices to save unnecessary costs in this ego-rich ecosystem is a political nightmare unless there is visible executive sponsorship. Suppliers and clients need to agree that nothing is out of 'innovation bounds' – and therefore understanding what innovations have been rejected needs sanction as much as those that are approved by the contract management team.

Our experience over the years of auditing and mediating in troubled outsourcing relationships has consistently underlined the importance of this formal innovation process. All too often we find during such audits that the customer is making statements along the lines of, 'We entered this agreement for innovation', when in fact it entered it for price first and quality second. Having achieved the shift from an in-house department that was both high cost and low quality, the customer has now developed a 'false memory' that it always wanted innovation (despite a lack of specific mention in the contract) – and this misconception has in turn become the basis for its heaviest criticism of the outsourcing provider.

Then, when we sit down with both sides during the formal audit, we generally find that the interface between the customer and supplier – the contract management team – has nobody left who was actually present when the deal was done. It is fair to say that in 95 per cent of failing contracts all the individuals who participated actively in the deal have moved on within 9–14 months of the agreement being signed. This means the people now involved in the critical interface between the parties, and in delivering the targeted benefits, can manage only to the letter of the contract. And, in all too many cases, the contract turns out to be mute on the subject of innovation.

The result is that the objectives have become company folklore handed down from a previous generation of managers – and, as with most folklore, it has changed in the telling. All too often the middle management on the customer-side contract team believe they have been put in place to contain costs, and that is what they do. When we examine the supplier side, we usually find there is a clear audit trail of innovation that has been put on the table and rejected by the self-appointed 'gatekeepers' on the customer side.

Breaking the gridlock

In such circumstances there is an absolute need to break this gridlock. The first step is to demonstrate to the customer CEO and board that innovation has been repeatedly offered and refused. This blockage is all the worse in cases where the provider's contract team has failed to negotiate an automatic 'right of reply' and escalation to customer board level.

Once these problems are pinpointed there are proven techniques for addressing them. Governance, reporting and escalation procedures need to be built, under which any innovation offering a given level of potential savings requires escalation to senior management or even board level on both sides.

Summaries of innovation offered, accepted or rejected should form a regular part of the six-monthly discussion sessions between the client and supplier executives. Joint continuous improvement programmes can also help to break the innovation logjam. However, they are not usually the primary route, since CIPs tend to focus on effectiveness and efficiency – primarily handling greater volume for the same price – rather than on driving ongoing quality increases.

Shared benefits from innovation

But innovation is not continuous improvement. Innovation is off-the-wall thinking generated by talking to the business, understanding its problems and coming up with fresh ideas and approaches that would speed up entire processes, take out headcount and so on. And a key characteristic of innovation is that both customer and supplier stand to benefit.

An example of this in action at a major oil company is described in the accompanying box overleaf. The key to such win/win arrangements is the fact that both sides should understand and take account of the strategic agenda of the other, enabling what they get from the deal to be complementary rather than conflicting.

Innovation: shared risk – shared benefit

A leading global oil company faced a problem during the 1990s with its petrol station network. Most of the outlets were franchised to third-party operators, and many were now opening up shops with their petrol stations. The problem was the franchise agreement included a clause enabling the operators to withhold payment of the whole invoice for a period if there were any mistakes in it – whether the error concerned revenues from sales of petrol or groceries. A further complication was that franchisees were often due retrospective discounts on fuel because of the group's commitment to maintaining price comparability with local competitors.

The petrol company's finance function was so concerned about triggering the delay clause on franchisee invoices that it was conducting manual spot checks and reconciliations on them. This in turn was slowing down the entire accounts process, and beginning to restrict the group's cash flow.

One of the oil company's outsourcing providers, incentivized by the opportunity to share benefits, came up with a solution. It suggested that it write a couple of programs to support an interactive enquiry routine, enabling finance personnel to check and validate petrol station invoices on-screen rather than via manual processes. The company liked the idea, but refused to bear the cost of writing the programs. Instead, it proposed a risk-sharing arrangement under which, if the initiative failed to produce any improvement, the provider would get nothing, and would have to bear the costs of the project. If it succeeded, the supplier would receive 60 per cent of the net improvement in year one, but nothing thereafter – and the customer would keep the IP to the programs.

The result was a win/win all round. The new routines delivered a major boost to the oil company's cash flow, triggering a large one-off payment to the outsourcing supplier in year one, and leaving the customer to continue to exploit the resulting savings on a continuing basis. The supplier, having received the one-off boost, was further incentivized to come up with more innovation in future. From both sides, this was outsourced innovation management at its clearest and most effective.

This sharing of benefits has implications for the whole approach to outsourcing on both sides of the deal. If we accept that the next generation of executives – both customers and suppliers – will regard the attainment of mutual corporate objectives with the same seriousness and commitment as in an M&A deal, then it follows that integration in outsourcing is not about either side losing control.

Instead, the real crux of the integration between customer and outsourcing supplier is around gaining new insights, new capabilities and potentially new directions for both parties, and leveraging these to the benefit of each partner. This means dispelling the preconception that there will always be a winner and loser in every outsourcing deal, but accepting – in M&A terms – the fact that a 'merger of equals' is possible, and that it can deliver demonstrable and lasting benefits to both sides, on a sustained but flexible basis.

A sharper tool

This gets to the nub of why we regard outsourcing as the sharpest tool in the executive team's box. Executed correctly, outsourcing enables a CEO and board to contemplate aspects of their company's future in ways they had never previously deemed possible. They get this ability through an open and forward-looking approach to 'partnering', encompassing both skill sets and the ability to underwrite results.

This forward-looking mindset includes an acceptance that needs and circumstances will change for both sides. The CEO of the customer needs to accept – as in an M&A transaction – that as the benefits of the agreement become apparent there may be aspects of a business or service that no longer fit. So the board needs to be prepared to do subsequent further deals that may be akin to the follow-on disposals in an M&A context.

For example, picture a utility company that runs its own fleet of vehicles and a fully employed workforce of drivers and maintenance staff. Once the idea of outsourcing takes hold, more and more possibilities emerge. Why not outsource maintenance of the vehicles? Then ownership of the fleet, supplying drivers to the outsourced entity? Then employment of the workforce? Then the garage premises? Ultimately the business will have freed up a large amount of property assets, removed significant staff exposure, moved a number of risks elsewhere and raised service levels to a point agreed and rigorously enforced with the outsourcing provider.

As the enablement from outsourcing flows through the business, it inevitably makes the board query its ownership of aspects of the business that were once perceived as core, or that it once thought would make the transformation journey along with the business. The liberating effect of a risk-carrying/sharing perspective lets the CEO ask questions that were once unaskable about what really needs to stay within the business. Our experience shows that this 'scope extension' usually comes to the fore around two years after the increase in enablement from an initial successful outsourcing deal.

From deal to life cycle

The flexibility to extend outsourcing underlines the key distinction between outsourcing and M&A as tools for corporate reshaping. While M&A is perceived as a discrete one-off deal with a beginning, middle and end, and with a sense of 'closure' and finality on completion, outsourcing is a philosophy that opens the way to a logical and progressive continuum of change. This is why outsourcing is actually more appropriate than M&A to the idea of a 'life cycle'. While the same skills apply in each case, a company engaged in ongoing outsourcing will find that it is applying all the skills at once in various initiatives, each at a different stage in its life cycle, rather than applying them in a sequential order as it does in an M&A deal.

The likelihood of continual progressive change in turn brings implications for the outsourcing contract. It needs to be crafted to allow leeway for the revelations that will come later to both partners. This is not easy. The art of writing an outsourcing contract lies in drafting an agreement containing principles that allow for change, which enables such change to be costed, and which gives the existing party comfort that it can be involved in this change without having to bid down to the lowest external price which might be offered by an aggressive incoming supplier.

These requirements make it critical that specialist external legal advisors are brought in to mediate on outsourcing contracts (see our specialist's section on legal issues on page 164). Often working closely with sourcing intermediaries, they are well versed in achieving the required balance – ensuring that the principles within the contract allow for further scope extension and innovation, even to the level of including guideline costings.

Underwriting the responsibilities

However, even the best-written outsourcing contract does not absolve the CEO and board from the need to stay constantly engaged with the relationship. True, you can contract for certain results to be underwritten, and for certain risks to be absorbed. But the pace of change in today's business environment, coupled with the potential for friction and blockages to spring up on either or both sides, means the agreement must be policed rigorously and continually. This will provide the bedrock for long-term success, and for the original objectives to be not only achieved but exceeded in ways the customer never conceived at the start.

Our experience highlights two best practice points through which outsourcing providers can use their wider resources to help customers exceed their expectations:

1 *Ongoing indemnity of strategy*: As the record of enablement grows, it empowers the board to become more adventurous. This changing perspective, given executional power by a resilient value-producing outsourcing relationship, allows the two parties to investigate increasingly sophisticated and challenging contributions that the provider can make to both the formation and delivery of corporate strategy. The robust relationship enables the customer and provider to stand overtly shoulder to shoulder to underwrite the strategy and targeted results in a very public way.

2 *Project drive*: Behind closed doors, the outsourcing provider can throw its weight and expertise behind driving the practicalities of the strategy in a project sense. Imagine an outsourcing provider who says: 'This may be a one-off, it's not part of the contract, but we know you want to go into China in a big way. We will contribute our best brains in the Greater China region to help you form your thinking and execution planning.' Given that this is outside the existing scope, the provider would then make a bid to run all, or just critical aspects, of the implementation approach.

This second area of best practice may potentially lead to a joint venture entry method between the customer and outsourcing supplier. Historically joint ventures have often failed because the common objectives that bring the two parties together tend to be transient and to dissipate over time. However, a robust outsourcing relationship is for the long term – so it can provide a sounder bedrock for sustainable joint ventures, since both sides already have a vested interest in the relationship. Secondly, both parties are already accustomed to working within an arrangement where one side is focused on containing costs and the other to maximizing value. And thirdly, the established strategic alignment and awareness between the two sides means there is much less of a learning curve to be negotiated than would be the case with a new joint venture partner. All of these factors mean that a joint venture with an existing outsourcing partner has a greater chance of success than a traditional third-party joint venture.

A venture that has benefited from this type of close alignment underpinned by an existing outsourcing relationship is the Fin-Force international payments processing utility created by Belgian bank KBC in partnership with EDS (see the case study on page 185 – and especially the comments by Fin-Force CEO Pascal Deman). The two organizations, which have worked together since the early 1990s, set out in 2000 to create a payments 'factory' with a non-banking culture. The expertise contributed by EDS, which has a stake in Fin-Force, was vital in driving the necessary industrialization, and in maintaining Fin-Force's momentum during the early years when third-party customers initially failed to come on board. Other banks have now caught on to the concept of Fin-Force as an industry utility – akin to several Formula 1 teams using Ferrari engines – and have started to sign up as Fin-Force customers. Germany's DZ Bank has even taken an equity stake. The mutual benefits for KBC and EDS are continuing to flow, as a direct result of the level of trust in their relationship.

The future: strategy, sourcing – and shareholder activism

So: what is next for outsourcing? To set the context, take a look at Figure 7.2, depicting the tools that a strategic outsourcing programme provides. And remember that most of the interactions in this chart will be undertaken personally by the CEO or CFO.

We have discussed how the combination of strategy and context creates a powerful lever for business transformation through outsourcing. We have shown the CEO, other board members and key stakeholders how they can *approach outsourcing by using M&A skills and techniques that are readily to hand through their existing experience and knowledge.* And we have illustrated how applying this existing knowledge in the context of outsourcing can shift the balance of probability from failure to success – with the determining factor being the CEO's *personal commitment to managing the process.*

Despite the greater maturity of M&A, the fact is that studies indicate its failure rate remains at about 65 per cent – roughly the same as for outsourcing. How come? The reasons for M&A failures have been well rehearsed elsewhere. But the point from our perspective is that if outsourcing is already on a par with M&A in terms of success, then combining outsourcing's inherent advantages in terms of focus and flexibility with a more disciplined and rigorous approach should push outsourcing's rate of delivery well ahead of M&A's.

We also argue that outsourcing is something no CEO can afford not to consider on strategic and commercial grounds. But there is a further

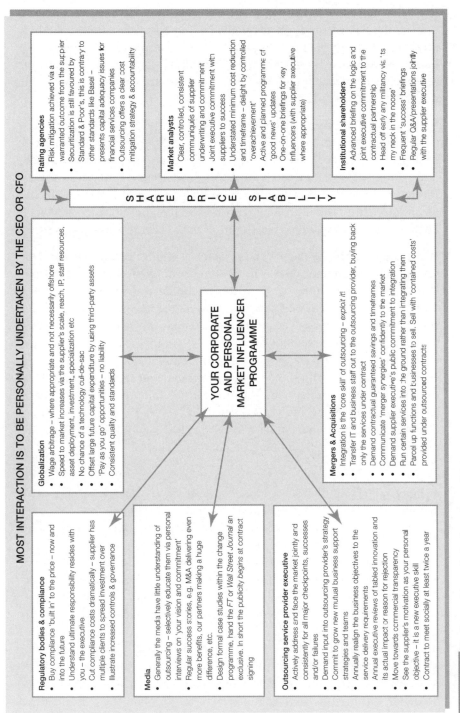

MOST INTERACTION IS TO BE PERSONALLY UNDERTAKEN BY THE CEO OR CFO

Rating agencies
- Risk mitigation achieved via a warranted outcome from the supplier
- Securitization is still favoured by Standard & Poor's, this is contrary to other standards like Basel – presents capital adequacy issues for financial services companies
- Outsourcing offers a clear cost mitigation strategy & accountability

Market analysts
- Clear, controled, consistent communiqués of supplier underwriting and commitment
- Joint executive commitment with suppliers to success
- Understated minimum cost reduction and timeframe – delight by controlled 'overachievement'
- Active and planned programme of 'good news' updates
- One-on-one briefings for key influencers (with supplier executive where appropriate)

Institutional shareholders
- Advanced briefing on the logic and joint executive commitment to the contractual partnership
- Head off early any militancy via 'its my neck in the noose'
- Frequent 'success' briefings
- Regular Q&A/presentations jointly with the supplier executive

S H A R E   P R I C E   S T A B I L I T Y

Globalization
- Wage arbitrage – where appropriate and not necessarily offshore
- Speed to market increases via the supplier's scale, reach, IP, staff resources, asset deployment, investment, specialization etc
- No chance of a technology cul-de-sac
- Offset large future capital expenditure by using third-party assets
- 'Pay as you go' opportunities – no liability
- Consistent quality and standards

YOUR CORPORATE AND PERSONAL MARKET INFLUENCER PROGRAMME

Regulatory bodies & compliance
- Buy compliance 'built in' to the price – now and into the future
- Understand ultimate responsibility resides with you – the executive
- Cut compliance costs dramatically – supplier has multiple clients to spread investment over
- Illustrate increased controls & governance

Media
- Generally the media have little understanding of outsourcing – selectively educate them via personal interviews on 'your vision and commitment'
- Regular success stories, e.g. M&A delivering even more benefits, our partners making a huge difference, etc.
- Design formal case studies within the change programme, hand the *FT* or *Wall Street Journal* an exclusive. In short the publicity *begins* at contract signing

Outsourcing service provider executive
- Actively address and face the market jointly and consistently for all major checkpoints, successes and/or failures
- Demand input into outsourcing provider's strategy
- Commit to grow new mutual business support strategies and teams
- Annually realign the business objectives to the service delivery requirements
- Annual executive reviews of tabled innovation and its actual impact or reason for rejection
- Move towards commercial transparency
- See the supplier's motivation as your personal objective – it is a new executive skill
- Contract to meet socially at least twice a year

Mergers & Acquisitions
- Integration is the 'core skill' of outsourcing – *exploit it!*
- Transfer IT and business staff out to the outsourcing provider, buying back only the services under contract
- Demand contractual guaranteed savings and timeframes
- Communicate 'merger synergies' confidently to the market
- Demand supplier executive's public commitment to integration
- Run certain services into the ground rather than integrating them
- Parcel up functions and businesses to sell. Sell with 'contained costs' provided under outsourced contracts

Figure 7.2 Tools provide a strategic outsourcing programme

Source: © Morgan Chambers plc 2006

irresistible force that is helping to drive the maturation of the outsourcing market: the activism and – increasingly – militancy of shareholders in their ongoing efforts to realize value from their investments. The overt link between investor activism and the interlinking commercial maturity of outsourcing suppliers to their clients may not be immediately evident. But it is there, and it is growing.

First, consider the rising global tide of instances in which investors have turned their sights on to CEOs in response to what they perceived to be poor strategic decisions or value-destroying M&A deals. This is hardly a new trend. In 1919, a group of US investors sued Henry Ford because they wanted to force him to pay them more dividends, and invest less in the business – hardly the most long-term perspective, but an understandable one. They got a sympathetic hearing from the Michigan Supreme Court.

What *is* new is the frequency and ferocity of similar confrontations. Not surprisingly the United States is in the forefront. Michael Eisner quit from Disney following running battles with shareholders, and Carly Fiorina was ousted as CEO of Hewlett-Packard as investors became increasingly disillusioned with the company's acquisition of Compaq and wider strategy. More recently, Phil Purcell of Morgan Stanley – another CEO renowned for controversial mergers – was ousted following shareholder pressure. All these events served to underline investors' commitment and aggression in seeking to drive changes in strategy and personnel in the topmost reaches of global companies. It hardly seems a coincidence that the Securities and Exchange Commission (SEC) is mandating new powers for shareholders to nominate directors and press their proposals on company boards.

A global shift

This trend extends far beyond the United States. And while much shareholder militancy is laid at the door of hedge funds, it is undeniable that traditional institutional investors are also flexing their muscles, both more readily and more often than before. In the United Kingdom, shareholders forced the departure of Sir Peter Davis as chairman of retail group J. Sainsbury in 2004 over perceived strategy failures – including problems with a major outsourcing programme – and boardroom remuneration (see the case study on page 193). These events coincided with a 'peace summit', held by the Confederation of British Industry and Investment Management Association, to try and cool the temperature between boards and shareholders.

The Anglo-Saxon economies present the longest-standing examples of investor activism – but they are no longer alone in experiencing it. In the heartlands of continental Europe, the chairman and chief executive of Deutsche Börse tendered their resignations following their failed and widely opposed bid for the London Stock Exchange. The episode saw overseas hedge funds branded 'locusts' by German politicians. Less widely reported was a suit filed by 15,000 investors against Deutsche Telekom in Frankfurt's Regional Court, and the introduction of new 'class action' provisions for German shareholders in late 2005.

Even Japan is not immune, with foreign shareholders now owning close to a quarter of shares on the Tokyo Stock Exchange – and foreign indirect investment via share ownership rising above 40 per cent in some sectors. Overseas and local investors are making their voices heard, pressing for companies to realize more value. An example came when shareholder pressure pushed Nippon Broadcasting towards a merger with Fuji Television.

Investor vigilance extends from M&A to outsourcing

To date, shareholder activism in the west has tended to focus on allegedly poor M&A deals. But it is only a matter of time before investors turn their attention to today's – and tomorrow's – major outsourcing deals, which have far more in common with strategic M&A than with traditional customer–contractor relationships.

For CEOs and boards, the message is clear. As outsourcing matures to the level of M&A, so the degree of public and shareholder scrutiny of these deals will rise to a similar level. Get strategic outsourcing right, and you can transform your business and be lauded by shareholders. Get it wrong, and you will be judged – and treated – every bit as harshly as Carly Fiorina in the wake of HP's acquisition of Compaq.

As with M&A, the attitudes of different investors and public commentators will be inconsistent and even contradictory. For example, investors' demand for maximized returns will tend to push offshoring – including offshore outsourcing – up the agenda. But public distaste for the apparent 'exporting' of jobs, and the socially ethical stance of some investors, will see companies criticized for going offshore in search of the type of competitive edge that actually makes businesses (and jobs) commercially sustainable.

Shoulder to shoulder

The heightened focus on outsourcing deals will bring major implications not just for client companies engaging in outsourcing but for outsourcing suppliers. As do participants in M&A, they will have to stand publicly with their clients, and exhibit comparable levels of transparency and commitment to the relationship. They will need to share the limelight, and the exposure when things go wrong. And they will have to treat clients – as some already do – as close partners rather than commercial customers.

In short, they will have to reach a new level of maturity. We have already discussed in Chapter 6 how we believe many senior executives of outsourcing suppliers will need to change their behaviour to reflect the needs of their clients' businesses and of their own. But this will be a symptom rather than a cause of maturity. We believe it is institutional investors and shareholders – through their vigilant monitoring of their investee companies' outsourcing deals – that will be the ultimate drivers of maturity in the global strategic outsourcing market.

Outsourcing and shareholders are two facts of life for today's CEO. But few have realized how closely – and increasingly – interlinked they are now, and will become in the future. This is not theory. As our case study on BP on page 199 shows, outsourcing can be used as a lever that simultaneously transforms performance, supports the execution of global strategy and manages the share price. We believe that, one day, most of the world's successful companies will be run this way.

Key CEO and CFO questions arising from Chapter 7

CEO

■ Do you believe that your strategic sourcing approach is fundamental to the long-term enablement and benefit of your corporation? Is it a policy and a philosophy that the whole board will sponsor both internally to ensure broad acceptance, and externally as a more flexible and controllable business model?

■ Whether this policy was originated in response to adversity and market challenges or by your foresight and design, do you see outsourcing as a tool to achieve a new corporate mindset, to reduce complexity and achieve tighter business focus and a faster, more responsive client lead set of solutions, services and/or products? In short, do you see this as a catalyst for change on an industrial scale?

■ Whether or not you consider the service provider to be a true partner, do you trust them to deliver at least to the letter of the contract; do you understand where you sit in their strategy and can you influence them at executive level; how open are you and their executive to establishing a one on one executive relationship?

■ Have you and your senior management understood that only by developing a mutual hybrid culture will the full flexibility and agility needed for reaping full business benefit and enablement be achieved? How will you contribute in the mid- to longer-term to ensuring this cultural change is given optimal encouragement?

■ Retention of the management who crafted the outsourcing deal and who are now the frontline interface to the supplier(s) is critical. How will you personally contribute to that continuity and thereby ensure motivation, direction, accountability and at least the minimum envisaged benefit collection?

■ Do you and the Board recognize that as your confidence and success with your sourcing strategy grows, that you will become more critical of non-performing parts of your business? And thus you are likely to be more adventurous in both the scope and reach of any future extension to the sourcing strategy and available structural/commercial options?

■ Have you begun to understand how the advantages of a cohesive and far-reaching outsourcing strategy play with analysts, institutional investors, rating agencies and regulators? Can you develop and communicate clearly and consistently the de-risking aspects, commercial flexibility, accountability and underwriting, access to scale, resources, intellectual property, leverage and experience of your contract and supplier(s)? Can you demonstrate the supplier commitment to your objectives?

CFO

■ Beyond the current contractual scope, can and will you be able to utilize consistently the suppliers' wage arbitrage advantages, scale and flexibility to flatten your unique economic cycles/seasonality and CAPEX requirements? Can you see how it really does stabilize aspects of the share price by offering new and additional flexibility and business enablement?

■ Do you recognize that as outsourcing services mature and become more sophisticated, risk and its mitigation via third parties will become a more usual part of the interdependencies of outsourcing arrangements? Are you and the chosen supplier(s) prepared for this? Will you pioneer or follow trends? What allowances for this is there within the contract and within your own functional responsibilities?

■ What role do you see yourself fulfilling in influencing of the multiplicity of stakeholders as to what an innovative sourcing philosophy could bring in the mid- to longer-term? Is this a step change or merely a tighter discipline to be adopted? Developing a hybrid service delivery culture with the supplier is one thing, how would you accommodate this approach within your own department? Is it possible and really relevant to aspects of your role or merely fanciful words to 'sell' the move to third party leverage to the wider corporate audience?

■ Do you recognise that these 'influencer' skills will be very useful to you as shareholder activism matures and takes hold?

■ What future risks could be underwritten by the suppliers and how can this be incorporated into the strategy and thinking of the executive? Would you become more orientated towards acquisitions if the very real issues of physical integration and cost synergies were contracted for? As outsourcing begins to deliver, will you become less tolerant of failing business units and move quicker towards disposal or radical surgery by using the suppliers as change agents and to mitigate risk?

■ Are you beginning to understand how your experience and expertise in M&A activities directly aids your ability to strategize and deliver on a comprehensive sourcing strategy?

8

Are you ready to outsource?

Outsourcing can be a great help in terms of helping both the chemical and pharmaceutical industries get out of the ruts we find ourselves in . . . when outsourcing works well, it allows companies to spend their resources on innovation, rather than on development or manufacturing infrastructure that already exists elsewhere. . . . the more important question to ask is . . . will outsourcing fulfill its promise in the future? My answer is . . . again yes.

Andrew Liveris, Business Group President, Performance Chemicals

We hope we have helped you to identify the inside track for deciding whether outsourcing is right for your business or a specific function, clarifying your objectives, creating the business case, building buy-in internally and externally, and establishing the right sort of ongoing supplier relationship under the right contractual terms.

However, before you start the whole process, the ultimate question can only be answered by you personally – it is an executive decision – are you *really* ready to outsource? Here is a self-check covering twelve areas, to determine whether you are still simply toying with the idea of outsourcing – or are all set and ready to join the game.

1 Knowing your own business
   Do you have sufficient granular knowledge about your full costs to enable you to slice, dice and compare operational performance data against various alternatives – whether driven by your own needs or by various constructs pushed by the service providers? Can the culture of your organization handle the concept of outsourcing? How about your fellow board members?

2 Strategic intent

Is it clear how outsourcing fits into your longer-term strategic and competitive planning – especially in the light of other large-scale change programmes in the pipeline such as M&A, restructuring, geographical expansion, legislative compliance, technology refresh requirements? How much and what kind of corporate flexibility would you like or do you need? What alternatives to outsourcing do you have?

3 Business benefits

Can you define – in a single sentence – what outsourcing will deliver to the business? Do you have clear priorities among the abilities to gain flexibility, cut costs or manage risk? Have you identified the trade-offs? What will success look like – and do you have enough certainty that it is realistically deliverable? How will you account for normal or unexpected change in your marketplace 'knocking on' to your defined benefits? Would a supplier guarantee some or all of the benefits you expect?

4 Scope boundaries

Which capabilities will you 'let go'? Will it be the back office and the technology, the process and 'business method', or the intellectual property unique to the service – its competitive differentiation? What about the knowledge and experience inherent in the staff and management? Should a pilot project be the first step, or will you outsource the business function holistically from day one? What about the assets – will you retain them or sell them? How will you value them? Are they potentially worth more than you think?

5 Deal construction

Will a disposal of the business function, together with a back-to-back service agreement for services, benefit your balance sheet and send positive messages to the market? How will you get 'gain share' into your ultimate model to ensure you benefit from, say, process innovation and new technology? Have you considered partnering through a joint venture structure? Do you want financial re-engineering to be at the heart of the deal, used for specific short-term issues, or kept to a minimum? How do you want to handle the staff – assure zero redundancies for a period of time and pay the supplier more, absorb or redeploy some ahead of the deal and transfer, or 'slim down' the function before the deal?

6 Supply market's capability

Have you developed a real understanding of the market's ability to deliver on the scope, criteria and objectives of your business plan? Are there truly global players out there? Can the selected supplier(s) deliver both the technology services and the necessary business function expertise? What measurements of success will they accept? What risk factors will they accept – even to the extent of regulatory and compliance responsibility – and at what price? What is the service provider's track record of staff attrition compared to yours? Does it truly understand your business? How many of your competitors does it work for already – and is that an advantage or a disadvantage?

7 Tender process and service provision options

Do you want a single supplier? Do you understand the issues, additional management time and costs of a multiple supplier model? What role will offshore play – what are the risks, and do you care which offshore destination your workload goes to? Should offshore economics be applied via an 'onshore' supplier to avoid direct offshore contracting? Do you need a competitive process to get the best value and innovation? Or if you go with a single or sole supplier – a non-competitive model – how can you illustrate to the board and/or powerful stakeholders that the negotiated price is fair and in line with the market? How will you contract for innovation and commercial/service flexibility? How quickly can you conclude the process?

8 Holistic communications planning

Who do you need to communicate with, and have you outlined a strategy for doing so? How will you ensure a single and consistent message for all stakeholders? What are the legal requirements on communicating with unions, workers' bodies, staff, investors, stock exchanges and regulatory bodies? How will you maintain security until the final decision, while simultaneously preparing the necessary data and facts to produce the tender and holding supplier discussions? What are the key messages to maintain morale? How do you handle any 'leaks' of information?

9 People skills

What skills will you need at each stage of the deal process – including to manage the contract? Do corporate legal or procurement have a role, if they have never done anything of this size, complexity, duration and criticality before? How will you acquire speciality support skills – in what areas and how early in the process? Will you expect specialist advisers to underwrite results or at least to be measured on performance? How will you ensure team motivation and longer-term retention of the contract management team? Will your supplier(s) make parallel commitments to keep their project team in place? Is your tax and accounting department sufficiently knowledgeable to analyze the implications of the current and future structure, or do you know where to get help and advice?

10 Governance, reporting and regulatory compliance

You cannot outsource fiduciary responsibility – so, after outsourcing, what compliance information will you rely on? What is the regulators' view on outsourcing, and do they need to be engaged and informed ahead of deal conclusion? At what point does governance become intrusive enough to impinge on delivery? How frequent should reporting be? What data will provide the essence for control, course correction, performance measurement and benefit collection?

11 Ensuring benefit collection

Statistically, only half of outsourcing contracts deliver the envisaged benefits – so how will you ensure that you are in that 50 per cent? What happens when business demand changes the service priorities, the investment profile or volumes? How will you track, measure and compensate for change? Can you raise the bar contractually, and for which criteria? Will your supplier agree to build relationships at the executive level? And will these relationships aid benefit collection – by enabling you to stand shoulder to shoulder publicly, and by ensuring the 'A teams' remain in place on both sides, that innovation is consistently put on the table, and that the supplier's leverage is focused for your benefit?

12 Commitment to manage – forever!

Ongoing relationship management is crucial – are you personally prepared to invest sufficient time and resources in it? Is this really an executive responsibility? What costs should you expect for the retained contract management entity? Does that cost skewer the economics of the business case? How will you motivate the retained team – and prevent them regarding their role as a career cul-de-sac? What information will you need to monitor your own commitment and performance as well as those of the supplier?

If you are ready and able to answer these questions, then you have faced up to the critical issues and decisions involved in preparing for outsourcing. In M&A terms, you are poised to do the deal. In outsourcing terms, we think you're ready – go for it!

9

Five key areas to focus on

'Many companies fail to realize you need different skills to manage an out-sourcing alliance rather than an internal IT department,' says Andy Chesnutt of Compass, a management consultancy which questioned 8,000 firms and found 58 per cent of IT and business process outsourcing (BPO) projects failed to meet expectations.

'Cost-Cutting Drives Outsourcing', IT Week, September 1 2005

Specialist section 1: Financial engineering

Sudhakar Balachandran of Columbia University notes how cost account-ing disciplines have migrated from manufacturing into the service econo-my .... As well as measuring the cash costs of providing a product or service, smart companies look at the assets tied up in the process. Such number-crunching focuses attention on balance sheet efficiency. If done well, he notes, it also yields a sophisticated view of which lines of busi-ness are truly profitable.

Simon London, 'The yin and yang of management', Financial Times, August 1, 2005

Overview

In our opinion, the best way to consider an outsourcing transaction from a financial point of view is to think about a financial derivative with two parts: one of service and one of financial flows. Financial data will fill sheet after sheet of Excel, in order to account for all the services at different times and volumes, accommodate cost curves (generally sloping down with time) and a variety of tax events. The result is that the parties face a maze of data.

Making sense of the financial data

Take a simple example in a seven-year desktop outsourcing project. One has to value the current hardware and software assets; estimate the time to the first refresh (which will allow the client to improve service and cut cost across the whole enterprise); price that refresh (hardware, packaged software, updated applications and labour); and then estimate the support cost (at various levels) until the next refresh. All this must cover the period up to the maturity of the contract, and potentially across several currencies if various services are sourced from offshore.

In all, this comes to 84 months of cash flows and no less than 250 lines per month. Any small variation in items such as the number of workspaces, the estimate of what a base mid-level desktop will comprise in year three, or the estimated cost of Microsoft Office in year five, will have an impact on the cash flows and can be tweaked to meet specific corporate targets of buyer or seller. It is worth noting that this process will probably involve many back and forth iterations with the suppliers to the client. In all, an extremely complex and time-demanding process that has to be run for each solution.

A sensitive equation

Therefore, just as in any financial derivative, relatively trivial changes to assumptions will generate significantly different results. Above we chose a simple example, but imagine the same fundamental structure in a large business process outsourcing transaction. The final analysis will cover hundreds of interconnected spreadsheets.

However, this analysis does need to be done. Having the underlying facts to hand and being able to manipulate the data will offer significant opportunities to create value and shift assets, liabilities and cash flows. Last but not least, outsourcing allows the parties to remain within Generally Accepted Accounting Principles (GAAP) but transform financial into operational and commercial contracts. How come?

The first and largest swing factor is the ownership of hardware. At the inception of a transaction, two key factors will determine whether a transfer of ownership is attractive: accurate knowledge of all the assets potentially transferred, and the difference between accounting (book) and market value. The transfer must be at fair market value and while many firms would want to use an outsourcing transaction to free up capital (and reduce total assets), they also have little appetite for write-offs, which has been the staple of technology investments. Moore's law is steeper than accelerated depreciation!

However, irrespective of the outcome at signing, the hardware will remain a key financial issue when considering refresh of the technology: should the assets be financed by the client, the outsourcing provider, or leased? Whereas total cost may not change materially, the outsourcing contract offers many opportunities to fine-tune cash flows each month. From the above comments, you might also infer that the same decisions would apply to labour restructurings. Deciding up front which party will pay for separation may have a significant impact on various financial ratios without changing the economic or human impacts one iota.

Bankable value

One aspect of outsourcing that has rarely been discussed is the ability of an outsourcing provider to guarantee results and therefore provide 'bankable' value. The best situation for this is in the case of a merger or an acquisition, where the outsourcing provider can substantially 'de-risk' the announced synergies that otherwise are substantially discounted by many financial analysts. Depending on the structure, the outsourcing provider can virtually write a cheque against the overall merger or acquisition.

In fact, using special-purpose vehicles or other sophisticated financial structures would actually make it possible to write such a cheque and participate in the financing of the acquisition itself. To the best of our knowledge this has not yet been done – the primary reason being that investment banks have not been prepared to bring outsourcing partners across the fire-wall.

To date this structure has been used to finance outsourcing transactions efficiently and turn the financial flows (client paying the outsourcing provider monthly) into a limited recourse structure generally funded by a bank. In the end the basis for the credit (beyond underlying assets) is the credit strength of the client and the outsourcing firm's ability to deliver services.

Conclusion: an era of sophistication

It is our opinion that recent events (Enron, Basel II, Sarbanes–Oxley and so on) have made such financial engineering more difficult. But they have also led to situations where financial engineering is an obligation, because of the weak financial condition of many firms in the outsourcing market. There is no question that the perception of commercial risk is very different from that of financial risk, and also that the risk perception changes when moving from 'generic' services (such as desktop outsourcing) to advanced BPO services such as securities or payments processing.

A key component of financial engineering is risk management – and when comparing the sophistication of risk management in a bank and the same practice in outsourcing, the reader will probably be surprised to hear that service outsourcing is far more sophisticated. Only complex limited recourse multi-tranche structures even come close to the level of sophistication in the typical multi-year large outsourcing contract.

Specialist section 2: Legal issues

When we think outsourcing we tend to think in terms of purchaser-provider and contract management. Now, and in the future, we will think much more in terms of contracts and relationships that look much more like strategic partnerships as a result of strategic sourcing.

Sue Vardon, Future of Public Administration in Australia and Outsourcing, 2003

Overview

There are five key areas of legal risk that typically emerge in outsourcing contracts. While the relative importance and relevance of these risks vary depending on the type of deal, location (onshore/offshore) and industry, each of them will apply to some extent. Certainly every one of these areas should be reviewed rigorously to ensure the appropriate legal risks are being managed not just adequately, but proactively. These five areas are: legal structure, regulatory risk, data protection, people, and information security.

1. Legal structure

The right legal structure is critical to realizing the targeted benefits under any outsourcing contract. Clients frequently go into the negotiations talking airily about partnering with providers and even about entering into formal joint ventures (JVs) with them. However, from a legal standpoint JVs are usually undesirable unless there are commercial or other considerations that outweigh the risks inherent in entering – and exiting – a JV. These considerations may include tax benefits or the need to ring-fence particular assets or the workforce of the outsourced operation for regulatory reasons (seen frequently in the utilities sector).

The choice of legal structure can be crucial in offshoring. The clearest division is between a 'captive' structure, which is created and owned by the business and therefore not actually outsourced; a relatively straightforward outsourcing deal involving paying a fee for a service; and a hybrid build–operate–transfer arrangement. The choice of structure is a tax-driven, operational or commercial decision that will determine much of the content of the contract.

2. Regulatory risk

Whatever the chosen structure, regulatory risk must be assessed, addressed and managed. While this consideration applies in all outsourcing deals, it is especially pivotal in highly regulated industries such as financial services.

The implications of regulation are profound. The UK Financial Services Authority demands that the senior management of the client firm must retain a clear line of responsibility for the outsourced operation. Other regulators across the world, including in the United States, are moving in the same direction, on the principle that while activities can be outsourced and offshored, regulatory responsibility for the outcome cannot.

The FSA's Principles for Business state that a firm must take reasonable care to control its affairs responsibly and effectively, with adequate risk management systems. In line with this, firms' directors and senior managers are responsible for assessing and managing risks, including those related to outsourcing and offshoring.

UK Financial Services Authority: *Offshore Operations: Industry Feedback*, April 2005

➤

Many outsourcing contracts fail to build in the kind of clear management and governance structures and reporting lines required to meet these requirements. Alternatively, they may not place the service provider under an obligation to provide the client's senior management with the necessary regulatory information. These types of provisions must be included. At the same time, a number of risks that might once have appeared to be outside the regulatory sphere now have growing regulatory implications. For example, financial regulators worldwide are increasingly focusing on whether the firms they regulate have taken geopolitical risks into account in their offshoring decisions.

3. Data protection

The issues of regulatory, geopolitical and cross-border risk converge in a further key area of legal risk in outsourcing: data protection. Here, companies may come up against conflicts between different national regimes. For example, the Indian Foreign Exchange Management Act gives Indian authorities certain powers that could potentially compromise the confidentiality of banking operations sited there. With this in mind, any offshore outsourcing contract needs to take account of such conflicts as far as possible, as well as demonstrating that the supplier is fully committed to helping its client comply with its onshore data protection obligations.

These onshore obligations include the manner in which data is processed, including restrictions on the movement of personal data between different jurisdictions. To ensure this compliance, outsourcing contracts need detailed provisions and mechanisms on the treatment, transfer and location of personal data.

4. People

The issue of human resources in outsourcing is something of a legal minefield. It is especially problematic in the context of the European Union's Acquired Rights Directive applying – contrary to popular preconceptions – in cases where operations are outsourced or transferred offshore.

In all outsourcing deals the compulsory transfer of staff remains one of the most difficult legal and commercial issues. Where problems arise it is generally because the outsourcing supplier and – perhaps surprisingly – the client prove unwilling to invest in proper due diligence to establish their legal liabilities and obligations under the law and the existing employment contracts. This omission is a false economy, often resulting in significant hidden costs and potentially massive liabilities for both sides.

The only solution is to carry out proper and extensive due diligence on the exact position in every affected jurisdiction, and to ensure there is clear allocation of responsibility for the resulting liabilities. This may not be easy, for example in situations where the outsourcing contract is switching between two suppliers, especially if they are located in different countries.

5. Information security

The issue of information security in outsourcing is especially pressing in an offshore context. The risks in this area were highlighted dramatically in April 2005, when three former employees at a call centre in Pune, India, together with nine of their associates, were arrested and charged with misusing financial data and illegally withdrawing funds totalling almost US$350,000 from the accounts of New York-based bank customers. Of course, offences of this type can happen at any time in any part of the world, and can occur in an in-house or outsourced operation. But the fact remains that stakeholders perceive these risks to be greater in more geographically distributed outsourcing arrangements.

To manage this risk, some outsourcing clients include highly specific requirements in the contract, tying the supplier to strict physical and logical security service levels and to providing detailed information and audit facilities to ensure that the required level of vigilance and monitoring is being maintained. Such a clause would usually include the right to step into, or terminate, the contract at little or no notice in the event of a breach.

Conclusion: a shifting landscape

As new outsourcing structures and techniques emerge, and as further offshoring centres come on stream around the world, the legal issues raised inevitably evolve at the same time. Similarly, new regulations affecting outsourcing will continue to emerge. However, for the foreseeable future the five key areas of legal risk outlined here are

➤

likely to continue to form the basis of a comprehensive approach to managing legal risk in outsourcing. As ever, the aim of legal advisers is to facilitate commercial activity within the bounds of the law – and as commercial and legal structures change, so the legal responses will change with them.

With thanks to Mark Lewis, Partner and Head of the IT and Outsourcing Group of Lawrence Graham LLP, London, and Director of Morgan Chambers plc.

Specialist section 3: Communication issues

Although Sprint has reduced its workforce by about 5,000 jobs in the past year, bringing it down to 65,000, many of those outsourced workers still work with other companies.

Gary Foresee, CEO and Chairman, Sprint

Overview

In outsourcing as in M&A experience shows that when problems emerge in a deal or in the delivery of the targeted benefits they usually come down to people issues. And, invariably, the root cause is a breakdown in effective communication. As a major organizational and cultural change programme, outsourcing will almost certainly fail if the interested and affected stakeholders are not kept informed and engaged in the process. If communications around the deal are not handled well the impact on stakeholders ranging from employees to investors can be dramatic, creating problems both for the operation of the agreement itself and for the share price.

Achieving the right level and quality of communication raises two major challenges for the CEO of the client organization. One of these – especially in the context of a listed company – lies in the tight restrictions on what the CEO can and cannot say, due to the three-way pressures of investor relations, scrutiny by regulators and labour regulations. The other challenge is the sheer number and variety of stakeholders to whom messages must be conveyed clearly, consistently and continually. The typical influencer programme depicted in

Figure 9.1 below gives an idea of the scale and range of effort required. The content and delivery of all the messaging needs to be closely coordinated – not only across all these channels and stakeholders, but also between the company and its outsourcing supplier.

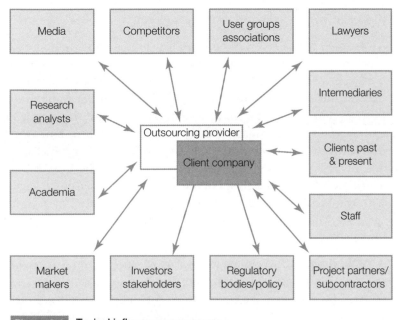

Figure 9.1 Typical influencer programme
Source: © *Morgan Chambers plc 2006*

However, perhaps the greatest pressure on the communications programme is created by its potential behavioural impact on the workforce – including both the transitioned employees moving to the outsourcing provider and the retained organization. All these people need information, reassurance and guidance throughout the process. And their goodwill needs to be sustained so the business can keep running during the upheaval, and move as smoothly as possible to the new operating model.

M&A comparisons

These pressures echo the communications issues arising in an M&A deal. The need for a holistic approach taking in all stakeholders, and for coordination and consistency of messaging not just across all these stakeholder groups but across both parties to the deal, mirrors the prerequisites for successful communications around a merger or disposal. Both M&A and outsourcing carry implications for the share price, and require clear communications with the media, investors and analysts. And political and regulatory issues are equally important in each case – especially where transactions are cross-border and involve the loss or transfer of jobs.

As a result, virtually everything we say here about the approach, processes and disciplines involved in communicating around an outsourcing agreement could equally be applied to M&A. However, in practice there are differences of emphasis between the communications around outsourcing and M&A, in terms of both the messaging and target audiences. In an M&A deal, the primary focus tends to be on the investment community, and slightly less on workforce issues, at least until the deal is completed. In outsourcing, there tends to be a greater and earlier focus on internal communications and engaging with employee groups, since workforce buy-in is central both to the successful completion of the deal and to the subsequent delivery of the targeted benefits.

A further distinction lies in the focus of analysts' and investors' interests. With M&A, the markets are keen to hear about planned cost savings, but are also eager to understand the strategic rationale, synergies and growth story going forward. With an outsourcing deal, analysts and investors are still primarily interested in how much will be saved, and by when. Their other concern – especially where offshoring is concerned – is to look at the risk management implications.

As we have already pointed out, we believe that there is substantial scope for the executive teams of both the client and outsourcing provider to support their mutual share prices by standing shoulder to shoulder, publicly affirming the mutual benefits of the relationship, and effectively leveraging one another's brand. As yet, the markets are not accustomed to seeing this happen. They still regard outsourcing largely as a cost play, much as companies used to in the past. As outsourcing becomes increasingly strategic this attitude in the markets may change – and we believe it is largely up to companies and their outsourcing partners to ensure that it does, thereby realizing the resulting benefits to each of their share prices.

Defining the risks as the basis for investment

Whatever the M&A parallels, it is clear that creating and rolling out a coordinated and well-planned communications strategy is a priority for a CEO entering an outsourcing agreement. The outsourcing supplier should hopefully be equally aware of – and committed to – the need for systematic communications, since outsourcing is its business. But for the client board, this may well be a one-off transaction in which experience is scarce. As a result, others on the board may not be as convinced as the CEO of the necessity of investing in communications – commonly regarded as a soft and fuzzy activity – at a time when there are so many other competing priorities with a clearer return. In many cases education is needed to overcome these doubts, and to create committed sponsorship of the communications effort across the board as an ongoing activity – lasting until well after the 'cut-over' to the new operating model.

One good way to build this buy-in is to approach communications from the angle of needing to reduce the 'people-related risks' that could hamper or even derail the outsourcing process. On the one hand, the deal must be sold to the market and regulators. On the other, if the necessary human capital becomes unavailable at any time or the people are simply pointing the wrong way, then the business grinds to a halt. These attitudinal and behavioural risks can only be mitigated and managed by targeting the right information and messaging at the right stakeholders at the right time. Once the board accepts that these risks are real, then investing in a strategy to address them becomes unarguable. Going forward, it is a good idea for the CEO to put a direct report 'on point' to ensure that communications activities are driven forward and remain a priority throughout the process.

Five steps to the programme

Once buy-in has been secured for the communications effort across both the company and outsourcing supplier, then the creation and execution of the communications programme is a five-stage process (see Figure 9.2 overleaf). The first step is to devise and agree the communications strategy itself on both sides of the deal. The second is to build the core framework for the programme, defining the central messages, standardized Q&A responses and information repositories that will lie at the heart of the communications programme.

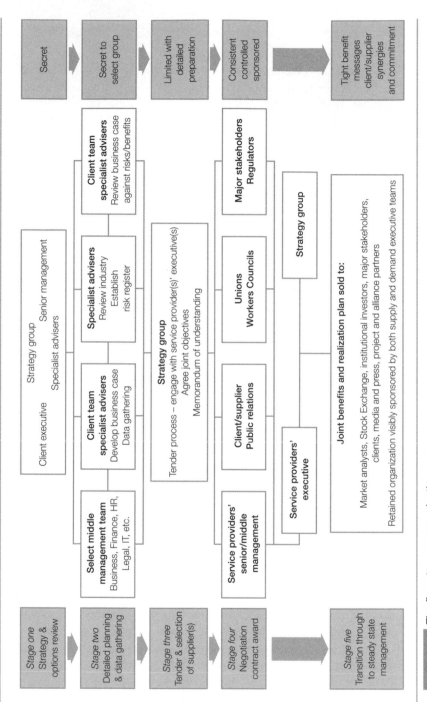

Figure 9.2 The five-stage communications programme

The third step is to roll these coordinated and consistent messages out along the various delivery channels in a planned and harmonized way, often with advice from legal, HR and regulatory advisers, and frequently via established channels such as the intranet, investor relations/public relations departments, external investor relations/public relations (IR/PR) advisers, corporate affairs professionals and public websites. At the same time, on the internal communications front, there needs to be a programme of specific workshops and meetings to roll out the messaging. These activities will be especially complicated in the case of a global organization, where cultural nuances have to be catered for.

The fourth stage is a carefully planned and structured feedback loop, ensuring that responses from stakeholders are taken on board and – where appropriate – acted upon. Finally, the fifth stage, which takes place after the deal itself, is steady state communications – which is built on the bedrock of the initial deal investment and approach to communications.

Timing and alignment

Two pressures may well be especially acute and unremitting throughout this five-stage process. One is time – since the communications strategy should ideally kick in as soon as possible after 'down-select' to one supplier takes place. At that point fear, uncertainty and doubt will be in full flow across the workforce. If a communications strategy has not been agreed in principle within three or four weeks of down-select then the CEO should be asking why.

The other pressure is the need for alignment and consistency across channels, geographies and the two organizations. Wherever a question comes from and whatever its entry point – be it to the company's Frankfurt office or supplier's headquarters in the United States – the answer must be the same every time. At the other end of the scale, the IR/PR teams and advisers on each side should be consulting and collaborating – something they are not culturally accustomed to doing. This alignment needs to be driven from the top, ideally by ensuring that a member of the tier one management on each side is explicitly responsible for the success of the communications strategy, and attends all the daily meetings of a jointly staffed communications team.

Where blockages occur – perhaps the IR teams refuse to talk to one another, or the client's regional head for Asia–Pacific decides that communications are not all that important – it may be necessary to bang some heads together. Plus the team must keep a close and responsive watch on the press, sure in the knowledge that a slightly off-beam or negative story in a trade newspaper will trigger a wave of concern and questions from the workforce.

Technology can be a valuable supporter of the necessary alignment. Shared websites, centralized Q&A lists, secure intranets, targeted and accurate distribution lists and regular electronic bulletins all help to keep everyone in line with developments and messaging. And the questions that must be handled go far beyond what many people might expect. In a recent global outsourcing transition only 30 per cent of the questions from the workforce related to HR issues such as pay and benefits. Two-thirds were about outsourcing in general, often questioning the capabilities of the outsourcing provider.

Channels to stakeholders

With the core of the programme secured, the messages need to be targeted and disseminated through the various channels. Getting the internal communications rolling quickly is clearly a priority, since the effect of uncertainty, disaffection and the rumour mill increases over time, and can be massively damaging for the project. Where staff are transitioning across to the supplier, a proven approach is to begin with 'town hall' workshops of 100 staff, and come down progressively via 50 or 25 to a 1:1 meeting with the individual's new boss. However, it is important to be aware that the stark differences in workforce regulation – contrast the hire 'n' fire culture in the United States or Asia with the European 'works council' model – create wide variations in the latitude for what management can say in different geographies.

That said, some principles hold true everywhere. It is imperative that members of *both* client and service provider organizations are present at the workshops, and that the representative from the outsourcing supplier is culturally attuned and has the right local language skills to handle the inevitable aggressive questioning from the floor. It is also imperative not to sugar the pill. People can accept being told that they are in for a rough time over the coming year, and that their longer-term career prospects will be better than before. They cannot accept feeling they are being lied to. And if issues such as pensions and benefits have not yet been decided, then there is no point pretending that they have.

IR and PR messages will be rolled out through the established channels in each organization to address these stakeholders, in close consultation with the core communications team and the IR/PR counterparts in the other company. Similarly, corporate affairs or regulatory specialists will take the messaging to governmental and regulatory bodies where appropriate. This may mean coordination of the timing of mutually price-sensitive announcements between the supplier's head office (say in the United States) and the client in Asia or Europe. Also, opportunities may arise to coordinate and cross-fertilize the messaging between various channels and stakeholders. For example, there may be a message that the companies want to address to institutional investors to support their share prices, but feel they cannot present directly. The solution may be to sponsor a research report from the academic community underlining the messaging, then get it picked up by the press, and thereby put it in front of the target investors.

Day one and beyond

As with the ongoing management of the outsourcing agreement and relationship, 'day one' of the outsourced operation is not the end of the communications strategy but the beginning of a new and continuing phase. The key from day one onwards is to ensure regular communications – something that may be difficult at first, as management will be largely focused on addressing any teething troubles and bedding in the contract. Continuing communications are especially important in a transformational outsourcing agreement, where reporting on performance improvements and internal HR messaging will be key.

In summary, the watchwords for communication around an outsourcing programme are not rocket science. They include:

■ top-level sponsorship, buy-in and engagement on both sides;
■ acceptance that the risks are real and that investment is needed to address them;
■ agreement on consistent messaging, and on a strategy for putting it across;
■ identification of the key internal and external influencers, and the delivery of appropriate information via the appropriate channels; ➤

- expecting and addressing broader concerns that will arise – these often demand direct executive involvement;

- throughout, synchronization and cooperation between the two organizations;

- deal-centric communication which must be used as the bedrock for 'steady state running' communications into the future

These principles are simple enough to communicate. As so often, the challenges lie in getting the messages right, fine-tuning them, and executing their delivery.

With thanks to Stephen Francis of EDS and Rachel Hirst of Hogarth PR.

Specialist section 4: Human resource issues

If a company or organization can show us a clear-cut business case which takes into account all the risks and true costs (managing remotely, effects on morale, all stakeholders, not just shareholders) of moving off-shore, not simply the financial gain, then the unions are not against it in principle. If, however, the justification hinges purely on the cost-cutting financial case, then companies will constantly chase the next cheapest operating environment and other third-world/developing countries will come on-stream.

Dai Davies, Director of Communications, UNIFI

Overview

If you overlay the concept and principles of an M&A-type approach on to an outsourcing agreement it is clear that the implications of HR are among the most significant of all those that arise. The message in each case is, get HR right – and you have a good bedrock for getting the deal right. However, the crucial importance of HR can itself cause problems in achieving the right approach. This is because, for the CEO and board members approaching the HR implications of an outsourcing agreement, it is all to easy to become fixated on the obvious areas such as redundancies, union issues, staff reallocation, benefits (including pensions) and the future headcount of the outsourced operation.

Clearly these are all important in themselves. But the key is to regard them in the context of – and not in isolation from – the wider agreement as a whole. Truly successful management of the HR aspects depends on the board's ability to use a 'wide angle lens' when looking at HR implications, ensuring that the multiple factors arising across systems, processes and people are all fully aligned, mutually manageable and in balance. Each should play its part in an integrated solution to achieve the overall benefits. A remorseless focus on – for example – achieving sharply reduced headcount costs by a particular stage, while ignoring the implications for service levels, will probably lead to a failed agreement.

Putting HR in context – at board level

Why is HR so critical yet so interconnected? The financial and synergy benefits for your business will clearly be central to the success of any proposed outsourcing agreement. But, as with M&A, it is the HR aspects that will ultimately determine how fully these benefits are achieved, and differentiate success from failure over time for the whole deal.

With this in mind it is vital to spend a considerable amount of board-level time considering HR issues during the planning stages. Assuming that there is a strong case for outsourcing in strategic value terms, there is then also a clear need to quantify and understand the roles and responsibilities during the transition and beyond, what type of human capital the business is giving away, and what kinds of costs and benefits will be transferred as a result to the outsourcing partner.

Maintaining the desire to serve

This understanding is equally critical from the outsourcing provider's point of view. All too often a company contemplating an outsourcing agreement may feel – consciously or subconsciously – that this is an opportunity to offload some lower-performing people, and make them the third-party provider's problem.

This is a hugely short-sighted approach, and a basic mistake reflecting the now-discredited 'my mess for less' approach to outsourcing. The people making the transition may be leaving the company's payroll, but they will still be in its ecosystem. They may even still be sitting at the same desk, albeit now receiving their payslip from the outsourcing supplier instead of the client company. If these people feel ignored and disenfranchised by the way the transition is handled, and have lost their allegiance and desire to serve the client, it is a problem for everyone – not just the outsourcing provider.

Involving senior HR people

So the challenge is to transfer and then integrate people in a way that reinvigorates and strengthens their commitment to, and identification with, the client's business. A crucial aspect is a communications strategy that engages the affected staff openly and early, the mechanics of which are examined more closely in our specialist section on communication issues around outsourcing.

Equally important is engaging senior HR officers, taking on board their insights and experience on the workforce's specific concerns – job security, benefits, pensions and so on – and then sharing these insights with the outsource provider to enable a joined-up approach to transition, acclimatization and translation of pay and benefits. This enables the client company to anticipate issues before they arise, shows the affected staff that they are still important to it, and helps both parties to engage the right people in the right way. The company's compensation committee or budget oversight committee is likely to be integrally involved in examining the long-term HR and financial implications of any decisions that are made in areas such as pay, pensions and other benefits.

Another important – but difficult – challenge is to give people choices during the process. The people who stay around, in both the leave-behind team and the outsourced workforce, should be those who want to stay around, and actively choose to do so. Ensuring that the right people stay is something of an art, requiring fine judgement and the application of relevant experience. But the chances of success are vastly improved by clear planning and messaging from day one.

Beyond the headcount numbers: sounding the alarm bells

We have already stressed the need to consider HR issues in the wider context of all the interrelated elements of the outsourcing agreement. This is especially the case when it comes to instances where headcount reductions are being presented as one of the main benefits.

Where this happens the focus on headcount is often driven by the client business – and generally reflects a lack of joined-up thinking at board level. The company might ask the outsourcing provider to take on all the relevant staff and provide a better service for a lower price over, say, eight years. Then the board thinks it has spotted a way to increase the benefit still further, and asks for the headcount to be cut by half over the first five years, with the cost reduction passed on to the business.

This should set alarm bells ringing on both sides. A CEO, CFO or any other board member who sees an outsourcing plan predicated on continuing headcount reduction coupled with an upturn in service levels should immediately demand further details. How will this conjuring trick be achieved? Through extracting more value from software? Server consolidation? Better leveraging of people? Offshoring? Or is it a question of crossing fingers and hoping something will turn up?

Planning – not hoping

Not surprisingly, crossed fingers are no basis for an outsourcing agreement. The whole range of factors – technological, process related, managerial, geographical – should be considered alongside the management of human capital to show how the targeted benefits will be achieved. If the numbers do not add up, then the outsourcing agreement will not either.

The best – indeed, we believe the only – way to ensure such pitfalls are avoided is to focus early and holistically on HR at board level. While it is important to get the legal details right in terms of people leaving, moving or transitioning, these are the means to an end, enabling a balanced approach that embeds the benefits by blending the management of the HR issues with the financial and systems considerations.

With thanks to Dan Brennan of EDS.

Specialist section 5: Tax issues

I think companies have to operate as efficiently as possible. So we make an efficiency decision to move the data center to Texas. We hire people in India. If we do a really good job in making decisions, we'll make a lot of money. The government then takes a lot of money away from us. It takes it away from us in taxes. And it's the government's job to take that

➤

money. The more money we make, the more money the government makes. The government shouldn't be mad that we're making money. The government gets a cut.

Larry Ellison, CEO, Oracle Corporation

Overview

Tax is an issue of ever-increasing importance in the IT outsourcing arena. Governmental organizations in many jurisdictions favour suppliers who are good taxpayers, contributing – in their view – appropriately to the social fabric of the country in which they operate. Companies seeking to outsource now focus not only on the 'real' after-tax cost of outsourcing – measured by reference to both earnings per share and cash flow – but also on the resulting opportunities in the tax environment.

In this section we will explore, from a UK perspective, the corporate imperatives and opportunities in the tax environment associated with IT outsourcing at every stage of the outsourcing process. However, while this is written from a UK standpoint, the principles and areas of focus are relevant globally. Of course, any reputable IT outsourcing company would consider it part of its normal due diligence process to discuss such tax matters.

'Greenfield' outsourcing

A greenfield outsourcing programme typically commences with an in-house IT department being benchmarked against external providers to evaluate relative costs and benefits. The associated tax costs and benefits are often overlooked in this assessment process. For financial services companies this can be a particularly difficult exercise as, in many cases, their current management information and reporting systems simply do not attribute the company's associated irrecoverable VAT costs with enough precision to enable the necessary like-for-like comparisons to be made.

The decision to outsource is often taken concurrently with the sale of various assets associated with the in-house IT department, together with the transfer of the relevant staff to the new service provider. Depending on the tax profile of the seller, significant tax benefits can be realized at this point in the form of tax-free gains on the sale of assets such as IT equipment, land and buildings. Naturally, transaction taxes – such as stamp duty land taxes in the UK – should be factored into any such arrangements.

Multi-country deals

Multi-country outsourcing transactions present their own unique opportunities and risks. As tax administrations globally legislate to protect their tax base, outsourcing providers should ensure that any cross-border arrangements are in full compliance with local laws and regulations. Pricing and invoicing arrangements are critical to ensuring satisfactory and demonstrable compliance with local law. Existing intercompany arrangements are now subject to a multitude of compliance and reporting obligations that are an often overlooked administrative cost. Properly structured outsourcing contracts can eliminate this hidden overhead cost.

In this context, an additional advantage of using a global service provider can be the removal of intragroup withholding tax costs that arise from the statutory invoicing by a centralized internal IT department. An outsourcer with truly global reach can facilitate local provision – and can therefore potentially eliminate these internal tax leakages.

A long-term perspective

Many companies entering an outsourcing agreement employ inter-mediaries at the time of contract negotiation. They do this in the belief that it will ensure not only satisfactory compliance with their tax obligations throughout the life of the contract, but also maximize their opportunities.

However, given that outsourcing arrangements are often for a duration of five or more years, focusing solely on the outset of an outsourcing contract often represents an overly optimistic approach. This is, first, because the scope and geographical reach of the business requiring IT support will change in that timeframe, as businesses may divest spare or non-strategic capacity and/or acquire new growth engines; and, secondly, because we live in a dynamic regulatory and tax environment that is fine-tuned to respond to political and budgetary imperatives.

What is actually needed is a continuing dialogue throughout the life of the outsourcing arrangement. This is why reputable outsourcing providers seek not only to include taxes in the ambit of their business change control clauses, but also to recommend separate tax cooperation clauses in their commercial arrangements. The less developed or less fiscally stable environments present particular risks here – witness the accession of additional member states to the European Union, and the overhaul of their tax systems that membership required.

VAT: a thorny issue

A current highly topical event in this arena is the recent European Court of Justice case lost by Accenture. This case centred on the outsourcing by an insurance company of much of its back office activities, including claims handling. While there was common agreement in the United Kingdom that an outsourced service of this nature would be VAT exempt, the Dutch tax administration did not share this view. The matter was eventually resolved in the favour of the Dutch tax authorities following lengthy litigation.

At the time of writing, many insurance companies will have concluded long-term outsourcing arrangements on the basis that the services thus provided do not attract VAT. This case law development, which many think will lead to the future imposition of VAT in some areas of insurance outsourcing, will have a dramatic impact on at least one of the parties to the outsourcing contract. To, at the very least, minimize losses from such developments and, at best, achieve a win/win situation, an upfront commitment by both parties to work together is a critical factor. Erosion of shareholder value because of poor planning on the taxation implications of an otherwise successful outsourcing transaction is clearly a lost opportunity.

Coming to termination

As has often been said, there are only two things certain in life – death and taxes – and this mantra should not be forgotten as an outsourcing agreement reaches its natural termination point.

A variety of decision points are faced by the service recipient. Should the current service provider have its contract renewed? Should the service be taken back in-house or indeed should another service provider be appointed? The costs associated with those decisions will have a tax impact on all affected parties.

The questions multiply depending on the precise circumstances of the termination. If the service is gradually transitioned in-house, will the previously VAT exempt supply continue to be exempt as activities are gradually insourced? Will any contract termination payments attract tax relief currently for the payer; or indeed will they crystallize a VAT charge? Will the transfer back of property leased to the outsourcing provider attract a stamp duty land tax? What will happen to the tax relief on the fixtures within such properties? All these factors require careful analysis to ensure adherence to the law and maximization of opportunities.

In taxation as in other aspects, an outsourcing arrangement should fundamentally be viewed as a partnership between service provider and customer, where the benefits to both – evaluated on an after-tax basis – are monitored and maximized over its life cycle.

With thanks to Judith Kent of EDS.

10

The outsourcing experience

The business issue

In today's international banking environment competitive, consumer, cost and convergence pressures have combined with currency issues and new cross-border regulations to create unprecedented challenges around payments. Internationally, payments have been strongly affected by the continuing evolution in banking. Competition and regulation have reduced payment costs to the consumer, placing an additional burden on banks. And while payments are a core competency, their processing can only retain a world-class level of efficiency if it is underpinned by high-performance systems, requiring substantial and continuous investment.

To achieve or maintain international leadership in such an environment, banks have to decide what they want to be and where they need to focus – and do it quickly. In the late 1990s this was a pressing issue for Belgium's KBC, a bank that is represented in 30 different countries and offers a full range of financial services to retail customers, businesses and multinational companies. Its commercial network includes nearly 4,000 bank branches, insurance agencies and brokers in its home country alone. The challenge facing KBC was to completely rethink its business processes in view of the changing financial reality. In the dynamic and complex international banking arena, KBC's goal was deceptively simple: to sift through the emerging threats, reduce the levels of risk, and find and exploit the new business opportunities.

There were some very specific strategic reasons why KBC needed to take action to address these issues. The bank had a strong starting position in payments processing, since it was already very active in European/ECU clearing. This effectively meant that, for its size, it was punching above its weight in this area, and had a healthy market share to defend. To do so, it first needed to build scale; and secondly, it needed to fund significant upcoming investment due to changes in factors such as regulation. In short, to maintain or improve its position KBC had to do something, and quickly. The route it selected was to create Fin-Force, a utility developed to provide global payments processing services to both KBC and other banks.

The chosen solution

Working together in 2000, in the wake of the launch of the euro, KBC and EDS identified a strategic opportunity that they both believed was ripe for the picking: creating a subsidiary that processed international payments. Two factors meant the partnership was uniquely well positioned to pounce quickly and gain first-mover advantage in this area. First, KBC already had a complete system that supported global payments in its International Banking System (IBS). IBS integrates all the financial systems of an international branch, from accounting through money markets to financial instruments. Secondly, it happened that EDS was already preparing to introduce a shared-service model into the financial marketplace that would provide clients with centralized back office support.

The deal structure

Fin-Force was launched in January 2001 as a joint venture between Belgian bank KBC, with a 90 per cent stake, and its outsourcing supplier EDS with 10 per cent. Since then the EDS share has been reduced to 5 per cent. Fin-Force is a utility that provides customizable back office processing services on a white-label or proprietary basis to financial institutions for international payments. It enables client banks – KBC included – to outsource international payments processing and a wide range of payment-related services, as well as management of payments-related databases. From the start of 2006, Fin-Force processes international payment transactions for Transaktionsinstitut, a daughter company of Germany's DZ Bank AG, which took a 10 per cent stake in Fin-Force as part of the deal.

The business results

KBC has reaped multiple benefits from the creation of Fin-Force. Outsourcing its own payments processing to Fin-Force helps the bank cope with increasing customer and government demands while removing the impact of dwindling international payments margins from its overall results. In fact, KBC expects Fin-Force will help quadruple its payments business within the next few years.

By 2003, two years in, Fin-Force was processing around 7.5 million international payments transactions annually for KBC. The initial success of Fin-Force convinced KBC that it should move its domestic payments processing across to Fin-Force as well, boosting Fin-Force's processing volume by well over 300 million transactions a year. As part of this agreement, almost a hundred KBC Bank employees were transferred to Fin-Force. By the end of 2004, Fin-Force's overall costs had decreased by 50 per cent from their level in the first full year of operation in 2001.

When KBC transferred its domestic payments across in 2003, Fin-Force's only client was KBC Group itself – a fact that the bank put down to the international banking market's lack of readiness to outsource payments processing to a specialized firm. This relatively slow start in attracting third-party clients also reflected the fact that some other banks had struggled to make a similar model work, and the market was sceptical over its long-term viability. For example, Deutsche Bank pulled out of its back office outsourcing joint venture with Wall Street Systems, called SOCX (Settlement & Operations Clearing eXchange), in February 2003, and ended up selling its 50 per cent stake in the company to founding partner Wall Street Systems.

A nervous time

Fin-Force CEO Pascal Deman admits that this background, and the slow response from the external market, resulted in a nervous period for Fin-Force – one that EDS helped it to get through. During 2002–3, when Fin-Force was delivering major internal benefits for KBC but was apparently failing to capture the imagination or confidence of the external third-party marketplace, serious questions were being asked. 'We had achieved dramatic cost reductions in a very short time, which had helped KBC achieve its internal objectives,' recalls Deman. 'That enabled KBC to remain competitive against some of the majors active in the clearing business. But after 18 months or so, we felt a bit of frustration on the external side. Costs were coming down, but new partners were not coming on board.'

However, the KBC board remained convinced that Fin-Force had a solid business model and would continue to demonstrate its efficiency in future, thereby attracting wider client interest.

'The relationship with our partner was very important to getting through that period,' says Deman. 'The EDS team worked closely with the KBC board to stress that this was a long-term strategic move, that they knew how it would work, and that the plan was supported by prior experience in both the UK and US markets. They said that the payments market would inevitably mature in continental Europe as well, and they have now been proved right. People at KBC were saying the same – but the strength of persuasiveness of EDS's

▶

viewpoint lay in the fact that they actually had experience of doing all this before.'

The strategy is borne out

This faith was rewarded in March 2005 with the announcement that KBC had concluded a deal to combine its payment processing activities with those of DZ Bank AG, Germany's fifth largest banking group. With Fin-Force processing 328 million transactions per year, and DZ Bank's Transaktionsinstitut für Zahlungsverkehrsdienstleistungen (TZD) handling over 3 billion (mainly domestic) transactions, the resulting combination created a powerful new force in cross-border payments service in Europe – the first of its type.

Under the deal, the companies agreed to combine their payment processing units – KBC's Fin-Force and TZD – from the start of 2006, with TZD processing all intra-European payments for the two companies, and Fin-Force processing all other international payments. DZ Bank agreed to acquire a 10 per cent stake in Fin-Force, while KBC took a 5 per cent holding in TZD. The combined company would process both corporate and retail transactions, involving transferring money between bank accounts in different countries and converting currencies. The targeted benefits include savings on processing expenses due to larger processing quantities, and a higher market share in their respective transaction areas for both companies. Both entities also committed to investigate the possibility of bringing a European multi-domestic payments solution to the market in the foreseeable future.

This commitment reflected the clear strategic growth rationale going forward. The main driver behind the partnership between DZ and KBC was the shared perception of what the future holds for the Single Euro Payments Area. Given the prospect that the single currency in Europe may lead to the abolition of national systems, KBC and DZ believed that the combined operation would be in pole position to lead the market for integrated cross-border services. Announcing the deal, the companies added that, given the fact that this process would inevitably involve huge investments in IT hardware and software, an increasing number of banks in Europe would be likely to outsource their payment processing activities to specialists such as Fin-Force and Transaktionsinstitut.

Lessons learned

Fin-Force CEO Pascal Deman says that much of the success of Fin-Force comes down to the relationship with the outsourcing partner – which he describes as 'certainly a partnership – not a transactional relationship'. He continues: 'EDS had the original vision, together with KBC. And during the difficult times, they continued to believe in Fin-Force and support us. And thirdly, from a purely technical and practical point of view in terms of things like resources and project management expertise, they have been of great assistance throughout – and still are today. They continue to give us a permanently up-to-date view of what is happening in the ICT marketplace. And Fin-Force is at least 50 per cent an ICT company.'

For Deman, the key learning from the Fin-Force joint venture is clear: 'What I have learnt is that you sometimes need to be patient,' he says. 'We were patient. But even for me at certain stages, around 2002 to 2003, questions were starting to arise about whether this market would ever really move. I knew this company was going the right way, and that it was a valuable utility for KBC. But the original idea was to get market share and convince other parties, and for a while I used to go home wondering whether it made sense to continue to pursue the external part. Sometimes you just have to wait for the market to mature – and this is what has now happened. We showed a bit of patience, the market caught up, and now I'm extremely optimistic about the future of Fin-Force.'

The verdict

Despite the slow take-up by third-party clients in its first few years, Fin-Force has underlined the benefits that can flow from a strategic outsourcing initiative – especially one that is implemented with a trusted supplier on the basis of shared and clearly identifiable strategic goals. Back in 2000, both KBC and their outsourcing partner spotted and targeted a potential gap in the payments marketplace, a gap they believed would become increasingly evident as current trends in cross-border payments played themselves out. In the wake of the DZ deal announced in 2005, Fin-Force is well placed for future growth, and is already in discussions with several other prospective partners, including some with whom negotiations are at an advanced stage. Overall, the achievements of Fin-Force to date have underlined the role that outsourcing can play in enabling a business to reinvent itself in an evolving marketplace, underpinned by the IT strength, resources and commitment of a trusted supplier.

The business issue

The US multinational General Electric has long been recognized as a pioneer in many areas of global business – and its use of offshoring is no exception. GE became one of the first multinational companies to shift its back office processing, data-centre and call-centre operations to India, when it set up GE Capital International Services (GECIS) in 1997 to enable it to centralize its back office operations in a low-cost country. The unit provided services including finance and accounting, customer fulfilment, e-learning and business analytics, as well as IT outsourcing and software development supporting in all nearly 1,000 business processes across GE's 11 business units. By 2004, GECIS's 12,000-employee operation represented one of the largest units of its type established by a western multinational in India.

However, priorities had changed during the seven years in which GECIS was in existence as a wholly owned GE subsidiary. While GECIS's services were working well, delivering the required services effectively and meeting acceptable cost parameters, GE believed that GECIS would generate more value as an independent company. It also decided that selling GECIS might release valuable funds for investment in other ventures and development, and specifically in high-growth areas such as security technology. The company said publicly that it thought GECIS should be able to compete in the outsourced back office processing marketplace on an even footing – and GE set about finding a way to free GECIS up to do that.

The chosen solution

In December 2004 GE announced that it had clinched the deal it was looking for, by selling a 60 per cent stake in GECIS for about US$500 million to a consortium of two venture capital investors. The plan was that GECIS would emerge from the deal as a recapitalized, stand-alone company, offering business support services to third-party client companies across the world, including GE itself – which would continue to be a client and major shareholder. GE's history in the offshore outsourcing arena made GE's sale of most of GECIS's equity especially significant in terms of the offshore industry's development. In the early 1990s Jack Welch, then CEO of GE, introduced a '70:70:70' rule for GE's offshore initiatives. This meant that 70 per cent of GE's work would be outsourced; of this, 70 per cent would be handled in offshore development centres; and of this, about 70 per cent would be sourced in India. As a rule of thumb, this equates to about 30 per cent of GE's work being outsourced to India.

The deal structure

Under the sale agreement, General Atlantic Partners LLC and Oak Hill Capital Partners LP agreed to buy a majority stake, totalling 60 per cent, in GECIS. The agreed structure was that GE would continue to hold 40 per cent of the equity in GECIS after the transaction, with the private equity firms each taking a 30 per cent stake in the business. After the divestment, GECIS would continue to provide services to GE under a multi-year contract, with GE continuing to use and expand on GECIS's services. GECIS would also continue to build and expand its global portfolio of third-party clients for BPO services.

The business results

Since GE's sale of a majority stake in GECIS to the venture capital investors, GECIS has continued to go from strength to strength. As of the first half of 2005, it is expected to more than double its revenues to some US$1 billion by 2007–8. There are also expectations that GECIS will go for a public listing within three years, on the back of rapid growth in its home market and China. At the same time, it expects to double its workforce in India and China over the same period, which would take it up to a total of 32,000 employees by 2008.

This continuing expansion will help GECIS to meet what it says is rising demand for business process outsourcing (BPO). 'With the combination of the GE brand and growth [in the industry], notably in China, we can now go out and sell to the rest of the world. After all, this is why we did the deal,' commented Pramod Bhasin, GECIS chief executive, in February 2005. The company's website continues to describe the business as being 'built on GE DNA', which is hardly surprising given that GE remains GECIS's single largest shareholder. The fact that GECIS also says it focuses on the 'highest global quality at lowest local cost', using Six Sigma and lean philosophy, underlines its common culture with GE.

However, GECIS now clearly has a life of its own. Mr Bhasin, in his February 2005 comments, described the sale as having 'energized' GECIS, enabling it to ease its level of dependency on GE. He went on to pre-announce the acquisition of two new non-GE clients, on top of the six GECIS had already won since the sale. GECIS added that it would set up a second BPO unit in China in 2005, increasing its workforce in China to 3,000 by 2006. In India, GECIS plans to double its number of staff to 24,000 by 2007, while increasing its workforce at a slower rate in its other BPO centres in Mexico and Hungary. At the same time, it is actively looking for acquisitions.

▶

Lessons learned

GE's strategic decision to sell off the majority of its stake in GECIS is not an isolated decision, in terms of either GE or the industry as a whole. It reflects an increasing trend under which multinational companies are tending to move away from having wholly owned 'captive' subsidiaries handling BPO services and software development in India, and are instead looking to outsource these operations to independent outsourcing providers, often indigenous operations based in India. In this sense, the view expressed in some quarters that GE was 'pulling out' of offshore outsourcing was very much wide of the mark. Instead, the deal shows GE evolving and advancing its strategy by shuffling its portfolio of risks, as well as locking in the gains it had already made from running and owning GECIS as a captive.

The sale also reflected wider industry developments. In the 1990s, multinational companies set up captive subsidiaries in India for BPO and software development, largely in response to the relative shortage of local third-party outsourcing companies capable of providing sufficient quality. Today, with a flourishing community of high-quality local providers underpinned by a well-developed skills base, multinationals are finding they can generate greater savings at lower risk exposure by using a third-party outsourcing provider rather than establishing a captive operation.

However, sceptics would suggest there are also other – more defensive – aims at play. While India still offers good wage arbitrage opportunities, it continues to carry a fair degree of political risk, notably at the state level, and its stock market is highly volatile. By selling off equity in their captives in the country, companies can cash in much of their investment and pass the management and the risk on to other parties, while continuing to benefit from the services provided by these operations. Remaining on board as a long-term shareholder also gives the former owner exposure to the business's future success, while also freeing up money for investment in newer emerging offshore markets such as China and the Philippines, which have not yet followed India up the wage inflation curve.

The verdict

GE's creation, management and ultimately majority divestment of its GECIS subsidiary reflects a life cycle that we may well see happening with increasing frequency in the future. GECIS has delivered significant commercial and competitive advantages to its parent company over the years. Now, with Indian assets in vogue and enjoying healthy valuations in the market, GE has figured that the time is right to sell up, reshaping its risk profile without losing the benefit of GECIS's services. The deal also creates one of the largest offshore

BPO operations in China, a country where GECIS has a workforce of around 1,500 people, and from where it provides outsourced support for GE's businesses in Japan.

So this was not a withdrawal by GE from the offshore outsourcing market. If anything, it represented a vote of confidence in the future of offshore outsourcing, given the ongoing contract under which the now largely independent GECIS is providing services to its former parent. In essence, what GE has taken is a calculated commercial decision based on the return on investment from this asset and its desired risk exposure in India and other markets. The fact that GECIS is continuing to expand rapidly in China reflects a similar rebalancing from its own perspective as an independent business.

Looking forward, the outlook for GECIS also appears relatively bright as an independent company. The GE heritage and investment over the years has given it the scale and mentality to compete with the world's largest BPO providers. The sale enables GE to gain access to – and progressively exploit – greater economies of scale, plus additional technological and financial resources. If India really is to succeed in the long term as a global provider of complex end-to-end business processes, then it is through businesses such as GECIS that it will do so. For GE, the beauty is that its risk exposure to this process is now greatly reduced.

case study 3   J. Sainsbury

The business issue

In 1999 the UK supermarket operator J. Sainsbury was facing an increasingly tough environment. Having been the London stock market's favourite mass-market food retailer for more than a decade, it suddenly found itself coming under increasingly intense competitive pressure from Tesco, a rival formerly more associated with the low-cost end of the market. To Sainsbury's dismay, Tesco appeared to be pulling off the seemingly impossible feat of moving its quality, branding and customer base up-market, expanding and improving its offer, and simultaneously keeping its prices down to a consistently keen level. Sainsbury found itself not only being challenged but overtaken in its core market – and needed to respond across a wide array of areas. These included not only cutting underlying operational costs, but also shortening its time to market, becoming more responsive to customer demand, refreshing its store portfolio, and widening the range and appeal of its outlets. Radical action was needed, and Sainsbury decided to take it.

▶

The chosen solution

That action came in the form of a £1.3 billion (US$2.5 billion) seven-year out-sourcing deal with Accenture that Sainsbury announced in December 2000. This amount was split roughly equally between a large-scale IT transformation project and the ongoing operational costs of running the fully outsourced IT function. At the time, Sainsbury's chairman Peter Davis commented: 'Driving change in our IT capabilities is a fundamental part of our business transfor-mation plans.' As well as outsourcing all of Sainsbury's IT operations, the deal involved transfer of about 800 Sainsbury employees to Accenture, with Sainsbury retaining a small in-house IT team to oversee the new IT strategy.

The deal structure

At the time, it was the transformational IT outsourcing and ongoing seven-year management agreement that made all the headlines. However, an aspect of the deal that was to prove equally significant in the long run was the fund-ing method used by Sainsbury. The company chose an off-balance-sheet funding structure that was to have long-term consequences for its own strategic flexibility, ultimately restricting its room for manoeuvre in the M&A market. Under the deal, the IT asset was securitized through a financing vehi-cle, with the majority of the financing being provided by Barclays Capital into a structure called Swan. This entity sat between Sainsbury and Accenture, handling the cash and financing flows.

The business results

At first, all went according to plan. The staff were transferred across to Accenture, which provided management and project bandwidth to Sainsbury's IT operation. The change programme forged ahead, and results began to come through. There were immediate operational cost savings from IT, as the delivery stream of beneficial change got under way. The vast majori-ty of the activities, funding and investment proceeded according to the fixed and agreed transformation plan, with a small additional fund set aside to cover extra requirements or scope changes.

The momentum continued into 2003. In March of that year Sainsbury rolled out new supply chain software, and in August it started using self-scanning checkouts. But, at the same time, the competitive environment in the UK supermarket sector was changing fast. In late 2003 Safeway, a top-four play-er in the market, was effectively put up for sale. Tesco, by now the clear num-ber one in the market, was effectively blocked from bidding by competition considerations. To Sainsbury the chance of acquiring Safeway presented a tremendous one-off opportunity to rebuild scale and reinvigorate its business. But the use of securitization in its IT and elsewhere in its business, such as new store construction, left it unable to gear up its balance sheet to finance a bid. In early 2004 Safeway was purchased by William Morrison, a rival supermarket chain. It can hardly give Sainsbury too much consolation that Morrison has encountered greater difficulties than expected in integrating Safeway.

By the time Sainsbury appreciated the limiting effect of securitization on its strategic M&A options it was too late to address the issue quickly enough to make a bid. In February 2004 Sainsbury simplified its contract with Accenture by buying the intermediary entity, Swan, for £553 million. By then the Morrison bid for Safeway was virtually a done deal. And at the same time, Sainsbury's outsourcing relationship – although not the whole contract – with Accenture began to unravel in a highly public way. In July 2004 Sainsbury's chairman, by now Sir Peter Davis, stood down because of the company's continuing poor performance, and by October the gloves were off between client and supplier.

'IT systems have failed to deliver the anticipated increase in productivity and the costs today are a greater proportion of sales than they were four years ago,' commented Sainsbury in a statement in August 2004, before going on to add: 'The contract with Accenture is being renegotiated to involve the company more fully in the selection and implementation of systems and IT solutions. Accordingly, the company is rebuilding internal capability.' However, while much of Sainsbury's IT was outsourced to Accenture, sources close to the deal pointed out that the four automated service depots where many of Sainsbury's difficulties had originated were actually outside its scope. Accenture responded: 'We are responsible for the IT transformation programme at Sainsbury's, including some of the supply chain systems. However, the IT automation systems within Sainsbury's four new automated depots are not, and never have been under the scope of the existing contract. We are not responsible for the strategy, development and operations of these systems.'

It is hard to avoid the conclusion that Accenture was taking the rap. In March 2005 it was reported that Sainsbury was planning to move its IT team back into its headquarters in central London. The company also reaffirmed that it was renegotiating its Accenture contract to drive efficiencies through its IT system.

Lessons learned

Sainsbury's experience highlights two main lessons. One is that by adopting securitization – effectively borrowing against its future revenue stream – and

▶

using the resulting cash to execute a whole range of transformational change, the company had effectively taken a significant group of its assets out of its books and off the balance sheet. This in turn made these assets entirely unleverageable in an M&A context. So while the fundamental change pro-gramme theoretically strengthened the business and reduced its risk profile, the funding method also reduced Sainsbury's ability to leverage its balance sheet. So this securitization was a single-use tool, and proved counter-pro-ductive when conditions changed. It remains a moot point whether Sainsbury could have succeeded in a bid for Safeway, but its inability to fund a bid means we shall never know one way or the other.

The other lesson is that, if you look at the implications for the balance sheet of taking money from above the line (either investment or asset), and moving it to a below-the-line operational cost for services, then you also remove the possibility of utilizing that debt to offset other liabilities within the company. The risk is that you may get to a point, say three years into a seven-year deal, where the benefit of having externalized the debt is outweighed by the down-side of not being able to put it on your balance sheet. In some cases the effect of having it on the balance sheet could create a tax benefit to the tune of several hundreds of millions of dollars a year for the remaining years of the contract.

These lessons from the funding of the deal were the subtext to Sainsbury's growing unhappiness with the deal, and underline the extent to which the outsourcing contractor may have been a convenient scapegoat for other problems. True, as a known and fixed transformation programme, the contract tended to put a 'glass ceiling' on investment, and also limited the company's flexibility and room for manoeuvre when conditions changed. But the underlying strategic rigidity came from the use of a single-purpose vehicle of a type not ideally suited to absorbing change. Today, with Swan reab-sorbed into Sainsbury and the outsourcing contract largely renegotiated, these structural issues have been addressed. But Sainsbury's new executive team under Justin King knows that it may well be a long time before a UK retailing asset akin to Safeway comes on to the market again.

The verdict

For clients considering transformational outsourcing, and even for the suppli-ers working with them, there are some profound messages to take away from the sequence of events at Sainsbury. One is to be extremely careful of single-purpose vehicles, and certainly only to use them for as far ahead as you can reliably see into the future. With the benefit of hindsight, the combination of the underlying rigidity of the funding structure with the seven-year span of the

Sainsbury/Accenture deal was almost bound to give problems sooner or later. As soon as the outlook becomes less certain, a greater degree of flexibility will be needed to handle it.

Repeatedly in this book we have stressed that much of the power of outsourcing as a tool for corporate reshaping and transformation derives from its flexibility, and its scope to enable and facilitate fast, agile and responsive change. It is ironic that in trying to harness the power of outsourcing Sainsbury inadvertently imposed a degree of financial inflexibility which had the effect of eclipsing the undoubted benefits that it was receiving from the outsourcing deal itself. It is a lesson which Sainsbury and the outsourcing industry will not forget.

case study 4   Aegon/GRE

The business issue

The Dutch insurer Aegon bought France-based rival insurer Axa's UK life and pensions business, branded Guardian Royal Exchange, for £702 million (US$1.33 billion) in September 1999. In completing the merger, Aegon faced some key issues over how it would absorb this new purchase into its business. Aegon wanted to complete the integration as quickly and smoothly as possible, and with the minimal disruption to its ongoing operations. A major positive consideration was that it was not critical to integrate the GRE products immediately into the Aegon portfolio, since much of the value of GRE lay in its client portfolio. What Aegon needed was a speedy, clean and controllable means of integrating GRE and getting it up and running within the Aegon group without tying up too much management time and resources.

The chosen solution

Aegon found the solution by applying its extensive experience and expertise in using outsourcing as a way of facilitating and driving corporate reshaping. It opted to take a 'straight-to-outsourcing' route for the whole of GRE's IT and telecoms infrastructure. The result was effectively an object lesson in the use of outsourcing to facilitate successful M&A integration, enabling the rapid and smooth acquisition and absorption of GRE. By going direct to outsourcing for the whole ICT infrastructure instead of trying to incorporate it into Aegon itself, the acquirer avoided the need to retrain and reskill significant numbers of in-house personnel and minimized the scale and length of the integration effort.

▶

The deal structure

The structure applied by Aegon to execute this straight-to-outsourcing was very simple. Taking on the role itself of core integrator for the project, Aegon drew on its existing experience to set up a series of outsourcing contracts and relationships to take over and manage the key elements of GRE's ICT base. BT was signed up as the outsourced telecoms supplier, Computacenter to manage desktop systems, and Fujitsu for mainframes. These agreements were all negotiated and put into effect in a rapid timeframe, bypassing many of the problems and bottlenecks traditionally associated with major merger integrations.

The business results

The outsourcing strategy around GRE's systems and telecoms delivered a string of benefits for Aegon. The clearest was that it enabled it to fulfil the strategic objectives it had targeted when deciding to conduct the M&A deal. Announcing the deal, Aegon had said the purchase would provide it with economies of scale and improve its distribution capabilities while also expanding its existing UK product range. 'Aegon UK's premium income will increase about 20 per cent, and funds under management by about 50 per cent as a result of the transaction', the company said. The principal GRE product lines that were acquired included its asset protection products, which the company said would complement Aegon UK's core asset accumulation products range.

Equally importantly, the use of a direct outsourcing approach minimized the extent to which management on both sides were distracted by the acquisition. It enabled both Aegon and GRE to get on with managing the process of merging the business organization, rather than getting tied up in the detail of integrating the underlying services. That element of the job was effectively taken off management's plate, to be managed effectively and efficiently in the background by the selected outsourcing contractors.

Overall, the outsourcing initiative enabled the merged business to hit the ground running in exploiting the planned synergies and efficiencies. So smooth was the resulting integration that by August 2001, within two years of the acquisition, Guardian Royal Exchange was ready to change its name to Aegon UK and come within the overall group branding.

Lessons learned

With its use of outsourcing in the integration of GRE, Aegon laid down a template that many other businesses might be well advised to consider. In this book we have drawn many parallels between the skills and approaches used in successful M&A, and those in outsourcing. With its GRE outsourcing approach Aegon demonstrated that outsourcing and M&A do not necessarily represent just alternative options for corporate reshaping, but can also be used in a complementary way to effect different parts of the same strategy.

Rather than getting its own management embroiled in the complexities of an internally driven systems integration effort, Aegon looked around to see what other tools might be available to achieve the same result. Given its existing sophisticated use of outsourcing in other parts of its business, it did not have to look very far.

The verdict

This case study is shorter than the others in this chapter, largely because when things go right there is less to say when analyzing the sequence of cause and effect in the deal. Aegon was smart enough to formulate and execute the outsourcing strategy for GRE from within its own management ranks, and had the requisite skills and experience to manage the integration of – and interrelation between – the various outsourcing contracts.

Many other companies may feel they are not so well provided with in-house supplier management capabilities. But that does not rule out a straight-to-outsourcing approach for a new acquisition. As we have described, there is now a wealth of top-class, independent and disinterested advice on outsourcing available to those clients ready and willing to seek it out and exploit it. With GRE, Aegon presented an object lesson in how to use outsourcing – and it is one that could be emulated even by companies without Aegon's outstanding prior track record of successful outsourcing deals.

---

case study 5   BP

The business issue

In our opinion, BP's CEO Sir John Browne is arguably the leading user and exponent of outsourcing as a strategic risk mitigation and corporate reshaping tool. The business issue he has faced since taking over as CEO in 1995 is clear but all-encompassing: to grow BP from a respectable but frankly mid-sized oil major into a global energy giant, to be regarded in the same bracket

▶

as industry leader Exxon and Royal Dutch/Shell. His success in achieving this highly ambitious objective, and his consummate use of M&A and management of risk throughout his pursuit of it, have established his reputation as one of the world's greatest corporate leaders.

Browne has built and maintained this reputation by delivering consistently on what he has promised – and this ability to deliver has been underpinned by outsourcing. Risk is pivotal to BP's strategy, and significant risk elements have been highlighted by analysts assessing deals ranging from the 1998 acquisition of Amoco to the creation of the TNK–BP venture in 2003, when BP pioneered the route into Russia for western oil companies. One of the hallmarks of Browne's corporate style is his skilful use of outsourcing to mitigate these risks, and to manage the knocks that may affect the company's share price if the hoped-for synergies from M&A are not delivered as fully or as quickly as hoped.

The chosen solution

While BP has been exploiting the efficient procurement of third-party IT services as a source of competitive advantage since the early 1990s, the beginnings of BP's finely balanced blend of M&A, risk mitigation and outsourcing under Browne's leadership can be traced back to August 1998. With the industry beset by a dramatic decline in the oil price, BP stunned it still further by swooping to acquire Amoco of the United States for US$52 billion, lifting BP at a stroke into the big league of oil majors. Amoco was just the first of a series of high-profile acquisitions across the world – a trail that now includes the purchases of Atlantic Richfield, again of the United States, for US$27 billion in 1999, the British lubricants business Burmah Castrol for US$4.7 billion in 2000, and then Germany's Veba Oel for US$4 billion followed by the US$8 billion investment in Russia's TNK in 2003. With each purchase BP leapfrogged further up the global corporate league table.

That acquisition trail has made headlines round the world. It also involved a lot of risk – and it is no coincidence that the roll-out of BP's daring acquisition strategy was accompanied by successive waves of outsourcing. What is equally clear is that Browne's strategic use of outsourcing, ably supported from 1999 by new CIO John Leggate, developed and evolved over the years, becoming increasingly sure-footed in the process. In 2001, speaking at Oxford University, Browne was quoted as saying: 'It was only really two or three years ago that we started to see IT as a set of integrated technologies with a real business potential.'

In Leggate Browne found an ally who understood BP's outsourcing philosophy, and who was ready and able to tackle issues head-on, mitigate risks proactively, cut costs, integrate systems – and use outsourcing to help achieve all these objectives. When Leggate become CIO in 1999 there were 10,000 different software applications being used across BP's operations. A year later 3,000 of these applications had been dropped, and management of a further 5,000 had been outsourced to third parties.

The deal structure

A key aspect of Browne's and BP's use of outsourcing is the exploitation of outsourcing's innate flexibility. This has manifested itself in the differing approaches and structures used during each wave of outsourcing activity, as Browne shaped and reshaped the approach in line with changing opportunities and circumstances. This facility with outsourcing reflects Browne's experience before he became CEO, when he was head of BP's exploration unit. During his tenure at the exploration business he reportedly used outsourcing to cut its IT budget from US$360 million in 1989 to US$132 million in 1995.

Having seen what outsourcing could achieve, he seized on it as a key element of his expansion strategy as CEO, with the first wave of strategic group-wide outsourcing coinciding with the 1998 purchase of Amoco. At that time, BP adopted a 'best of breed' policy of seeking out and using specialist suppliers with specific skills for defined areas of the business, rather than looking to use more generalist outsourcing providers to handle a range of activities.

The first major outsourcing wave involved a triumvirate of IT providers, each of which was contracted to manage a particular aspect on a global basis – thereby simplifying the task of merger integration from the Amoco deal onwards, and mitigating the resulting risks for the group. BT Syncordia took over telecoms provision worldwide, SEMA was awarded the contract for desktop services, and EDS was appointed as outsourcing provider for the mainframe systems. While other providers continued to handle discrete elements for divisions such as exploration, the majority of IT activities firm wide were divided up between these three global suppliers.

The big three IT deals all made headlines – but a parallel move, which went unreported at the time, was equally significant. This was BP's decision to effectively close down its in-house finance and administration services, and outsource them to Accenture. This was one of the first times that a European-based company had taken such a step, and it was every bit as ambitious and forward-looking as what BP was doing on the IT side.

In 1999 BP hit the headlines again, with news of a US$600 million deal to outsource many of its human resources processes to Exult – a fledgling supplier that then had just one major client of similar standing, Bank of America. Under the deal, 100,000 BP personnel worldwide would access a wide range of HR services via computerized self-service, run remotely from Exult's outsourced shared service centres in the United Kingdom and United States. Much has been written about the subsequent ups and downs of this groundbreaking deal, but less has been revealed about one of its key strategic drivers: the need to establish a basis for consistent internal communications across BP.

Sources suggest that shortly after BP took over Amoco Browne was shown figures stating that fully 34 per cent of the total group headcount had no access to a computer during their working day. One of Browne's renowned strengths as a leader is his ability to communicate – and he knew that a key success factor for the acquisition trail on which he had just embarked lay in the ability to get clear and consistent corporate messaging across to all staff worldwide, irrespective of their legacy organization and of their functional or geographical location. This could only be done via technology – and it required everyone to be using a computer. A further beneficial effect would be to increase the level of computer literacy across the business.

So, the question was: how do you make everyone use a computer? The answer was clear: make them want – and need – to use it, by turning it into their sole source of access to information about their salary, accumulated benefits, tax position, vacation allowance, company cars and so on. That in turn would turn the desktop computer into the ideal channel for consistent corporate messaging across the unified group. So the route to effective communication lay via outsourcing and automating HR – and Exult's 'kiosk' technology was ideally suited to the task.

As the Exult deal rolled out and then rolled on – with a few well-publicized hiccups along the way – BP was preparing for the second major wave of IT outsourcing, four years on from the first. Continuing reviews of the original 'triumvirate' agreement with BT Syncordia, SEMA and EDS suggested that BP was not getting the keenest possible pricing for the contracted services. So, in a change of tack away from the original 'best of breed' approach, the company awarded contracts on a global basis to IBM and EDS, with EDS mainly handling telecoms and communications, and IBM the mainframe and desktop systems.

While these deals were widely reported, what was not revealed at the time was that a significant proportion of the resulting cost synergies were underwritten by the vendors, thereby de-risking the deals significantly from BP's point of view. This reflected Browne's clear understanding – already exhibited in the finance and administration outsourcing deal with Accenture – that integration is a key skill of outsourcing providers. So, he reasoned, the suppliers would be willing to accept the risk of underwriting the targeted benefits, on the basis that a truly world-class provider should be able to exceed those targets.

Large-scale outsourcing remains pivotal to BP's operational and risk management. Third-party vendors provide services including data centres, telecoms, helpdesks and development of applications. While this level of maturity means the pace of its outsourcing programme has inevitably slowed down, BP is constantly reviewing all its deals. It usually keeps its outsourcing contracts down to a relatively short term of three years, and tries not to require external suppliers to create alliances with one another, as tended to happen in its 'best of breed' days. This approach in turn helps to avoid potential political problems between vendors.

The statistics on BP's global positioning under Browne's tenure speak for themselves. BP was ranked 27th in the Global 500 in 1996, as Browne completed his first year as CEO. By late 2003, at the time when BP made its move to invest in TNK, BP ranked fifth in the Global 500. It has also outperformed most of its peers in terms of shareholder returns. The ability to manage and de-risk the M&A process and to integrate large acquisitions smoothly and rapidly has been central to this performance. And this ability is underpinned by BP's outsourcing strategy.

Lessons learned

While M&A is clearly at the heart of this book, there are few companies that exhibit as clearly as BP the power that can come from combining a well-planned M&A strategy with equally well-thought-out strategic use of outsourcing as a risk mitigator and integration enabler. The lesson from Sir John Browne's linkage of M&A and outsourcing, effectively making them two sides of the same coin, is a positive one: just look what can be achieved. Interestingly, outsourcing is not yet a significant element of BP's Russian strategy. One day it probably will be – but only when the outsourcing supply market in Russia has developed sufficient sophistication and quality to live up to BP's requirements.

The verdict

Few companies have a better track record in successful outsourcing than BP. The charismatic CEO's clear direction and strategic vision together with his consistent and overt support for his senior management drive the rate of change and the certainty of benefit collection. Outsourcing is used by BP to facilitate the integration of acquisitions and ensure that the predicted cost savings match the market's expectations and aid the stability of the share price. This planned and strategic use of outsourcing's ultimate potential is something of which all CEOs should be more fully aware.

case study 6   Nextel Communications

The business issue

US-based Nextel Communications is a leading provider of fully integrated wireless communications services. It has built the largest guaranteed all-digital wireless network in the United States, covering thousands of communities across the country. Nextel customers now include 95 per cent of the FORTUNE 500, and Nextel and Nextel Partners Inc. – its affiliate for rural and mid-sized markets – currently serve 297 of the top 300 US markets, where approximately 263 million people live or work. In December 2004 Nextel consolidated its leading position in its marketplace by confirming plans to merge with Sprint.

The expansion of Nextel's business during the past decade has been consistently strong. After signing up its millionth customer in October 1997, Nextel's market penetration accelerated dramatically. Within nine months, its customer base had grown to 2 million. Nine months after that, a further 1 million subscribers had signed on. The risk with such headlong growth is that it may raise problems such as a reactive approach to IT and a sprawling information infrastructure supporting literally hundreds of applications.

By 2001 Nextel needed to develop an efficient information environment to meet the ongoing growth in its demands. At the same time the company was facing rising costs because of its above-industry-average rates of customer churn. It needed to stem these costs quickly, while also improving its standards of customer care to maintain its rate of revenue growth.

The chosen solution

Both of these challenges lay outside Nextel's core competence in rolling out wireless data services. So, to find the rigour and discipline needed to tackle these issues, it decided to seek out partners capable of providing the right capabilities and experience. In choosing its vendors Nextel looked at more than merely price or capabilities. Instead, it realized that truly successful partnerships require a similarity in cultures, a willingness to communicate and a dedication to making the relationship mutually beneficial.

Nextel's choice of IT partner 'was a decision based not solely on cost and not solely on technical capabilities', comments Nextel CIO Dick LeFave. 'We found a company we felt we could work well with – and that has proven to be true. We feel that is probably one of the most important components.'

The deal structure

In early 2002 Nextel turned over its data-centre operation, helpdesk support and desktop services to EDS. In the same year it outsourced its entire customer care operation to IBM and its partner TeleTech.

Under the helpdesk and desktop agreement, approximately 300 Nextel employees moved to the outsourcing supplier and Nextel's data centre was also transferred. The first task was to stabilize and then improve service levels across the board. Following this, the teams identified 46 separate categories, from server availability to application response time, and set ambitious performance targets. At the start of the contract, benchmark performance in many areas was unacceptable; more than half of the categories had unsatisfactory ratings. Within two years, that number had been reduced to just 11 per cent.

Rather than meeting to review performance, the Nextel/outsourcing supplier team now meets to discuss strategy. This has turned a previously informal part of many outsourcing relationships into a standardized procedure that helps to keep all parties focused on the same goal: helping Nextel position itself for further growth.

At the time of writing, the diamond team is primarily focused on process improvements and technological innovations. A recent innovation at Nextel has been the implementation of a remote desktop takeover, which allows helpdesk staff to handle many computer problems without physically dispatching a technician. EDS has also partnered with Nextel to use its BlackBerry® handhelds to improve field support for those problems requiring onsite assistance. The technology not only accelerates service delivery but has proved to be a source of valuable insight into common performance issues.

The business results

By halfway through the five-year contract Nextel had already realized approximately 70 per cent of the cost savings the company anticipated from outsourcing. Further, IT cost as a percentage of total revenue has decreased by almost 10 per cent in less than two years.

Nextel has been able to achieve these savings during a period when its customer base has been continuing to expand. In the past, a rising number of subscribers meant rising costs as the company worked to accommodate them. In 2003 Nextel gained approximately 2.3 million new subscribers, while its IT cost per subscriber dropped by nearly 9 per cent. These cost savings have come primarily as a result of making Nextel's information systems more

▶

reliable, with these systems now achieving an average uptime ranging from 99.2 to 99.9 per cent.

Other developments in the business point to the parallel success of the customer care outsourcing agreement with IBM. Just a year on from that deal, the annual J.D. Power & Associates survey of wireless customer satisfaction awarded Nextel the top customer satisfaction ranking in three of the four regions of the United States in which it was evaluated. At the same time Nextel's level of customer churn fell to the lowest levels in the industry. During the eight years of the contract Nextel expects to achieve cost savings totalling around US$1 billion.

Lessons learned

For Nextel, the results have confirmed the wisdom of the decision to outsource. Nextel CIO Dick LeFave sums up the benefits to the business resulting from the desktop services agreement: 'Nextel's growth has been very consistent. With each growth spurt, we've needed enhancements for our IT platforms. We need that capability to grow. Our outsourcing supplier provides the management; they provide us with oversight; they provide us with technical innovation; they're giving us services we were not able to provide for ourselves.'

Henry Green, vice-president I/T Operations at Nextel, is equally positive: 'It was very important that Nextel pick a partner that we could work closely with,' he says. 'As fast as we're growing, there are always challenges to be met. Our relationship has built a high degree of trust that allows us to provide the very best service for our clients.'

The verdict

The IT partnership has clearly achieved the level of cost savings and productivity improvements that lay at the core of Nextel's reasons for moving to an outsourced arrangement. However, the most striking aspect of Nextel's experience is probably the way in which the relationship continues to deliver value to both parties in new and unexpected ways.

For example, a dedicated Nextel/EDS account alliance team put in place to collaborate on joint market-facing activities has exceeded the projected five-year revenue targets in just 14 months. Additionally, EDS has deployed more than 12,000 Nextel devices throughout its own organization to improve the efficiency of its call centres and helpdesk operations for its clients. And Nextel's willingness to move to centralized, overnight distribution of replacement computers and peripherals helped minimize their outsourcing partner's internal support costs.

Not surprisingly, Nextel remains committed to outsourcing as it continues to grow its business. The company comments on its website: 'The focus on key industries enables Nextel to pinpoint customer needs. Collaboration with market-leading partners such as IBM, EDS and Raytheon also enables Nextel to offer unique solutions and improve the way business gets done.'

case study 7   JP Morgan

The business issue

In July 2004 JP Morgan Chase – a global leader in investment banking, financial services for consumers and businesses, financial transaction processing, asset and wealth management and private equity – executed the latest phase of its strategy through its merger with Bank One. The roots of this strategy can be traced back to the early 1990s, when JP Morgan (as it then was) adopted a pioneering approach to outsourcing. Its experience in the years since then has underlined the importance of governance to successful benefits realization from outsourcing, and the value of the external discipline that outsourcing brings to the drive to reduce costs. The underlying benefits from its outsourcing strategy in terms of lower costs and higher shareholder value continue to be evident today.

The stimulus for JP Morgan's outsourcing strategy lay in a number of issues facing the firm in 1991. The business had arrived at a point where its annual technology spend had risen above US$1 billion a year. At the same time there was a feeling at senior levels in the firm that it was failing to get full value from that investment. There was also a realization that, as the business continued its transformation from commercial to investment bank and trading firm, there was a need for continued investment in technology – especially in fixed income and equity trading and broking.

The chosen solution

As a result, JP Morgan began a fairly aggressive search for ways to contain costs and improve value from its IT spend. Outsourcing was seen as an attractive option from two angles. One was the potential for exploiting economies of scale. The other was the chance to create greater accountability in terms of sticking to budgeted spending levels – something that was proving to be particularly problematic with the existing in-house approach.

▶

Further investigations indicated that these benefits could be achieved, so in 1992 the company moved ahead with an outsourcing strategy masterminded by new CIO Peter Miller.

The deal structure

JP Morgan's first major ICT outsourcing contract – set up in 1992 – was a network outsourcing agreement with AT&T. At the time JP Morgan had a number of different communications protocols. AT&T offered a solution based on Cisco multi-protocol routers, and provided a way to deliver more efficient and cheaper network communications across the business, on a consistent and global basis. Inevitably, the deal made global headlines, as one of the largest and most ambitious network outsourcing transactions seen up to that time.

Another area of focus for the outsourcing strategy was JP Morgan's data centres. In late 1992 the company entered negotiations about a proposed deal with IBM International Shared Service Center (ISSC), which was offering an outsourced solution providing cost reductions of 10 per cent and a 50/50 split of savings beyond that level. In the event JP Morgan decided not to proceed with that agreement – not because of the deal itself, but because it was felt at the time that the firm was not culturally ready for the transition of a significant number of personnel to an outsourcing provider. In contrast, the outsourcing deals it had done before that had involved the transfer of either very few personnel or none at all.

However, the pressure for more outsourcing continued – largely because IT spend was continuing to grow at a rate of around 15–20 per cent, which in hard cash terms was around US$200 million a year. Debate in the firm focused on governance issues between the business organization and the technology organization. A number of initiatives were undertaken, including the introduction of 'horizontal' centres of excellence to provide skills and technology to multiple businesses across the group, enabling better sharing and leveraging of knowledge and clearer career paths for IT specialists. However, there was a growing sense that internal solutions could never deliver the rigour, discipline and accountability needed to keep costs down to budgeted levels.

By 1994 JP Morgan was ready to contemplate a fairly complete IT outsourcing solution for virtually all its businesses, apart from private banking and investment management. The proposal was to outsource about 70 per cent of the IT organization including the network, infrastructure and applications, a move that would involve the transition of a significant number of JP Morgan staff. Three consortia lined up initially, led respectively by IBM, EDS and CSC, with each consortium including AT&T for the network, since that element (outsourced in 1992) was continuing to run well.

Personality differences between the IBM bid team and JP Morgan saw IBM drop out of the bidding fairly soon, leaving a close run-off between EDS and CSC. In late 1995 the deal went to CSC, which signed up as the master contractor with Accenture (then called Andersen Consulting) handling the applications, and AT&T managing the communications network element. The deal with the 'Pinnacle Alliance', as the consortium was termed, was a seven-year agreement estimated at more than US$2 billion, making it one of the largest outsourcing transactions ever.

Under the deal, targeted to deliver aggregate savings of about 15 per cent on technology costs, the Pinnacle Alliance undertook to manage JP Morgan's data centres in New York, London and Delaware; distributed computing operations (such as desktop support and local area networks) and voice and data services in New York, Delaware, London and Paris; and some internal corporate applications in the United States and Europe. About 900 Morgan employees in areas covered by the agreement remained in their existing roles, but transitioned across to become employees of one of the Alliance firms.

In a statement at the time Peter Miller commented: 'The Alliance will give us access to the bench strength of leading firms to meet the growing technology needs of our global business. It also will free up our internal technologists to focus on strategies and innovations that give Morgan a competitive edge.' The subtext was a view at senior level in JP Morgan that the only way to control IT costs would be to have governance that imposed real accountability – and that this in turn represented the only route to increasing the market value of the business without disrupting its operations.

With the in-house approach, it had always been possible for the IT function to make excuses for why spending targets had been exceeded, ranging from volumes being higher than expected to simply 'we tried but failed'. By introducing the discipline and governance of an external supplier arrangement a policy of 'no excuses' could be put into effect and fully enforced. The Pinnacle Alliance deal did deliver the targeted benefits, prompting a positive market reaction that helped JP Morgan's market value rise significantly.

However, while the deal succeeded from JP Morgan's viewpoint, tensions were beginning to arise between the members of the consortium. Rising processing power and falling desktop prices saw the contract pricing come down, along with positive variance in the cost base for CSC. But Accenture, which was providing the applications element, found itself squeezed between falling contract pricing and rapid salary inflation for the type of human capital it needed for the contract: capable, experienced programmers with sound business knowledge. So Accenture initiated conversations with CSC and JP Morgan about repricing to reflect the changed circumstances, while JP Morgan began to become dissatisfied over the staffing of some projects. Pretty soon the well began to get poisoned – and in late 1998 Accenture launched legal proceedings against CSC for allegedly failing to defend Accenture's interests, and thereby affecting the interests of JP Morgan.

Ultimately a settlement was reached under which a large chunk of the contract was split off, and some of the work became direct between Accenture and JP Morgan rather than going via CSC. At the same time JP Morgan was continuing to enjoy the benefits in terms of cost, service, stock price and shareholder value. So in early 2000, when Chase acquired JP Morgan, the CSC contract stayed in place.

It was here that a further strand of JP Morgan's outsourcing and IT strategy under Peter Miller came to the fore: offshoring. Back in 1992, following a systematic review of operational costs, JP Morgan had moved to set up regional processing hubs. For example, Singapore became the regional hub for Asia, with processing from other centres including Japan moving there. At the time JP Morgan also had a minority holding in the Indian investment institution ICICI, and this encouraged it to become an early entrant into the Indian back office processing market. After setting up some operational capabilities in India in the late 1990s, JP Morgan Chase – as it had now become – moved some equity research capabilities there in 2001, as part of a controlled and ongoing expansion of its Indian operations.

In 2002 JP Morgan Chase went out to tender for a major IT outsourcing contract widely regarded as the biggest ever in the financial services sector. With CSC stepping back or set to assume the role of subcontractor, the lead bidders were IBM and EDS – and EDS's well-publicized credit problems at the time helped IBM Global Services to clinch a seven-year deal to take over a range of the company's IT functions including data-centre operations, helpdesk support, day-to-day operation of the distributed computing resources, and voice and data *networks*.

However, about a year later in January 2004, JP Morgan Chase agreed to buy Bank One for about US$58 billion. This merger ushered in a new leadership team that was more distrustful than its predecessor about the cultural and business benefits of outsourcing. Later that year the IBM contract was cancelled, and the staff who had transferred from CSC to IBM were brought back in house as JP Morgan employees.

The business results

JP Morgan's twelve-year progression through the cycle from in-house IT solution via outsourcing and ultimately back to in-house illustrates many of the benefits of outsourcing – and some of the pitfalls, especially for suppliers. Crucially, it delivered precisely the long-term and sustainable rise that the company hoped to achieve in its stock price. This widened its strategic options and strengthened its bargaining position in the rapidly consolidating financial services market, and ultimately enhanced the value delivered to its shareholders.

Lessons learned

Despite the speed-bumps along the way, such as the legal dispute between CSC and Accenture, JP Morgan's successful use of outsourcing underlines the value of external accountability and governance in implementing a rigorous cost control strategy. Like an executive who cannot get up at 6am to go to the gym without arranging for a personal trainer banging on the door, JP Morgan used the discipline of an external third party to whip its IT costs into shape.

There were also clear lessons in the company's switch from CSC to IBM, and in its ultimate exit from IT outsourcing when it cancelled the IBM contract in 2004. A lot of companies instinctively believe it is not possible to change or drop suppliers where an outsourcing project of this size and complexity is involved. But JP Morgan showed that if a major client wants to bring its IT in-house, or run a proper competitive tendering process, it can be done. At the time the cancellation of the IBM deal was seen as a loud wake-up call to suppliers not to be complacent. It also underlined the fact that when a client signs a contract it should already have a divorce mentality in mind, so it is ready to contain its liabilities when the two organizations part company.

The verdict

Irrespective of the vendors' viewpoint, JP Morgan's experience and exploitation of outsourcing were both positive and successful. It used outsourcing to create real accountability where this had previously been lacking, and – alongside the operational and cost benefits – succeeded in its aim of driving its market value upwards. Overall this is a great example of what outsourcing can deliver in strategic terms, and of how the starting point for this delivery is effective governance.

The business issue

When British Telecommunications (BT) was privatized by the UK government in 1984, the former state-owned telephone monopolist had already embarked on the much-needed transformation into a lean and leading-edge global communications business. One key area of focus was its human resources function. In 1990 this consisted of 14,500 HR professionals servicing BT's 250,000-strong workforce. By the late 1990s the discipline and rigours of the private sector had seen BT reduce that workforce to less than 100,000, and its HR function down to less than 2,000, through a sweeping change programme underpinned by widescale process re-engineering and innovation throughout the business.

As well as getting smaller, BT's HR function had also been reshaped radically in line with the business as a whole. Starting in 1991 with the consolidation of its former 26-region HR administration structure into customer-focused functional units, BT then went on to concentrate its HR transactional services in nine centres and to rationalize its HR systems. By 1998 BT's HR was moving to a shared service structure for transactional services, opening the way for HR to move to higher ground and focus on strategic and operational issues facing the business. BT also wanted to commercialize its HR transformation capabilities and knowledge base, which it saw as potentially having a competitive edge in the external marketplace for HR services.

The chosen solution

BT's chosen solution combined two radical elements into an approach that was ground-breaking for its time – especially in Europe. One element was to outsource its transactional HR services to a third-party provider. This in itself was a major step. However, BT also wanted to go further, by outsourcing those processes to a joint venture that BT would part-own, and into which it would inject its collective wealth of HR transformation expertise. This joint venture would then seek other clients, offering world-class outsourced HR services to major companies.

The way was paved in 1998 by the move to shared services for transactional HR, which enabled BT to improve the quality of HR service across the business, lower the cost base and enhance the levels of productivity from the function. It also enabled BT to go out into the market and talk to potential partners about the creation of the joint venture to which it would outsource its HR processes.

At the time, another organization looking closely at the potential of the HR outsourcing (HRO) market was Accenture. In 1999 the two entered serious discussions about teaming up to combine BT's operational expertise in HR transactions with Accenture's strengths in technology and business transformation.

The deal structure

In 2000, BT and Accenture announced the creation of e-peopleserve, a 50/50 joint venture set up to provide HR services to both companies and to other customers. Over 1,000 BT employees transferred across to the new entity, leaving BT's retained HR organization at just 600 people, a far cry from the 14,500 its HR function had employed just a decade earlier. Employees of all three organizations – BT, Accenture and those newly recruited into e-peopleserve – then collaborated on the creation of a comprehensive, end-to-end HR factory capable of handling HR transactions throughout the employee life cycle.

In press comment on the creation of e-peopleserve, BT executives have repeatedly stressed the importance of cultural fit in doing the deal. Stephen Kelly, BT senior vice-president of HR, quoted in 2003 in *HRO Today* magazine, commented: 'Not all providers could grasp our complex culture. Cultural fit was important, since we needed to build a relationship with the supplier. It's a bit like a marriage – you have to be clear going in that it's someone you will be happy with several years from now. That requires a leap of faith grounded by trust.' Other BT executives highlighted the fact that technical competence was just one consideration alongside the right attitude and commitment.

At the launch, everyone involved in the e-peopleserve joint venture foresaw a bright future for it. With the excitement of being part of an innovative new company and belief in the heady market predictions for take-up of HR outsourcing, management and employees alike were optimistic about the exciting future ahead.

The business results

However, as ever in a major transformation of this kind, there were some initial issues. The switch from an internal shared services function to an outsourcing provider was a difficult cultural barrier to cross. For many e-peopleserve employees it was not easy to see what impact the new joint venture had achieved. They remained in the same building, doing the same job for the same people, so there was minimal change to their day-to-day position. The

▶

continuing tendency to push through ad hoc projects and activities for 'my colleague John in department X' – as and when they asked for it – would have repercussions for the company later into the contract.

Nevertheless management were making great strides forward, with e-peopleserve designing an operating model and investing time and money in partnerships and alliances to create a best of breed solution for the HRO market. By 2001 e-peopleserve had picked up its first third-party customer – though BT, not surprisingly, remained its biggest single client by a substantial margin. However, within little more than a year, wider strategic realities came into play. In March 2001, following a series of ambitious deals worldwide and the bursting of the dotcom bubble, BT's debt mountain stood at some £28 billion, creating real fears over the company's long-term stability.

In response, the management team of chairman Sir Christopher Bland and incoming chief executive Ben Verwaayen set about an aggressive debt reduction programme. Within a year a successful £5.9 billion rights issue and an £8 billion disposal programme – including selling its stake in the directory service Yell, unwinding the Concert joint venture with AT&T and spinning off the mm02 mobile business – had halved the company's net debt to £13.7 billion.

The 50 per cent stake in e-peopleserve was always unlikely to survive the sell-off. In February 2002, just two years in, BT agreed to sell its stake in e-peopleserve to Accenture, for US$70 million in cash. Under the agreement BT would receive additional payments from an earn-out arrangement based on e-peopleserve's revenues from customers other than BT and Accenture over the subsequent five years. Following this deal e-peopleserve was subsumed and repositioned by Accenture as a core Accenture service offering, focusing on the HRO market – Accenture HR Services – and continued to provide BT with HR services.

In a statement at the time Philip Hampton, BT Group finance director, said: 'The sale [of e-peopleserve] is in line with our strategy of focusing on core activities, and reflects our continued success in reducing BT's net debt. We believe the future of e-peopleserve is best served within the Accenture organization which is looking to accelerate the growth and development of the business globally. BT will also retain significant value and interest in the future success of the business through the earn-out arrangement.'

Throughout this period there were also some other notable changes occurring at Accenture HR Services. It was on to its third CEO since its inception and was heading for its fourth. In fact it was not just the chief executive who would leave with the sell-off, since the CFO and Chief Operations Officer (COO) also left the organization. The majority of the founding BT management team was to be replaced by senior Accenture partners.

At this time Accenture HR Services was finding the embryonic HRO market tougher than expected. It had struggled to sign up any significant new clients and operating costs were rising. With the new management team on board it now needed to renew its focus on operational effectiveness – so it was not surprising that the next programme implemented within the company was voluntary redundancies. With new management and a slimmed-down organization, the focus on winning new business could start.

However, these changes coincided with some high-profile issues over the costs of the service to BT. Reports said that BT's expected spending for 2002 under the contract was around £75 million, but that additional costs had pushed the company's HR spend up to £80 million, and there were suggestions that BT was unhappy with this. With the harder than expected battle to pick up new clients and the real possibility that BT could walk away from the outsourcing agreement at the end of 2005, it was clear that Accenture needed to take immediate action. So renewed focus was given to the BT contract – for the first time truly addressing it as an end client rather than a parent. A vast amount of effort was put into building the relationship and enhancing the service BT was receiving, as well as managing the costs effectively.

It worked. In February 2005 BT renewed the existing HRO and transformation contract with Accenture for a further ten years for £306 million, with effect from August 2005. This was one of the largest renewals of an HRO contract to date anywhere in the world. BT said the deal would provide it with 'higher levels of workforce management and performance services' in 38 country operations worldwide, in tandem with 'further cost savings'. In addition Accenture HR Services has now won a number of new clients across the globe – and has emerged with a stable management structure and a healthy financial outlook.

Lessons learned

In a statement at the time of the signing of the new ten-year agreement in 2005, BT Group human resource director Alex Wilson summed up the benefits from his company's point of view: 'This agreement will allow our staff to concentrate even more on the strategic role of human resources management to our growing global business,' he said. David Clinton, president of Accenture HR Services, added: 'British Telecom's bold decision in August 2000 to undertake large-scale human resources outsourcing has been validated with this new agreement.'

While this looks like a fair assessment there were plenty of cultural speed-bumps along the way. One of the biggest was getting people within e-people-serve to see BT as a client rather than an employer or a parent. Another was

▶

the need to manage the expectations of both the management and employees within the organization. As with many new ventures, the initial great hopes for the future ended up leading to a path that was longer and more difficult than expected.

The verdict

There is a common thread running through the five-year life cycle that has taken the BT transactional HR function from an in-house operation, via the e-peopleserve joint venture, to a new ten-year outsourcing agreement with Accenture. This thread is that HRO does work for BT. At the same time the company has realized its original objectives of achieving cost-effective, world-class HR services, freeing up its HR professionals to focus on strategy, and exploiting the commercial potential of its own HR expertise. Accenture, for its part, now has a market-leading HRO operation to show for its efforts. In short, both companies ended up getting what they wanted, albeit via a roundabout route.

However, what the e-peopleserve experience also demonstrates is that BPO providers often overestimate the willingness and readiness of the potential client base to leap across to new and innovative operating models. As with the Fin-Force joint venture between EDS and KBC Bank (see the case study on page 185), e-peopleserve found that its customer base grew more slowly than it might have expected. In each case this was not down to shortcomings in the offering, but rather to potential clients' reluctance to face the radical change that would be necessary in their own businesses. And HR, being so pivotal to human capital management, is an especially sensitive target for this kind of change. BT and Accenture's original vision has largely been realized. But not quite in the way, or at the pace, that they might have envisaged at the start.

Index